AREAS OF
ECONOMIC STRESS
IN CANADA

Proceedings of a Conference
Queen's University, at Kingston, Ontario

Editors
W. D. WOOD, R. S. THOMAN

Published by

INDUSTRIAL RELATIONS CENTRE
Queen's University
at Kingston, Ontario
1965

FOREWORD

Although the writings of recent decades have manifested deep concern over the problem of regional economic development, that concern has not brought forth a sound analytical base for study of this subject. This neglect is doubtless traceable in part to the overriding interest during the 1930's and '40's in serious national aggregative economic problems such as the severe dislocations of the Great Depression and the formidable task of mobilizing national resources for World War II and its aftermath. With the emergence of difficult problems in the Canadian economy in the mid '50's, localized and regional aspects of economic and social problems received greater attention at both the theoretical and policy levels. In view of the pronounced difference in rates of economic growth between regions, it became increasingly necessary to study the stresses associated with regional development. We are now finding that broader aggregative concepts and approaches need to be re-examined in order to better understand these problems. We have become acutely aware of the need to analyse the interdependence of national and regional problems: on the one hand, how do national developments affect the regional situation; on the other hand, how do regional stresses influence national activities?

This conference on Areas of Economic Stress in Canada was projected in the belief that a sound treatment of regional economic problems requires a more comprehensive understanding of this subject, and that the time has come for a more thorough examination involving several viewpoints and approaches. The Conference was planned by a committee consisting of Professor Richard S. Thoman, Department of Geography, Professor David W. Slater, Department of Economics, Professor W. Donald Wood, Department of Economics and Director, Industrial Relations Centre, and Professor Stewart Fyfe, Department of Political Studies, Queen's University. In making these plans, the committee benefited from the suggestions and counsel of officials of the Department of Industry, Ottawa, and the Department of Economics and Development of the Province of Ontario. These departments also generously assisted in the financing of the programme. The conference, held at Queen's University on January 21st and 22nd, 1965, was attended by 130 invited experts in this field, including representatives from universities in Canada, the United States and Britain, from federal, provincial and local governments, and from industry and labour.

The objective of the conference programme was to bring together academics and policy makers from different disciplines and backgrounds to study both the theoretical and policy aspects of this subject. The first day of the two-day conference was devoted to general and theoretical considerations. In his banquet address, Dr. Mackintosh traces the evolution of regional economic developments and provides a valuable historical perspective for the study of contemporary regional problems. Professor Graham's paper examines the basic problem of economic stress in the Canadian federal context. The study by Professor Berry brings a geographer's viewpoint to bear on the identification problem by means of multivariate analysis. Professor Scott presents a theoretical economic approach for developing policies for declining regions. The general problem of regional disparities in Canadian economic growth is the subject explored by Professor Brewis.

Specific public policies in the field of regional development were studied on the second day of the conference. Mr. Reckord's paper outlines the experience in this field in the United States, while Professor Manners analyses developments in the United Kingdom. The vital policy issues in the study of regional aid in Canada is explored in Professor Pleva's paper. Finally, we have an appraisal of development policies at the provincial level by Mr. Gertler. These papers and the discussions that were put before this conference do not, of course, solve all the problems of regional development. It is our belief, however, that they bring into sharper focus many issues, concepts and approaches in this important field.

A number of individuals and organizations contributed greatly to the proceedings of this conference. First, we wish to express our sincere appreciation to all the authors and discussants for preparing their papers for publication. We are also indebted to the Department of Industry, Government of Canada, Ottawa, and to the Department of Economics and Development, Province of Ontario, for providing generous financial assistance which made this conference possible. For final preparation of the manuscript, we are grateful to the staff of the Industrial Relations Centre, particularly Mrs. Carol Williams.

W. DONALD WOOD,
RICHARD S. THOMAN.

Queen's University
at Kingston, Ontario.
September 1965.

TABLE OF CONTENTS

FOREWORD v

BANQUET ADDRESS

Growth and Stress: Some Historical Notes 3
        Dr. W. A. Mackintosh,
        Vice-Chancellor,
        Queen's University.

I THE BASIC PROBLEMS — IDENTIFICATION

Areas of Economic Stress in the Canadian Federal Context 7
        Professor John F. Graham,
        Head, Department of Economics and Sociology,
        Dalhousie University.

  • Discussants:

        Mr. S. E. Chernick,
        Economic Council of Canada. 17

        Professor André Raynauld,
        Département des Sciences Economiques,
        Université de Montréal. 19

Identification of Declining Regions: An Empirical Study of the Dimensions
        of Rural Poverty 22
        Professor Brian J. L. Berry,
        Department of Geography and
        Center for Urban Studies,
        University of Chicago.

  • Discussants:

        Dr. Pierre Camu,
        Vice-President,
        St. Lawrence Seaway Authority. 67

        Professor Donald Kerr,
        Department of Geography,
        University of Toronto. 69

II THE BASIC PROBLEMS — TREATMENT

Policy for Declining Regions: A Theoretical Approach 73
        Professor A. D. Scott,
        Department of Economics,
        University of British Columbia,
        (1964-65, University of Chicago).

• Discussants:

Professor Clarence L. Barber,
Department of Economics,
University of Manitoba,
(1964-65, McGill University). 93

Professor K. G. Crawford,
Department of Political Studies,
Queen's University. 96

Growth and the Canadian Economy: The Problem of Regional Disparities .. 99

Professor T. N. Brewis,
Department of Economics,
Carleton University.

• Discussants:

Professor Yves Dubé,
Faculté des Sciences Sociales,
Université Laval. 114

Dr. W. R. Dymond,
Assistant Deputy Minister,
Department of Labour, Ottawa. 118

III POLICIES IN THE UNITED STATES AND THE UNITED KINGDOM

Federal Redevelopment in the United States: Concept and Practice 123

Mr. Gordon E. Reckord,
Assistant Administrator for Program Development,
U.S. Area Redevelopment Administration.

• Discussants:

Dr. Sar A. Levitan,
W. E. Upjohn Institute for Employment Research,
Washington, D.C. 134

Professor Maurice J. Boote,
Department of Economics,
Trent University. 137

Areas of Economic Stress: The British Case 139

Professor Gerald Manners,
Department of Geography,
University College, Swansea,
(1964-65, Resources for the Future, Inc.,
Washington, D.C.).

- Discussants:

    Dr. E. P. Weeks,
    Executive Director,
    Atlantic Development Board. 155

    Professor Richard Lawton,
    Department of Geography,
    University of Liverpool,
    (1964-65, University of Southern Illinois). 159

IV REGIONAL POLICIES IN CANADA

Vital Issues in the Study of Aid 167

    Professor Edward G. Pleva,
    Head, Department of Geography,
    University of Western Ontario.

- Discussant:

    Professor A. L. Levine,
    Department of Economics and Political Science,
    University of New Brunswick. 172

Development Policies at the Provincial Level 176

    Mr. L. O. Gertler,
    Head, Planning Department,
    H. G. Acres & Company, Limited.

- Discussants:

    Professor Pierre Harvey,
    Ecole des Hautes Etudes Commerciales. 192

    Mr. W. Hugh Flynn,
    Ontario General Manager,
    Canadian Industries Limited. 195

    Mr. Stanley A. Little,
    President, Canadian Union of Public
    Employees and Vice-President,
    Canadian Labour Congress. 198

Appendix A: Programme 204

Appendix B: List of Participants 208

Banquet Address

Growth and Stress:
Some Historical Notes

by

Dr. W. A. Mackintosh,
Vice-Chancellor,
Queen's University.

GROWTH AND STRESS: SOME HISTORICAL NOTES

Dr. W. A. Mackintosh,
Vice-Chancellor,
Queen's University.

Mr. Chairman and Gentlemen:

I appreciate greatly the honour of speaking to this group which has been devoting its collective mind to the problems of areas of slow growth and of depression and stagnation.

When some weeks ago I offered the title "Growth and Stress" for this talk, I did not realize how ambiguous it might be for you who have just finished so ample a dinner. I did add for my own protection the phrase, "Some Historical Notes", as I wished to free myself from the necessity of keeping up with the young by offering a multivariate analysis of something or other, or presenting a dynamic model of the stationary state. What I have to say is simply some comment on the place of growth in economists' thinking and a few reflections on some implications of historical changes.

In contrast with a few decades ago, growth is now everybody's word. Economists insist on it, they predict it, they assign it a function, build a model, and write prescriptions for it.

In fact, however, over the centuries, economists have given only intermittent attention to growth. For long periods they have left it to the care of the businessman and the politician. The Mercantilists, who were admittedly special pleaders, gave great attention to it and, broadly, growth and national security were the ostensible objects of Mercantilist policy. They rarely defined growth. They were able to measure it only crudely in terms of population, the money value of trade, the number of artisans, or the growth of the King's treasure.

Adam Smith, among all the economists, put it in its proper context. His "Inquiry" was really a quest to find what conditions and policies promoted increase in national income per capita and how the free market effected a moving equilibrium of prices and distributive shares.

After Smith, there was a long digression in which much was said about equilibrium and distribution and very little about growth or national income. The possibility of increases in national income which would provide increased shares to the factors of production was always present but over some generations, economic analysis seemed bound to end dismally in the tendency of profits to a minimum and the stationary state.

In the 19th Century, growth and change were left largely to Karl Marx for whose analysis they were the important elements but who, to a decisive degree, misread his learned researches.

The national dividend reappeared with Alfred Marshall but for many decades it was a concept rather than a measure and such statistical enquiry as was made usually ended in highly tentative statements that the national income for 1893 or

1908 could not well be less than so many millions. It was not until Simon Kuznets set up adequate measures just before World War II and J. M. Keynes persuaded the British Treasury that this was a useful expository tool even though it still wavered as an objective measure, that the gross national product emerged in its present guise as a sacred image for all economists, bureaucrats and states-men.

I recall that at the Dominion-Provincial Conference in 1945, some of us feared that the most shaky proposal was that to adjust Provincial grants annually in terms of changes in the G.N.P. We found to our astonishment that each Provincial premier seemed completely satisfied that the mysterious processes of the Dominion Bureau of Statistics would produce an unassailable and, to him, advantageous figure.

It is well to note that if growth were often neglected by the economists, it was in North American history an object to be sought by every possible means. Political speeches could not be made without reference to random evidence of growth. There was at all periods a consensus that it was to be desired. It was the substance of politics and the hope of the landowning citizen.

For an economy as a whole, depression and stagnation may seem to alternate with growth. Looked at more broadly, depression and stagnation in particular regions or countries are most frequently the concomitants of growth elsewhere. This, again, is something which Karl Marx understood, for he saw capitalism, not only as a creator of new ways, but as the great destroyer of the obsolete and the redundant. In the annals of the hand-loom weavers, the cottage workers, the small landowning farmers and the agricultural labourer, he had abundant records of the destructive power of capitalism. Indeed, one may argue that much of his strategy or historical science, if you prefer that phrase, was to have capitalism carry out the necessary destruction and be replaced by a beneficent socialism. Indeed, one may speculate that Lenin's modification of his theory was an assumption that socialism could by-pass this destructive phase of capitalism but Stalin seemed to demonstrate that destruction was necessary and that socialism could be a more effective and ruthless destroyer.

The destroyer indeed is not capitalism, but technological and social change. The historical answers are mobility, migration, adaptability and new skills. In terms of the lifespan of one man, however, they may be slow and partial. History has proved Marx's general projection wrong but there are many, many examples regionally and sectionally of the destructive aspects of growth and change.

If one looks at particular areas which have become depressed, depleted or stagnant, one is struck by the variety of circumstances which have occasioned these conditions. Exhaustion of resources, poor resource management, inability to compete with superior resources or new discoveries or techniques, the enlargement of market areas and the eroding of natural protection, loss of initiative or loss of managerial skill through selective migration — these are some of the more common but their roots may be deep and complex. Particular cases are made more stubborn by the rapidity with which a transformation can come about. A region dependent on an export which has now failed suddenly finds that the local market for goods and services no longer affords to producers the price in outside markets plus the cost of inward transportation but offers for surpluses the price in outside markets minus the cost of outward transportation. There is not simply a decline to be reversed but an abrupt drop which requires a stiff ascent by entirely new paths.

On general policy, I offer only some random comments. There is danger, I think, in defining full employment as that which leaves only a 3% unemployment, not because this is unattainable but because it sets the problem in the wrong light. Three per cent is not very meaningful when it is the average of widely varied regional percentages. What needs to be understood is that somewhere in the area below 5% unemployment, conditions will be encountered in which the increase in demand by monetary and fiscal expansion as a policy must be supplemented and to a degree replaced by measures to increase the availability and adaptability of labour. So that with increasing efficiency in the labour market, full employment may require lower and lower percentages of unemployment.

Most studies of economic growth unavoidably point to the crucial importance of initiative and managerial ability and all regional projects must be directed toward increasing and strengthening them.

If we look back at the history of the capitalist system or, if you prefer, the system of free enterprise, we must accord it an excellent mark for its decentralization of economic decisions. One must give it very good marks for its allocation of resources. It ranks well in providing effective rewards for innovation and initiative. It draws a very bad mark indeed for its allocation of the penalties of the destructiveness of change. We have clearly entered an era in which rapidity of change and growth of social conscience must produce a consensus which will promote at one and the same time productive change and greater skill and justice in distributing its penalties.

PART I

THE BASIC PROBLEMS — IDENTIFICATION

• Areas of Economic Stress in the Canadian Federal Context

>   Professor John F. Graham,
>   Head, Department of Economics and Sociology,
>   Dalhousie University.

Discussants:

>   Mr. S. E. Chernick,
>   Economic Council of Canada.

>   Professor André Raynauld,
>   Département des Sciences Economiques,
>   Université de Montréal.

• Identification of Declining Regions: An Empirical Study of
the Dimensions of Rural Poverty

>   Professor Brian J. L. Berry,
>   Department of Geography and
>   Center for Urban Studies,
>   University of Chicago.

Discussants:

>   Dr. Pierre Camu,
>   Vice-President,
>   St. Lawrence Seaway Authority.

>   Professor Donald Kerr,
>   Department of Geography,
>   University of Toronto.

AREAS OF ECONOMIC STRESS IN THE CANADIAN FEDERAL CONTEXT

JOHN F. GRAHAM,
Head, Department of Economics
and Sociology, Dalhousie University.

It is useful at the outset of this conference to consider, in view of their ambiguity, the operative terms "areas" and "economic stress", even though this ambiguity does not likely present any serious problems, as it would probably be possible to reach agreement that particular situations could appropriately be designated as "areas of economic stress".

"Areas" could be construed as meaning geographical regions, large or small; or economic sectors such as agriculture, mining, and secondary manufacturing; or sub-sectors, such as dairy farming, coal mining, and manufacturing electronic equipment; or cross sections of society, such as the unskilled worker and the indigent aged. "Stress" in itself is so broad and imprecise a term as to require some clarification as to how it is to be construed in this instance.

For most purposes, the geographical area is the most pertinent for economic analysis and public policy. It is with respect to geographical areas that economic stress will usually be identified and with respect to which remedies must be devised, whether such remedies call for outward migration of labour and capital, for revitalizing declining industries, or for developing new industries. If the diagnosis shows economic stress to originate in particular economic sectors, then it is necessary to analyse the state and prognosis of these sectors. Sectoral analysis is, then, essentially a part, often the crucial part, of the diagnosis of and prescription for economic stress.

On the other hand, economic stress might occur in cross sections of society common to all geographical areas in a country and not be revealed by the usual indexes, such as income per capita and unemployment as a percentage of the labour force, or be related to any particular economic sector. The indigent aged are an example. In such a case, the prescription is likely to call for social security measures rather than for economic adjustment by migration or industrial development.

The ambiguity of the term "economic stress" can be resolved in part by simply selecting the particular notion of "economic stress" that seems most useful. The notion of economic stress chosen here is one of strain that develops among identifiable groups of people in our society that gives rise to dissatisfaction, whether justified or not, with the way in which the economy is functioning. This notion, though useful as an initial working concept, would have to be accompanied by some means of objective measurement and some criterion of intensity to make it "operational". Whatever the notion of stress chosen, judgment must inevitably be made as to whether the stress is serious enough to require action and, if so, as to what kind and degree of action are required to eliminate it. The responsibility of the economist lies in determining whether and in what ways the stress impairs efficiency and in analysing the effects on efficiency of the alternative means of eliminating it.

It should be emphasized that the concern here is not with the creative kind of stress that challenges the individual to develop his constructive potential as fully as possible and leads to his and therefore to society's fulfillment, but rather with areas of economic distress that frustrate the fullest development of our society's potential. The distinction is not always clear, and there is bound to be argument as to whether some instances of stress are on balance productive or destructive.

It is important, too, to recognize the inherent deficiency in limiting the discussion to *economic* stress, for both the origins and the consequences of economic stress may be largely non-economic. One of the problems that plagues the social scientist is that he is trying to contribute to an understanding of society in the round, but is forced by the magnitude of this task to focus on one aspect of society if he hopes to contribute anything of moment. Ideally, the social scientist should first be thoroughly trained as a philosopher, but that too is more than a life's work. The good social scientist strives both to see society in its full historical and contemporary context and to master the technical side of those aspects of it relevant to his chosen discipline, but he inevitably approaches questions primarily from the point of view of that discipline. While this conference is concerned with the economic aspects of stress, acknowledgement is made of the shortcomings of this one-sided approach.

It is instructive to list some of the areas of economic stress, prior to narrowing the focus to ones deemed to be of particular concern. The items are not mutually exclusive.

1. *Disparities in levels of unemployment and underemployment.*

2. *Disparities in income, wealth, and expenditure per capita among provinces and localities, and therefore in levels of public services or in rates of taxation.*

3. *Disparities in industrial development and in rates of growth of income per capita.* It is important to emphasize that unless efficiency considerations are to be ignored, disparities in average income and rates of growth among provinces and localities are practically inevitable, for even with perfect mobility of resources there would be differences among provinces and localities in average income because of differences in occupational distribution appropriate to areas of diverse natural resources and differences in wealth. Geographical disparities in average income are likely, however, to be due in large part to misallocation of resources, i.e., to imperfect mobility.

As Professor A. D. Scott has pointed out, in the very long run, if there were no sociological impediments, occupational differences in income would be ironed out, except for differences necessary to compensate for the degree of training required. There would still be differences within occupations reflecting differences in native ability. To the extent that such income differences are reduced, so also are differences in average income, in equilibrium, and, *ipso facto*, differences in fiscal capacity. While there is little reason to expect that these very-long-run conditions are more likely to be achieved in the future than they have been in the past, they are still something to aim for.

4. *The strains arising in public finance from the great disparities in the revenue-raising capacities of the provinces and municipalities, their limited tax bases (especially in the case of the municipalities), and the pressure on*

them to provide higher and higher levels of public services. One of the most marked developments in Canada since 1945 has been the swing from a powerful centralist emphasis in the confederation to the powerful fragmentary one of the present. Perhaps it would be more accurate to stress the increasing power of the provinces, for if there has been a decentralizing tendency at the federal-provincial level there has been an equally strong centralizing tendency at the provincial-municipal level with the provinces assuming more and more direct responsibility in the fields of education, social welfare, health and hospitals, and community planning.

One has only to recall the Dominion-Provincial Conference on Reconstruction of 1945-46, with its strongly centralist emphasis, abortive though it was, and consider how futile it would be even to call such a conference today, to realize how far we have veered from the centralist path.

The shift is borne out by the simple statistics that the provincial-municipal share of total expenditures by all governments, excluding intergovernmental transfers, grew from 46.3 per cent in 1948 to 54.1 per cent in 1963. (See Table 4.)

5. *The rapid poorly-planned metropolitan urbanization that virtually imprisons people in large cities and denies them easy access to the countryside and all the healthy amenities associated with it, and that makes it more and more difficult to provide the basic civic services efficiently.*

6. *Related to the enhancement of provincial power, and in large part a cause of it, is Quebec's determination to control its own economic and social destiny, in order to do which it feels it requires a high degree of fiscal autonomy with respect both to the raising of revenues and the provision of public services constitutionally under provincial jurisdiction.* Quebec's moves to increase its autonomy are mainly responsible for federal-provincial relations becoming the salient area of economic stress in Canada in the post-war period.

It is interesting to speculate about what would have happened if we had had a strong federal government through the post-war period which was able to prevent the loss of momentum of economic growth and, what is more important, to establish in concert with the provinces a set of social and economic goals backed by a strong national concensus, and to develop a set of policies designed to implement them systematically. Possibly the fragmentation actually experienced was inevitable; certainly the causes were not of recent origin; but there is no doubt that the failure of federal leadership, and the breakdown of what semblance of Anglo Saxon-French Canadian rapport there had been, made the outcome a virtual certainty. The failure of Quebec governments to develop the province's educational institutions in accordance with the requirements of an advanced industrial and commercial society of the mid-Twentieth Century was also a crucial, if irrational, factor in explaining the present cleavage. One lesson to be learned is that the Canadian penchant for lack of policy, for a series of often unrelated patchwork programs, that is, for bumbling "ad hockery", is a luxury this country can no longer afford, if indeed it ever could.

At the same time, it is necessary to acknowledge the federal government's increasing interest in regional problems, as evidenced by the payment of Atlantic Provinces Adjustment Grants, and the quite recent establishment of

ARDA (Agricultural Rehabilitation and Development Act), ADA (Area Development Agency), and the ADB (Atlantic Development Board). It is also envisaged that the Economic Council of Canada will give considerable attention to regional problems, even though there is not much evidence of this in its first report. The apparent intention of ARDA to consider the problem of inter-sectoral coordination in implementing its program, which in the first instance is concerned with the primary industries, is encouraging; but ARDA is hampered, if not hamstrung, in its efforts by the lack of a clear focus of federal policy and by inadequate federal-provincial coordination of programs. The situation can still be fairly described as one of programs without policy.

7. *The differential impact of public policy, such as tariff and transportation policy.* The arguments about this have become hackneyed, but there is no denying, for example, that the tariff policy has discriminated against the Atlantic and Western Provinces and that the St. Lawrence Seaway is of greatest benefit to Central Canada and is detrimental to the Maritimes.

8. *The introduction of public programs such as medicare and universal pensions in conflict with the private interests of doctors and insurance companies.*

9. *The decline of industries in one-industry communities, such as Elliot Lake, the coal mining communities in Alberta and Nova Scotia, and the iron ore community of Wabana on Bell Island, Newfoundland.* It is in these cases where economic stress is probably most apparent and most difficult to alleviate; for if the decline is not arrested, the only economic solution is the harsh one of emigration and abandonment of much private and social capital that is physically sound. Still, it is less cruel than the alternative of debilitating economic and social stagnation.

The communities concerned have generally been prosperous at one time, when their main industry flourished and adjustment to economic expansion took place relatively easily. But our economic system, probably any type of economic system, is inefficient in dealing with declining industries. Economic adjustment is much harder in the downward than the upward direction. People cling tenaciously to such communities long after any chance of establishing a new economic base has gone. It is quite understandable that public policy should be concentrated on these problem areas of the economy, since they stand out like sore thumbs and can usually marshall considerable sentiment against adjustment by migration, which politicians are unlikely to ignore.

10. *Rural poverty.* The most prevalent sort is a legacy of subsistence farms settled in the days when a self-sufficing rural economy was typical. This problem has been accentuated by the growing income disparities between such areas and other areas of the economy and the technological revolution in agriculture from which these farms have failed or been unable to benefit. Such farms are especially common in, although are not confined to, eastern Quebec and the Maritime Provinces. They are often characterized by poor soil, small size, unsuitable topography for the use of machinery, and a poor location in relation to markets. The obvious prescriptions of farm consolidation, where economically feasible, and abandonment of farms and the reversion of farmland to forest where consolidation is not feasible, are being

followed in a hit or miss way; but their implementation is impeded by the consequent displacement of people who would be virtually incapable of coping with life in any other environment. Much the same can be said for some of the small scale fishing and logging activities in the eastern provinces.

At the same time, one must be wary of urban-rural comparisons, for investigators of rural areas generally have a strong urban bias, since they are themselves usually strongly oriented towards urban living. There is the opposite pitfall, not unrelated to the first, of assuming an idyllic view of the life of the country dweller. While some country living may conform to this picture, no one who has seen the unrelieved poverty of, for example, some of the rural areas of northern New Brunswick would be misled by it.

One type of rural dweller, who is no doubt found in all provinces but seems to be most prevalent in the eastern provinces, is what might be called the "happy low-income casual worker", who works occasionally at various jobs in the primary industries and has no desire for full-time employment even when it is available. He does not want to be pinned down and has no desire to move to where permanent employment is available within his province or elsewhere. Many in this group have a great liking for their way of life. Many are also very much aware of and quick to accept benefits from social assistance programs. One might argue that as long as such people are satisfied with their outdoor lives and do not wish to change, they should be left alone; but their existence is to some extent parasitic in that they are a burden on their fellow citizens who must pay the taxes for the welfare benefits they are glad to receive. Even so, it is possible that the low-income casual worker is not really misallocated, in that he and his family may be less of a charge on the rest of the community if he is left where he is, where, one way or another, he provides for most of their needs; whereas, if moved to an urban area, he might not be fit for steady work and might even become a complete charge on the community. If change is to come under these conditions, it must depend upon providing good education and training for children and young people and will come only slowly, perhaps over a generation.

11. *The actual and anticipated upheavals caused by automation and the current concern, justified or not, about the need for a universal income and consumption maintenance structure that would not require contributions or even a willingness to work from the recipients.* Such a program would eliminate most of the economic stress, however defined, but it would imply not merely an affluent, but a super-abundant society, which is not likely yet in sight even for countries like the United States and Canada, and is, for the foreseeable future at least, quite fanciful in the global context of a world in which poverty is still the condition of the bulk of the people. This reference to stress stemming from automation calls to mind also that classic, not unrelated source of economic stress: the conflict between labour and management.

12. *Canadian-American tensions arising from the Canadian dilemma of whether to reap the tangible rewards of more rapid economic development and higher levels of living or opt for the psychic satisfaction of having domestic control over our industry, a satisfaction that might vanish if people were well-informed about the alternatives.*

One could extend this enumeration of "areas of economic stress" much further, to include such things as the developing trade rivalry among provinces, the swing of immigration from Northern to Southern Europe and its concentration in the heavily industrialized urban centres of Ontario, the alleged "brain drain" from Canada to the United States and from the Atlantic Provinces to the rest of Canada, and the acute population pressure in Newfoundland; but it has been carried far enough to illustrate the various conditions encompassed by the term, the overlapping of the spatial and sectoral aspects, and at least to mention many of the areas with which this conference is likely to be concerned.

The cause of all economic stress is ultimately the basic economic problem of scarcity. Given the insufficiency of resources to satisfy all wants fully, economic stress among the members of society is inevitable, although the more productive the economy the more it should be possible to reduce it. The inevitability of stress does not excuse a society from taking all possible steps to minimize it whenever it is destructive rather than productive.

The lack of any clearly established and generally supported objectives in this country makes systematic discussion of regional problems an almost hopeless task. It is necessary to assume at least rudimentary objectives before one can proceed with a meaningful discussion. It is therefore assumed that the primary economic objective is to ensure that resources are utilized to maximize the total production of the nation as a whole in order to permit the maximum achievement of social objectives at all three levels: federal, provincial and local. This approach begs the question of what constitutes the good society we might aim to achieve; rather it puts the emphasis on providing the means for achieving practically any set of social objectives that might be chosen.

This simple statement of objectives implies the general criterion of efficiency in the utilization of resources that is inherent in the economist's focus on society. This is interpreted here to mean efficiency in the broad sense of utilizing resources to maximize social welfare.

In a modern industrial society, efficiency requires not only considerable mobility in terms of willingness of people to move geographically, but also a great deal of occupational flexibility and adaptability in adjusting to rapid economic change, which in turn requires public institutions that will facilitate this adaptability. At that same time, the criterion of efficiency does not mean uprooting a whole depressed community without counting the psychic cost to the individuals concerned, nor does it necessarily preclude subsidizing industrial development in an area of chronic unemployment and underemployment.

It is of interest to look at the Atlantic Provinces with reference to the efficiency criterion, since they constitute one of the most generally acknowledged, and historically one of the most intractable, areas of economic stress in Canada. These provinces, as Table 1 shows, have average incomes considerably below those of the other provinces. They have also a long history of chronic unemployment and underemployment in excess of that for the country as a whole. (See Table 3 for figures on unemployment.)

The relatively low average incomes of the Atlantic Provinces are in part inherent in the occupational distribution appropriate to the natural resource base and location, in part due to the lack of internal economic adjustment, particularly in the primary industries, and in part to a chronic labour surplus in the form of both unemployment and underemployment.

Historically, since 1871 at least, emigration has been the most important economic corrective for the three Maritime Provinces; yet it is surprising that so much economic adjustment remains to be made in the primary industries. It may be that the passive reliance that has long been placed on migration from the region as a means of economic adjustment has obscured and retarded the very considerable adjustments that could be made within the province. Lack of sufficient capital to move by those with very low incomes in the rural areas is also partly responsible for the slowness of adjustment. And no doubt continual emigration of the more vigorous and ambitious members of the communities has left people behind who were slow to effect adjustments that should have been made within the region.

The dilemma of the Atlantic Provinces is that their population and labour force are increasing quite rapidly in spite of continued and substantial emigration, from the Maritimes at least; at the same time, employment opportunities in the primary industries have been declining and will likely continue to decline if these industries become more highly rationalized, as they must if they are to yield competitive returns to labour and capital. The service sector already contributes a much larger part of total production than in the rest of the country. There are probably opportunities for expansion of the tourist industry, although the short season of only two months severely limits the amount of capital it is profitable to invest and means that the industry provides little of the year-around employment that is sorely needed.

There are two avenues for preventing or eliminating a large and persistent surplus of labour: (1) even larger movements of population from the provinces than have been taking place in recent years and (2) a considerable expansion of primary and secondary manufacturing industries. To most economists, particularly those unfamiliar with the region, the first alternative would seem to be the obvious economic solution. In large part, it is. There will likely continue to be considerable net emigration from the region as well as considerable internal migration from areas of unemployment within the region to areas where jobs are available in other parts of the region. Such mobility is essential in a modern industrial society and there is no cause for regretting it. The important thing is whether *people* are better off if they move, not the survival of stagnating localities as such. Yet, experience indicates that after allowing for all the migration that can be expected to take place, even with ample employment opportunities in the rest of the country, a condition not very common in recent years, there will still be a large residue of employed and underemployed labour. If such a surplus is in fact inevitable, there is a strong argument on efficiency grounds for the use of federal subsidies, at least for a limited duration, in such forms as low interest loans, grants, tax concessions of various sorts, and perhaps transportation adjustments, to encourage the expansion of secondary manufacturing industries, provided the value of the contribution to production of the otherwise unemployed and therefore wasted labour exceeds the cost of the subsidies and provided the funds cannot be more productively utilized elsewhere. In fact, the value of the contribution to production might not have to be even that great, if account is taken of the completely unproductive social assistance payments and the publicly contributed portion of unemployment insurance that would have to be paid if the employment were not provided. The success of such a program would still depend upon a considerable degree of occupational adaptability of the region's people and their willingness to move at least within the region to those localities ("growth centres") where new industries can be established with the best prospects for success. It is, of course, necessary to set against the gains in production from the utilization of otherwise wasted resources the losses resulting from some blunting of incentives to inter-regional mobility as a result of the subsidies; but, in view of the likelihood of the Atlantic region becoming relatively more attractive economically with the rapid general growth of the population of the country, there is a good chance that the policy would in fact be self-justifying and, in the long run, even self-financing. The main hindrance at present is the narrowness of the existing secondary manufacturing base and the limited range of industries interested in locating in the Atlantic Provinces far from the large Central Canadian markets.

The kind of program of rationalization of primary industries and expansion of primary and secondary manufacturing envisaged here requires carefully formulated and highly coordinated federal and provincial policies. There is too much room for costly mistakes to take the usual path of proliferation of uncoordinated *ad hoc* programs. The virtue of the efficiency criterion nationally is obvious, but it is crucial for the region that its economy be put on a sound footing, not only so that it can make its maximum contribution to social welfare, but also so that it will be more attractive to the vigorous and able men and women upon whom the level of development and the quality of society largely depend than would a basically sick economy that must be perpetually bolstered by subsidies.

If all parts of the country are to accept the efficiency criterion, then all must share equitably in the fruits of the economy's production and growth. What does this mean? It does not require equality of income distribution of individuals or equality of average incomes of provinces and localities; but it would require that all provinces and their localities were able to provide comparable levels of public services at good standards with comparable burdens of taxation. To achieve this would require federal-provincial and provincial-municipal fiscal equalization transfers on a much larger scale than at present. Such transfers would be in accord with the efficiency criterion, for without them the heavier fiscal pressure in the form of inferior services or heavier tax burdens that will be exerted on individuals of any given economic circumstances in a poor province will be conducive to some uneconomic movements of labour and capital from poor to rich provinces and impede some economic movements of labour and capital from rich to poor provinces. The geographical neutrality of the resulting fiscal structure would be consistent with optimum resource allocation; it would not in itself assure it. To the extent that market forces failed to bring about the most efficient utilization of the nation's resources, selective public policies could be used to that end.

The proposed transfers would greatly enhance the ability of the poorer provinces, including Quebec, to pursue their particular economic and social objectives. At the same time, the acceptance of the desirability of income redistribution on a national scale with respect to the provision of public services, would be a powerful unifying force in the nation, and, combined with a program developed by federal and provincial governments acting in concert to maintain high levels of employment throughout the nation, or at least to maintain incomes, would make possible the elimination of most of the destructive areas of economic stress in our society. (Rural poverty might be an exception, except for education of children.) It is likely too that the enhancement of public services in the poorer provinces, particularly education, would yield rich economic rewards from which the whole country would benefit.

The alleviation of economic stress in this country requires a coordinated approach to the interrelated problems of growth, stability, and structural change. The problem of developing effective policy in these spheres is no easy task in any country; it is considerably more difficult in an economically and socially heterogeneous federal country like Canada, with its divided jurisdiction. It is a problem with which this country, in its typical aimlessness, has never come to grips. The closest the federal government has come to making the effort was at the Dominion-Provincial Conference on Reconstruction of 1945-46.

Problems of stability, growth, and structure almost invariably relate to particular industries or groups of industries and usually to particular communities in which the industries concerned are concentrated. The more heterogeneous the economy, the more specific the problem area. It follows that, to be effective, policy must be capable of being geared to the circumstances of local communities, as well as operating over larger areas, possibly the whole country when the problem is a general one. The current discussion of coordinated federal-provincial countercyclical budgeting is highly relevant, although other even more selective devices may be required as well. The successful implementation of such policy requires that the federal, provincial, and municipal governments act in concert to a degree never before attempted or perhaps even seriously envisaged, at a time when provincial autarky is the order of the day. Ironically, one valuable by-product of this autarkic trend may be that in making a nationally aggregative policy politically unacceptable, it will force the rethinking and the reworking that should logically lead to a regionally sensitive set of policies. We may at last be rid of the simple-minded Keynesianism that has epitomized federal fiscal policy in most of the period since the end of the Second World War.

STATISTICAL APPENDIX

Table 1

Per Capita Personal Income

	1948	1953	1958	1961	1962	1963	Mean 1961-3	Mean 1961-3 as % of Unwtd. Mean	Mean 1961-3 as % of Wtd. Mean
Newfoundland	472[a]	632	794	937	979	1029	982	68	59
Prince Edward Island	505	653	850	971	1028	1075	1025	71	62
Nova Scotia	664	891	1068	1195	1240	1283	1239	85	75
New Brunswick	637	771	947	1065	1107	1151	1108	76	67
Quebec	779	1047	1238	1378	1444	1504	1442	99	87
Ontario	1069	1459	1714	1842	1928	2019	1930	133	117
Manitoba	980	1166	1442	1510	1672	1664	1615	111	98
Saskatchewan	927	1319	1242	1223	1689	1890	1601	110	97
Alberta	1030	1357	1534	1593	1684	1747	1675	116	101
British Columbia	1090	1478	1696	1815	1876	1957	1883	130	114
Unweighted mean	815	1077	1253	1353	1465	1532	1450	100	
Weighted mean (Canada)	916[b]	1235	1445	1562	1660	1734	1652		100

Source: Dominion Bureau of Statistics, *National Accounts Income and Expenditure,* 1926-1956, 1962, 1963.

a Value for Newfoundland is for 1949.

b Incorporates 1948 data for Newfoundland.

Table 2

Percentage Increase in Per Capita Personal Income, 1948-1963

Newfoundland	118[a]
Prince Edward Island	113
Nova Scotia	93
New Brunswick	81
Quebec	93
Ontario	89
Manitoba	70
Saskatchewan	104[b]
Alberta	70
British Columbia	80
Unweighted mean	88
Weighted mean (Canada)	89

Source: Calculated from Table 1.

[a] Comparison for Newfoundland is for 1949-1963.

[b] 1963 was not a typical year for Saskatchewan. Percentage increase from 1948 to mean of 1961-3, was 73%, compared with 78% for all of Canada.

Table 3

Unemployed as a Percentage of the Total Labour Force

	1948	1953	1958	1963
Atlantic Provinces	4.5	5.5	12.8	9.7
Quebec	2.4	3.8	8.8	6.9
Ontario	1.7	2.1	5.4	3.8
Prairie Provinces	2.3	2.0	4.1	4.6
British Columbia	3.4	4.0	8.7	6.5
CANADA	2.3	3.0	7.1	5.5

Source: *The Labour Force.*

Table 4

The Percentage Distribution of Government Expenditure in the Post World War II Period among Federal, Provincial, and Municipal Governments

		Expenditure on Goods and Services	Total Expenditure Excluding Inter-Governmental Transfers
1948	Federal	37.5	53.7
	Provincial	26.0	24.6
	Municipal	36.5	21.7
1953	Federal	57.8	63.1
	Provincial	15.7	17.7
	Municipal	26.5	19.2
1958	Federal	46.2	55.9
	Provincial	19.8	20.7
	Municipal	34.0	23.4
1963	Federal	36.2	45.9
	Provincial	21.6	26.3
	Municipal	42.2	27.8

Source: Dominion Bureau of Statistics, *National Accounts Income and Expenditure,* 1926-1956, 1962, 1963, Table 37.

COMMENTS

S. E. CHERNICK,
Economic Council of Canada.

Professor Graham has covered a lot of territory in relatively few pages. The coverage, however, is very uneven. I wish he had had more time to order and explore further the many complex issues which he raises in his paper. I also wish I had been given more time to consider his views with deliberation.

For different reasons perhaps, I arrive at the same point as Professor Graham when he suggests that the central concern is with areas of economic *distress* rather than stress and with the individuals or groups of individuals ultimately affected. This focus is correct, particularly if we want to formulate appropriate policies for its alleviation.

I would not, however, employ Graham's definition of economic stress. "Dissatisfaction among identifiable groups of people" is not a very useful criterion and is void of operational content. Indeed the author himself appears to abandon this definition in drawing up his list of areas of economic stress. Otherwise, how could he possibly omit the classic area of economic stress that would be embraced by his definition, namely, the clash of labour and management. Clearly, a quantifiable notion is essential here.

There is fairly wide agreement, by now, that a univariate index for identifying areas of economic distress is not adequate. I think that a measure of productivity or income for a region, an economic sector, or group of individuals must be one of the elements included in any index. We would want to consider both the relative level of the index and its rate of change over time. It is of interest to be able to say, for example, that an economically distressed region is characterized not only by a relatively low level of income per resident at the time, but also one which has in the face of a general economic advance persisted over some period of time past and is likely to persist over some time into the future.

If we do not apply strong criteria for identifying distress, we run the risk of failing to distinguish the disparities in productivity and income that are inevitable and transitory features of the process of efficient resource allocation, from those that characterize a "true" state of economic distress. The former can be termed a form of frictional economic distress and the latter can be thought of as structural economic distress. It is the real or imagined fear of interfering with the natural forces of competition that frequently makes an economist hesitate in making a judgment. He cannot always be sure whether a declining activity is a Schumpeterian catharsis or downright permanent obsolescence.

Unless we are satisfied with identifying only the extreme case of economic distress in each possible economic distribution, say Newfoundland among the provinces, or the east coast fishing industry among the sectors of economic activity, or the low tail percentile income group, a judgment inevitably has to be made as to what is a relatively low level and a relatively low rate of growth of income.

The income criterion does not help us very much, however, with the increasingly important area of economic stress represented by the spatial concentration of economic activity and the growth of the urban area. The problem here is better revealed in such terms as the average availability of residential and recreational space, fresh air and water, and the travel costs for the inhabitants.

Identifying areas of economic stress is all very well, but for policy formulation we want to know the causes of distress. Professor Graham suggests that "the cause of all economic stress is ultimately the basic economic problem of scarcity". While this may be true in a philosophical sense, there is an alternative approach which is likely to be more fruitful. In my view, the source of economic distress is to be found in the changes that are inherent in economic growth. The leading edge of economic growth is generally confined to a relatively narrow range of economic sectors and is limited in its initial geographic impact. An area of economic distress emerges because the force of the economic advance that reaches it is weak or non-existent, or in the face of a strong force, it is unable to adapt rapidly to the requirements of economic growth. We want ultimately to isolate the impediments to adaptation and focus policies on their removal or at least a reduction in their severity. Successful achievement would mean a fuller and more efficient use of resources in the area of economic distress.

In common with other developed countries, the Canadian economy has experienced significant economic changes. There has been a dramatic shift in the structure of its output — from agriculture to industry and services; major substitutions in fuel inputs; and a sharp increase in the utilization of "brain power" in the productive process. Accompanying these changes has been the increased geographic concentration of both population and economic activity.

Many of the areas of economic distress that we commonly think of would emerge clearly as consequences of these broad economic changes. The problems of urban growth, declining industries and areas in which they are located, rural poverty, the group of unemployables, and even the Atlantic region taken as a whole are among those which would yield to an analysis focussed upon the process of adaption to economic change and impediments to it.

The notion of distress, as applied for example, in Professor Graham's discussion of the Atlantic region lends a bias in favour of a conservative, or even negative view of the problem. This attitude, in turn, affects the formulation of policy. In the minds of many, the region has been written off, and we rely on equalization grants and other forms of transfer to achieve national objectives in providing minimum standards of public services. I wonder whether the chronically lagging region does not at some stage become an underdeveloped area. It might at least be a useful stratagem for policy purposes to proceed as though it is. Approached as a problem of development, objectives have to be set out explicitly, possible future contours of development have to be evaluated as much as, if not more than, past experience, and the policies ultimately recommended must have an internal consistency and harmony in relation to the set of objectives. A similar approach and procedure seems to have been adopted in Quebec, for some of the activity sectors, if not for all. And the terms of reference of the Atlantic Development Board encompass the possibility of approaching that region's problem in this spirit.

By way of final comment, I would strongly support Professor Graham's plea that public policies at all levels of authority be re-examined and evaluated from the standpoint of their regional impact and that new policies display a keener sensitivity to regional requirements. I would extend this further by suggesting that policy formulation at all levels be better attuned to future requirements.

COMMENTS

Professor André Raynauld,
Département des Sciences Economiques,
Université de Montréal.

The study of regional development is itself a large area of distress in economic literature. It follows that the major task that confronts us is still in this field to define and explain what we talk about.

Quite rightly in such circumstances Professor Graham has chosen not to restrict the subject. But my first reaction, which is never the appropriate one, was really that the subject was too wide. The areas of economic stress of Professor Graham are almost unlimited. We feel the wind of the Prairies rather than of the Maritimes. The same is true of his notion of stress. I had not realized how much stress I was suffering from myself. Living in a large city and being deprived of the beauties of the countryside, being the victim of an income differential as anyone is with respect to someone else, and, what is more, recognizing myself in this "happy low income casual worker" who is described in the paper, I thought I should revise my set of values.

And so it is that I came to want, even if the other procedure is perfectly valid, to narrow the notions in my present comments in view of the discussions that will follow.

Let me assume first of all that our subject in this Conference is regional or local economic development so that we may be permitted to understand the word area in its geographic or physical sense and leave the problems associated with a particular industry to another Queen's Conference. It seems to me that the analysis and policies that can be devised to deal with a declining industry for example are to a large extent different from regional development.

My second objective is to limit the proportions of economic stress. Given my general assumption, I would propose to submit the Canadian regions or localities to two criteria (to give them the stress benefit) namely unemployment and out-migration. My particular assumption here is that our only professional interest in depressed areas lies in a more or less obvious need for correction. Some of the sources of economic stress, as they are listed in Professor Graham's paper, need not or cannot be corrected. Wage differentials for example fall into this category, I believe, whereas when unemployment and/or out-migration exceed a certain figure, we might reasonably wish to call an area, a depressed or a distress area where a corrective action is called for. It will be realized however that average income as distinct from average wage has some close relationships with the two measures proposed.

I am not in a position to state what the relevant figures should be, that is, from what point should one consider an area as depressed. But I thought it would be somewhat illuminating to examine a particular case with respect to both unemployment and migration.[1]

---

[1] With a high figure of unemployment, a low out-migration figure means that the adaptation process does not work and conversely that some adaptation is taking place but at too slow a rate. With little unemployment and high out-migration, the area is relatively poor, but would not give reason for concern unless the rate of out-migration is deemed too high to be socially tolerable.

This case is the Census Division of Bonaventure, in Quebec, and the study from which I quote the figures was prepared for the year 1962 by the Economic Research Bureau of the Department of Trade & Commerce. The figures are derived from a special field survey. As far as I can ascertain, the results are fairly reliable. On the question of unemployment, in the Census Division of Bonaventure in 1962, 49% of the male labour force was unemployed at one time or another during the year (for a minimum of one week). A second figure which is more significant tells us that if we take the total number of man-week during the year, 26% of the time was lost by lack of jobs. The average duration of unemployment was found to be 28 weeks, that is, more than half of the year, and lastly 6.4% of the labour force was unemployed during the whole year. One might say that, perhaps, these workers are living on the farms so that the figures are highly misleading. The break-down is given however between the part-time farmers and the other workers. In fact, the figures are only slightly lower where the calculations are limited to out-of-farms workers.

What is the significance of such a situation in relation to our subject? Although Bonaventure may be an extreme case, the figures for an area to justify as depressed could be set fairly high. And this is as it should be, in my opinion. Despite the low opinion in which "simple-minded" Keynesianism is held by Prof. Graham, it is worth remembering that unemployment goes up and down in depressed as well as in other areas along with demand conditions prevailing in the Economy, so that it is quite possible that a major part of the so-called structural unemployment is just and no more than cyclical unemployment. We must make sure that we have exploited to the fullest the resources of the old fashioned pumps available to step up demand before we turn to long-term and costly corrective policies.

But, we cannot rely exclusively on unemployment figures to take care of everything because the unemployed may go away. In the end, every Canadian might choose to cross the border and nobody be left to keep the discussions going on unemployment. For this reason, I suggest out-migration as a second rule by which to define an area of economic stress.

In the Bonaventure study, an attempt was made to measure migrations. On the basis of the total male labour force, it was found that 3.2% had left the region definitely during the last three years. An additional 2.6% were away nine months in a year, 1% had moved within the region, and surprisingly perhaps, 3.7% had come into the region from the outside. The measure of the gross migration would thus be 10.5% of the labour force, of which 6% more or less, could be considered as net out-migrants.

Quite frankly I cannot say whether a figure of 6% is high or low in this matter once due account is taken for the size of the area and for the number of years to which the flows apply, etc. I have never read comparable studies so that I will leave this point to your consideration. Furthermore, I am not as confident as in the case of unemployment on the reliability of the figures I referred to and the way they were arrived at.

Figures or no figures nevertheless, it seems to me that migrations and unemployment provide us with a good if not a sufficient basis for the identification of areas of economic stress.

*   *   *

Once the areas of economic stress have been defined and located one might wish to consider other problems some of which are listed in Professor Graham's paper, in order to discriminate between various types of policies according to the various situations.

Suppose that as a point of departure, we make three classes of depressed areas:

1 — The classical economists' areas: a subsistence economy with surplus labour and where agriculture, fisheries or trapping predominate.

2 — Areas characterized by one or two declining industries (*except agriculture which goes under No. 1*) or to use an American terminology, areas where industries are in a stage of "increasing retardation".

3 — Areas where Government action or inaction prevent development.

These three classes of depressed areas are of course hand-made. The first two are understandable in terms of economic analysis but the third one is not. This is done on purpose. With the help of this new category, I would like to get rid of a large number of problems to the solution of which a great deal of energy is spent in using sophisticated economic analysis and principles where they are not needed at all. I do not want to mention cases here, but surely everyone is aware that in this or that particular region or locality in Canada, development does not take place simply because basic public services are not available in spite of an abundant labour force and population. Tourists do not go because there are no roads and no information bureaus. Industry does not go because the territory is closed to prospection or use on Government orders. Other regions or localities are depressed rather than inhabited because some years ago people were moved into those regions at public expense. The idea I wish to convey by these trivial examples is simply that in many cases, regions or localities do have some potential (I up-dated my vocabulary recently) that could be exploited economically if useless obstacles were removed. I call this *administrative development*. In underdeveloped countries, to cover the same ground, one would say that a stable and sensible Government must precede economic development.

Under the heading of Government, it might be advisable to put also those positive policies which may promote development in given areas, but are justified on social rather than economic grounds. I am not sure if one should always try to reconcile these social objectives and associated policies with economic criteria. Equalization payments are ready examples. This is not to say that the economic effects of these policies and objectives do not matter, but that regional economic development is in another chapter of the manual of instructions.

Of the first two classes of depressed areas presented above, it is essentially the first which we are concerned with. I will not repeat the description of the situation. It is contained in the paper. Suffice it to say that if it is true that this is the typical case of an area of economic stress, as I have tried to show by the elimination process, then we are really dealing with regional development or underdevelopment. And then again we are in fact dealing with the same problem that confronts all the underdeveloped countries of the world. The same theories, the same techniques, the same strategies apply with only minor changes.

IDENTIFICATION OF DECLINING REGIONS:
AN EMPIRICAL STUDY OF THE DIMENSIONS OF RURAL POVERTY

B. J. L. BERRY,*
Department of Geography and
Center for Urban Studies,
University of Chicago.

Where economic development occurs unequally across a country, regional differences in levels of welfare are likely to become urgent political issues.[1] Such is the case in both Canada and the United States, where there is a growing concern for areas of economic distress that frustrate the fullest development of society's potential. In both countries a variety of public agencies are involved with definition of distressed areas, and with the development and execution of remedial courses of action. Canada's Area Development Agency used unemployment criteria to designate distressed local office areas of the National Employment Service, whereas the Agricultural Rehabilitation and Development Agency makes use of income and demographic criteria to identify rural areas which are socially and economically disadvantaged. In the United States the Area Redevelopment Administration relies upon unemployment criteria for designation along county lines of journey-to-work areas of at least 15,000 workers, and uses both income and unemployment criteria for defining rural distress. In neither Canada nor the United States do we sense, however, any real political awareness of the fact that "where the manner in which economic space is organized affects the pace and structure of economic growth, national policy must turn to strategies of spatial evolution to further the general development objectives of the economy".[2]

Following Friedmann and Alonso, we would argue that:

> "Human activities are distributed over the national territory in certain rhythms and patterns that are neither arbitrary nor the workings of chance. They result rather from the interdependencies that give form to economic space. Spatial patterns will shift with shifts in the structure of demand and production, in the level of technology, and in the social and political organization of the nation. The economic and social development of the nation is reflected in its patterns of settlement; its systems of flow and exchange of commodities, money, and information; its patterns of commuting and migration; and its reticulation of areas of urban influence. And if there is a spatial pattern corresponding to each 'stage' of economic development, it may be further suggested that there is an optimal strategy for spatial transformation from one stage to the next. In the early period of development, marginal returns of the factors of production differ greatly among regions. With economic

* Several other persons made major contributions to this paper, and I wish to acknowledge my debt to them while also making it clear that they bear no blame for the ways in which I have misused their assistance in the manuscript. In addition to the major contributions made by Mrs. Cooke and Mr. Ray, data were provided by the Economics Branch of the Canada Department of Agriculture through the good offices of V. Gilchrist, Chief of the Farm Organization Efficiency Section, and Figures 1-6 were drafted by the branch cartographers. The Dominion Bureau of Statistics had Peter M. Neely of the University of Chicago prepare the grouping programs. Robert A. Murdie and Larry S. Bourne edited and processed the data at the University of Chicago's Computation Center, and Marston Case aided in interpretation of some of the results.

[1] Friedmann, J. R. P. and W. Alonso, *Regional Development and Planning*, Cambridge, The M.I.T. Press, 1964, p. 2.
[2] *Ibid.*, p. 2.

advancement, economic factors become more differentiated in space, and the relevant scale of many functions will increase. At an advanced stage of development, the national economy will appear as a fully integrated hierarchy of functional areas, with most of the population and activities polarized in metropolitan areas and, in effect, with national markets for labor, capital, and commodities."[3]

In this vein, we show in this paper that Ontario's rural poverty is distributed in certain rhythms and patterns that are clearly results of the forces and inter- dependencies giving form to economic space. In particular, the analysis which we summarize points out that economic disadvantage among rural residents has two quite distinct, independent patterns, and that social disadvantage forms yet a third and equally distinct dimension. Some areas, for example in Eastern Ontario, appear particularly unfortunate because they occupy the lowest levels in all three patterns. Other areas may fare well upon one and poorly upon another, for the study shows the three patterns of poverty to be independent of each other, with no reason therefore to expect throughout the province the consistent behaviour dis- played by Eastern Ontario.

What are the three patterns? The first is that of *rural farm poverty*, with a distribution which mirrors the spatial pattern of agricultural resources; rural farm poverty is at its most intense along the Frontenac Axis where the thin soils and upland areas of the shield extend southwards into Eastern Ontario. The second pattern of economic disadvantage is that of *rural non-farm poverty,* which is at its most intense in the areas which are least integrated into the hierarchy of Ontario's functional economic areas and which do not have resources to exploit for recre- ational purposes; such areas are located along the divides which separate zones of urban influence. The third pattern is one of *social disadvantage* which appears to result from the cultural differentiation of Ontario's population. Those areas which have the highest proportions of their residents French Canadians are also areas with the lowest levels of education, the highest infant mortality rates, and the like.

Identification of three different types of economic and social disadvantage, with three distinct regional patterns, and three equally distinct sets of causes, should be some contribution to the poverty debate. Regional differences in wealth do indeed appear to have the rhythms and patterns that are part of the inter- dependencies giving form to socio-economic space, but no single index, such as average income per capita, or unemployment, will capture these differences in all their variety. Differences in resource endowment provided by the land imprint themselves upon the human condition, yet men from divergent cultural back- grounds will use the same piece of land in different ways. Behaviour is also patterned with reference to urban nodes, which thus serve as central places in the organization and use of space. Such patterns change and may be changed as the interdependencies change and are in part themselves a function of change. Yet if change is to be directed towards achievement of a society's fullest potentials, each pattern of interdependency may have to be manipulated in a different way. No single set of policies may be able to reach all the economically and socially disadvantaged. Strategic location of new industries at important "growth poles" may facilitate the movement of society to higher levels of integration in metro- politan systems of functional economic areas, and may affect positively rural non-

---

[3] *Ibid.*, p. 2.

farm poverty by reducing the isolation of the inter-urban periphery, but such policies may be quite ineffective for tackling problems of social disadvantage. Educational planning may affect the socially disadvantaged, but touch hardly at all poverty-stricken farmers trying to eke out a marginal existence on the poor soils of Renfrew or Frontenac counties. Some policies may be appropriate to once-dynamic economies now facing hard times. Others may be more important to zones of meager natural resources. Yet others may be most apposite for the inaccessible peripheries. We hope that the exercise in definition that this paper essentially comprises will be a useful contribution to the poverty debate, by distinguishing the different types and regional patterns of rural poverty.

The Measurement and Identification Problem

By what criteria should areas of economic stress be recognized? How are relative differences in regional levels of welfare to be measured? In reviewing the theoretical, empirical, and practical literature we are impressed by the ferocity of the arguments and the lack of any general agreement either about ways to identify areas of stress or methods of measuring its intensity.

Lord Kelvin's dictum, much debated and frequently excoriated in the social sciences, is nowhere more applicable than to these studies of the regional differentiation of poverty. Whatever they may be named (and we certainly name them many apparently synonymous things: study of areas of economic stress,[4] of distressed areas, of declining regions,[5] of regions of social and economic disadvantage,[6] of economic health,[7] of local viability,[8] of underdevelopment or of economic development,[9] and many more), these studies have comprised many poorly-integrated strands. There has been but little dialogue between theoretical-deductive and empirical-inductive analyses, and both of these have, in turn, been neglected or avoided by those concerned with public policy. Little wonder, then, that there is still no clear concept of the object of study, let alone of the costs and consequences of alternative forms of public action.

A variety of ingenious ways of indexing economic and social disadvantage has been developed using single or multiple criteria, but one is left with the feeling that causes, characteristics and consequences are being confused. Is a single object being considered, or do the discussions frequently run at cross purposes because poverty comprises more than a single syndrome? How can the

---

[4] Taken from the conference title. See also Thoman, R., "Areas of Economic Stress in Canada", paper presented at the Conference on Regional Development and Economic Change held by the Department of Economics and Development of Ontario at Toronto, February 15-17, 1965.

[5] See the companion conference paper by Scott, Anthony, "Policy for Declining Regions, A Theoretical Approach".

[6] A.R.D.A. folder of maps on areas of *Economic and Social Disadvantage in Canada*, Canada Department of Forestry, October, 1964.

[7] Bell, W. H. and D. W. Stevenson, "An Index of Economic Health for Ontario Counties and Districts", *Ontario Economic Review*, 2 (1964), No. 5.

[8] Hodge, G., "The Prediction of Trade Centre Viability in the Great Plains", paper presented at the 1964 Annual Meetings of the Regional Science Association, and forthcoming in the *Papers and Proceedings*.

[9] Berry, Brian J. L., "An Inductive Approach to the Regionalization of Economic Development", in Ginsburg, N., ed., *Essays on Geography and Economic Development*, Department of Geography Research Paper No. 62, University of Chicago, 1960, pp. 70-107.

problem of regional differentiation of welfare be addressed if no clear answers to this simple question are available? The dialogue would, we suspect, be furthered by some careful comparative classification and measurement.

In what follows we take a large number of criteria, all of which have been used at one time or another to study rural poverty, and by using a combination of factor analysis and certain other forms of dimensional anlaysis, we are able to conclude: (a) how many different *types* of social and economic disadvantage are actually being embraced by these many original criteria, and (b) what *regional pattern* of poverty is evidenced by each type. Then, by a process of interpretation which depends upon our understanding of the principles by which a socio-economy is organized spatially, we determine what relationships these types and patterns bear in the interdependencies giving form to space, so that we can then argue about causes and evaluate the potential effects of proposed policies. These steps, we would submit, solve the *identification problem.*

Factor analysis is a process with two distinct parts. Every factor analysis involves a "boiling-down" operation in which we find out how many underlying dimensions of variation express the "meat" of a much larger number of initial variables, many of which tell related stories and are therefore highly correlated. Secondly, factor analysis includes a "rotation" process by which the underlying variables are transformed mathematically so as to have the maximum intrinsic meaning. In the analyses which follow we always select a rotation such that principal factors (the underlying variables) as nearly as possible summarize mutually exclusive subsets of the original variables (the criterion of "simple struc-ture").[10]

Dimensional analysis supplements the factor analysis, first enabling precise measurements to be provided of the location of all original observations on the principal factor scales (the underlying dimensions of variation), and second allowing discriminatory analysis to be undertaken: (a) to find out the degree of similarity of observations on each scale and simultaneously on several of the scales, and (b) whether distinctive regional patterns exist.

The combination of factor and dimensional analysis, we would further submit, solves the *measurement problem* we identified earlier.

Measurement Methods

The complete process of analysis, combining factor and dimensional analysis, is as follows:

Given a matrix X of order n by m, in which the n refers to observations (say, countries, counties, municipalities, or census tracts) and the m to variables (say, proposed measures of social and economic disadvantage), form a matrix Z, again of order n by m in which the original variables have been normalized if necessary and then in which every variable has been expressed in the standardized form of zero mean and unit variance. Also form R, the m by m matrix of zero-order correlations among the variables based on Z. Then perform a principal axis factor analysis of $[R-U^2]$, where U^2 is a diagonal matrix containing the unique portion of the variance of each of the m variables. Generally, any u^2_i is estimated

---

[10]For an elaboration of this description of factor analysis see Tukey, J. W., "The Future of Data Analysis", *Annals of Mathematical Statistics*, 33 (1962), pp. 1-67. The rotation option selected is Kaiser's "normal varimax" criterion.

as $[1.0-h^2_i]$ where h^2_i, the communality of variable i, is approximated by computing the coefficient of determination resulting from the regression of i on the remaining $[m-1.0]$ variables in the set.

The principal axis factor analysis produces a matrix A of order m by r, such that $[R-U^2] =AA^T$ and $A^TA=\Lambda$. Any a_{ij} is a correlation coefficient, of variable i with factor or dimension j, there being r dimensions of variation underlying the original m variables. Λ is a diagonal matrix containing the λs, eigenvalues associated with each factor. An eigenvalue expresses that portion of the total common variance (given by the trace of $[R-U^2]$, which also equals the trace of Λ and of AA^T) accounted for by each of the underlying dimensions of variation. Since Λ is diagonal, the cross products of the factors are zero, i.e., they are not correlated, so that each dimension expresses an independent, additive part of the original whole given by the m variables. Which part of which of the original m variables has gone to constitute which of the factors may be determined by examining the factor loadings a_{ij} in the matrix A. In addition, one can compute the n by r matrix F by a pseudo-inverse method such that $F=ZA^{-1}$ and then scale the column vectors of F to zero mean and unit variance. Each f_{ij} is a factor score, the score given to observation i on factor j. The spatial variation of each factor can be seen by mapping the factor scores.

What is the degree of similarity of each pair of observations? This may be computed as distance between observations i and j in the r-space given by the dimensions, which since they are independent are also orthogonal, i.e., the dimensions intersect at right angles. Thus $d_{ij}=[\Sigma_r (f_{ir}-f_{jr})^2]^{1/2}$. This is simply the straight-line distance between the observations located as points in the scatter diagram of r dimensions, and distance increases as does the dissimilarity of the observations. If every pairwise distance is computed, it is possible to prepare the array D of order n by n, an inter-observation similarity matrix. A stepwise grouping procedure applied to this matrix will provide a near-optimal classification of the observations into as many subsets as are required. If a contiguous regionalization is required, this stepwise procedure is modified by use of a simple contiguity constraint. Iterative multiple discriminants will force the near optimal classification to converge to the optimal classification or regionalization, such that within-group distance (and therefore variance) is minimized and, by definition, between group variance (and therefore differentiation) maximized.

Examples

These methods were developed in a progressive series of studies. The first of these was at the international level. Forty-three proposed indexes to the level of economic development of ninety-five countries had been assembled as part of a larger project at the University of Chicago.[11] Berry was able to show by means of principal components analysis that these proposed indexes represented only four distinct dimensions along which the countries were differentiated (i.e., m = 43 but r = 4, a considerable simplification by elimination of redundancy).[12] The

[11]Ginsburg, Norton, *Atlas of Economic Development*, Chicago, University of Chicago Press, 1961.

[12]Berry, *op. cit.* In his study Berry drew inspiration from the earlier work of M. G. Kendall, "The Geographical Distribution of Crop Productivity in England", *Journal of the Royal Statistical Society*, 102 (1939), pp. 21-62; also M. J. Hagood, "Statistical Methodology for the Delineation of Regions Applied to Data on Agriculture and Population", *Social Forces*, 21 (1963), pp. 287-297.

dimensions were interpreted as: (a) the general scale of economic development which each of the proposed indexes had supposedly represented; (b) a dimension of demographic variation in birth, death and infant mortality rates; (c) a scale indexing countries by the extent of dualism in their economies; and (d) a measure of the effects of size of country.

Berry's approach was used by P. R. Gould and others in a study of economic health in New York State. The analysis was replicated by Bell and Stevenson in a study of Ontario using counties as the units of observation (n = 54) and sixteen variables (m = 16).[13] Among the variables used in the Bell-Stevenson study were measures of size, income level and accessibility, and indexes of change in population, economic activity, and the like. The authors expressed interest only in the first principal component resulting from the analysis, however, since this component showed the extent to which the original variables combined to form a vector of economic health, the creation of which was the object of the analysis. Among their conclusions was the fact that this vector appeared to differentiate counties on an urban-industrial to agricultural scale. However, they lamented the fact that use of county data shrouded much important and interesting intra-county variation for which smaller area data were not available. Fortunately, in the analysis reported below we have been able to correct this situation.

In a similar study undertaken using identical procedures in Saskatchewan Hodge analyzed the 473 trade centres of that province in terms of some thirty-five variables.[14] He found that six components summarized the variability of the centres as originally expressed in the thirty-five variables. These were interpreted as: (a) urbanism, or size and functional complexity of urban centres, indicating their position in the urban hierarchy; (b) agricultural adaptation, distinguishing those locales which have adapted themselves to the exigencies of a highly mechanized and commercialized agriculture; (c) underdevelopment, the classic syndrome with high negative loadings on private investment, agricultural land potential, community assets, and population over 65; (d) rural centredness; (e) isolation; and (f) peripheral development. Trade centre viability he found to be largely a function of rank on the urbanism scale; the lower the rank the greater the probability of decline.

Spatial Variation and Regionalization

In the international studies analyses were also undertaken of the spatial variations of countries using the factor scores computed for each country on each of the four dimensions of economic development.[15] Maps of each of the dimensions showed spatial variations in the classic way. Scatter diagrams locating countries as points in graphs by means of scores in the factor space revealed degrees of similarity and difference of the countries, and initial experiments with discriminant functions were made to provide means of grouping the countries

[13]Bell and Stevenson, op. cit. I am indebted to Mr. D. W. Stevenson, Director of the Economics Branch of the Ontario Department of Economics and Development for providing me with a complete set of the original data he used. The Gould study was originally published in the Annals of the Association of American Geographers and is now available as Development and Planning, Cambridge, The M.I.T. Press, 1964.

[14]Hodge, op. cit.

[15]Berry, op. cit., and Ginsburg.

into regions which had some formal properties of maximum internal homogeneity (minimum internal variance). Parallel explorations by Stone into use of distances as measures of similarity,[16] and by Ward into grouping algorithms designed to approximate minimum variance solutions[17] facilitated an initial statement of procedures for deriving optimal uniform regions.[18]

These procedures are as follows. Given the matrix D of order n by n, containing $n(n-1)/2$ distinct measures of interpoint distance (i.e., of similarity of the observations):

1) Identify that pair of observations for which d^2_{ij} is a minimum.[19]

2) Combine the row and column vectors of D represented by these observations into a single row and column vector representing the new group. The elements of these new vectors are the squared distances from the group centroid to all other points. The matrix D is now of order (n-1) by (n-1).

3) Repeat the process through a complete series of steps until a final pair of groups is linked into the entire population of observations. If, in forming distances between group centroids, the different sizes of groups are taken into account, groups will as nearly as possible be of uniform size. However, they may vary greatly in size if simple averaging of pairs of distances in vectors representing groups is undertaken.[20]

The result is a complete "linkage tree" which may be drawn to display the entire hierarchy of groups of observations.

The tree proceeds from n outermost branches, through (n-1) and (n-2) to i and (i-1) to 4, 3, 2 and finally the main trunk 1. It is possible to select that level deemed most desirable for a particular problem, and know that an optimal minimum-variance stratification has been achieved, subject only to previous steps in the group process. Where the observations have location in geographic space, the groups may form compact regional clusters, and thus indicate the presence of *multi-factor uniform regions*. However, where no constraint is imposed to ensure regional clustering, they may also indicate the geographic arrangement of *regional types*, such as type-of-farming areas. If the choice of the research analyst is for aggregation of observations into uniform regions, a simple contiguity constraint may be imposed upon step (1) of the grouping process, requiring that

---

[16]Stone, R., "A Comparison of the Economic Structure of Regions based on the Concept of Distance", *Journal of Regional Science*, 2 (1960), pp. 1-20. Also see Moser, C. A. and W. Scott, *British Towns*, Edinburgh, Oliver and Boyd, 1961.

[17] Ward, Joe H., Jr., "Hierarchical Grouping to Optimize an Objective Function", *Journal of the American Statistical Association*, 58 (1963), pp. 236-244.

[18]Berry, Brian J. L., "A Method for Deriving Multi-Factor Uniform Regions", *Przeglad Geograficzny*, 33 (1961), pp. 265-282.

[19]The squared distance is normally used because of its formal equivalence with the variance.

[20]Berry, Brian J. L., "Alternative Regionalization Algorithms under Contiguity Constraint", in preparation. Group size effects are taken into account as follows: Let d_i be a vector of squared distances for group i which had p members, and d_j be the same for group j of q members. Then the vector for the combined group of $p + q$ members is $d_{i+j} = \frac{1}{p+q}(p.d_i + q.d_j)$. Actually, a variety of objective functions is possible: (a) minimize contribution to within-group squared distance; (b) minimize within-group distance; (c) minimize average distance . . . etc. Each of these alternatives is included in The University of Chicago's Grouping Program for the IBM 7094, written by Peter M. Neely for the Dominion Bureau of Statistics.

the minimum d^2_{ij} selected only be from the subset of pairs which are geographically contiguous. The updating procedure then requires simply the statement that if any observation was contiguous to any of the group members before the group was formed, it must be contiguous to the group.[21]

The entire analytic procedure is illustrated in a study of the 120 census counties of Quebec and Ontario in terms of 88 cultural, demographic, housing, agricultural, urban and manufacturing variables, plus special income measures derived from income-tax returns.[22] Separate analyses were completed for each major group of variables and for the entire set together, and it was found that just three basic dimensions of social and economic differentiation repeated themselves: (a) differences between French and English Canada; (b) variations on an urban-rural scale; (c) contrasts between northern shield and more southerly lowlands. In addition, the agricultural variables indicated three type-of-farming dimensions (dairying, fruit and vegetables, and wheat and poultry), and the manufacturing variables located the Canadian manufacturing belt. A great amount of repetition was thus indicated in the many census variables normally reported for counties. Maps were provided of the spatial distribution of each of the factors. Scatter diagrams showed the regional differentiation of Ontario and Quebec. Finally both the unconstrained and the constrained grouping procedures were illustrated and the results contrasted in an example case in Eastern Ontario.

The regionalizations reported in the Ray-Berry study were near-optimal. Procedures and computer programs for iterating the near-optimal results to an optimal grouping using iterative multiple discriminant functions were recently provided by Casetti.[23] The analysis has also been extended to data matrices in which the observations are flows or connections between places (vector variables) instead of properties of places (scalar variables). Regions produced in this vectorial case are *multi-connection organizational regions*, the second of the classic types of geographic region. Use of vector variables, thereby specifying connectivity, eliminates the need to use any form of contiguity constraint.[24]

---

[21]Practically, the step is to code the squared distance $+$ if the observations are contiguous and group only positive distances. In combining vectors the following sign combinations become plus: $++$, $+-$, $-+$.

[22]Ray, D. Michael and Brian J. L. Berry, "Multivariate Socio-Economic Regionalization. A Pilot Study in Central Canada", in Rymes, T. and S. Ostry, eds., *Regional Statistical Studies,* Toronto, University of Toronto Press, 1965.

[23]Casetti, E., *Classificatory and Regional Analysis by Discriminant Iterations.* Technical Report No. 12, ONR Task No. 389-135, Contract NONR 1228(26), Department of Geography, Northwestern University, Evanston, Illinois, 1964. The full procedure of principal axis factor analysis, distance scaling, hierarchical grouping and discriminant iteration is utilized in a study of Indian cities forthcoming in the Department of Geography Research Series, University of Chicago, by Q. S. Ahmed, in 1965.

[24]For regionalizations based upon factor analysis of flow data see Berry, Brian J. L., "Structural Components of Changing Transport Network Flows", portion of a report submitted to the Army Transportation Command, Fort Eustis, Virginia, by the Transportation Center, Northwestern University, 1963. Also Garrison, W. L. and D. F. Marble, *The Structure of Transport Networks,* Department of Geography, Northwestern University, 1962. A study of the organizational regions of Ontario using census data on rail and truck flows is being completed as part of a study of reasons for the differential development of various sectors of the Canadian manufacturing belt by D. Michael Ray. This study will also be published in the Department of Geography Research Series of The University of Chicago in 1965.

Rural Poverty in Ontario

These methods, combining factor and dimensional analysis, may now be used to explore rural poverty in Ontario.[25] Five hundred and fifty-five municipalities were selected for study (all Ontario municipalities except certain large urban centres, Indian reservations, and undeveloped areas). They can be located on the maps which follow. For each of these municipalities, the Canada Department of Agriculture provided information concerning thirty-one separate variables. Since the Department of Agriculture work was ARDA-related, the variables correspond closely to those published on a county basis for the entire area of Canada by that agency in its folder of "Graphic Indicators of the Location and Degree of Economic and Social Disadvantage in Canada"[26] which in its approach evidences a multivariate consideration of the problems of poverty. From the thirty-one variables an additional sixteen were created by taking percentages and computing certain kinds of ratios. See Table 1, which also provides the "computer-code" names of each variable.

To save space, the tables of descriptive statistics and matrices of zero-order correlations for these variables in raw and normalized form will not be presented, although all were necessarily computed as a step prior to the factor analysis.

Factor Analysis

Tables 2-4 present results of principal axes factor analyses of the municipality data, in each case after rotation according to the normal varimax criterion.[27] For ease of reading, loadings lying between plus and minus 0.40 have been eliminated.

Aggregate Municipality Data

Tables 2 and 3 show the dimensionality and factor structure of twenty-six aggregate variables, in the first case untransformed and in the second normalized. Attention will be focussed on Table 3, since in it the variables satisfy the normality assumptions of factor analysis. The first table is included simply for comparative purposes, to show that transformations make enough change in detail of the factor structure to make satisfaction of the assumptions of normality important in subsequent interpretation of results.

---

[25] Note that a study of manufacturing development of Ontario is also being undertaken, footnote 24 above. In addition, as part of the Urban Renewal Study of the Metropolitan Toronto Planning Board, Robert A. Murdie is conducting a study of the changing socio-economic differentiation within that area using both census tract and very detailed enumeration area data. He has found that, as in all other North American cities, the inner differentiation may be expressed in terms of only three patterns, conventionally called social rank (or economic achievement), family structure, and segregation. The spatial variation of the former is sectorial with respect to the city centre, of the second radial, and of the third highly localized. Poverty and overcrowding are summarized by the first factor, densities by the second, and deterioration usually by the third, although certain special features of the pattern of deterioration are now being studied in detail. Murdie's study will also be one of The University of Chicago's Department of Geography Research Papers in 1965.

[26] *Op. cit.* Maps in the October 1964 folder are: counties and census divisions, distribution of population, low urban wages, low income farms, low rural non-farm wages, low non-farm family incomes, registrations for employment, low educational levels, and infant mortality rates.

[27] For further discussion of the procedures and terminology of factor analysis see Harman, H., *Modern Factor Analysis,* Chicago, University of Chicago Press, 1961.

TABLE 1

LIST OF VARIABLES*

1.	AVINCOME	Average total income per farm operator.
2.	FARMERS	Total farm operators.
3.	UNDER1TH	Number of farm operators with income under $1,000 per year.
4.	UNDER2TH	Number of farm operators with income under $2,000 per year.
5.	UNDER3TH	Number of farm operators with income under $3,000 per year.
6.	UNDER4TH	Number of farm operators with income under $4,000 per year.
7.	UNDER5TH	Number of farm operators with income under $5,000 per year.
8.	TOTFARMS	Total farms less residential farms and institutional farms.
9.	HRDCORE1	Index of "hard core" poverty farms: number of farm operators having capital investment of less than $25,000, gross sales of agricultural products of less than $2,500, works less than 25 days off the farm, and less than 55 years of age.
10.	SMALFRMS	Number of small-scale farms.
11.	LD+BLDGS	Total value of land and buildings on farms.
12.	MACHINRY	Total value of machinery on farms.
13.	LIVESTCK	Total value of livestock and poultry on farms.
14.	HRDCORE2	Number of Type 2 hard core poverty farmers: number of farm operators with capital investment of less than $15,000, gross sales of agricultural products of less than $2,500, works less than 25 days off the farm, and less than 55 years of age.
15.	INFANTMY	Infant mortality rate (county rates assigned).
16.	NONFRMFA	Number of non-farm families.
17.	NFUNDER1	Number of non-farm families with income of less than $1,000.
18.	NFUNDER2	Number of non-farm families with income of less than $2,000.
19.	NFUNDER3	Number of non-farm families with income of less than $3,000.
20.	NFUNDER4	Number of non-farm families with income of less than $4,000.
21.	NFOVER5$	Number of non-farm families with income of over $5,000.
22.	TOTPOP+5	Total rural population 5 years plus not now attending school.
23.	VARSITY1	Number having one or two years university education.
24.	VARSITY2	Number having three or more years university education.
25.	VARSITY3	Number reporting university degree.
26.	4THGRADE	Per cent reporting 4th grade or less education.
27.	8THGRADE	Per cent reporting 8th grade or less education.
28.	TOTHOMES	Total occupied dwellings.
29.	FLTOILET	Number reporting flush toilet.
30.	H+CWATER	Number reporting hot and cold running water.
31.	FURNACE	Number reporting furnace heat.
32.	PC UNDER1TH	Percentage of farmers with incomes of less than $1,000.
33.	PC UNDER2TH	Percentage of farmers with incomes of less than $2,000.
34.	PC UNDER3TH	Percentage of farmers with incomes of less than $3,000.
35.	PC UNDER4TH	Percentage of farmers with incomes of less than $4,000.
36.	PC UNDER5TH	Percentage of farmers with incomes of less than $5,000.
37.	PC HRD CORE1	Percentage of hard core poverty farmers type 1.
38.	PC SMAL FRMS	Percentage of small farms.
39.	M+L/L+B	Ratio of value of machinery and livestock to land and buildings.
40.	PC HRD CORE2	Percentage of hard core poverty farmers type 2.
41.	PC NF UNDER1	Percentage of non-farm residents with incomes of less than $1,000.
42.	PC NF UNDER2	Percentage of non-farm residents with incomes of less than $2,000.
43.	PC NF UNDER3	Percentage of non-farm residents with incomes of less than $3,000.
44.	PC NF UNDER4	Percentage of non-farm residents with incomes of less than $4,000.
45.	PC VARSITY	Percentage of population reporting university degree.
46.	PC FL TOILET	Percentage of population reporting toilets.
47.	PC H+C WATER	Percentage of population reporting hot and cold running water.

* Note: All definitions correspond to the last Census of Agriculture in Canada.

TABLE 2

FACTOR LOADINGS FOR ANALYSIS OF MUNICIPALITY AGGREGATES,
DATA UNTRANSFORMED

FACTOR NUMBER (BEFORE ROTATION)		1	2	3	5	4
SUM OF SQUARES		7.996	6.146	2.496	2.127	1.977
PER CENT 26 FACTORS		30.8	54.4	64.0	72.2	79.8
5 FACTORS		38.6	68.2	80.2	90.5	100.0
NO.	NAME	COMMUNALITY				
1	AVINCOME	0.711	—			—0.787
2	FARMERS	0.899	0.748			—0.500
3	UNDER1TH	0.835	0.868			—
4	UNDER2TH	0.904	0.920			—
5	UNDER3TH	0.933	0.934			—
6	UNDER4TH	0.925	0.919			—
7	UNDER5TH	0.914	0.900			—
8	TOTFARMS	0.884	0.729			—0.517
9	HRDCORE1	0.842	0.891			—
10	SMALFRMS	0.836	0.893			—
11	MACHINRY	0.429	—			0.478
12	HRDCORE2	0.783	—0.779	—		—
13	INFANTMY	0.219		—		
14	NONFRMFA	0.869		—0.831		
15	NFUNDER1	0.878		—	0.913	
16	NFUNDER2	0.687		—0.487	0.533	
17	NFUNDER3	0.718		—0.561	0.492	
18	NFUNDER4	0.818		—	0.882	
19	NFOVER5$	0.852		—0.809		—
20	VARSITY2	0.592		—		—0.637
21	4THGRADE	0.661		—		0.749
22	8THGRADE	0.800		—		0.830
23	TOTHOMES	0.954		—0.899		—
24	FLTOILET	0.934		—0.919		—
25	H+CWATER	0.937		—0.917		—
26	FURNACE	0.927		—0.928		—

TABLE 3

FACTOR LOADINGS FOR ANALYSIS OF MUNICIPALITY AGGREGATES,
DATA TRANSFORMED

FACTOR NUMBER (BEFORE ROTATION)		1	2	3	5	4
SUM OF SQUARES		8.290	4.725	4.468	1.976	1.949
PER CENT 26 FACTORS		31.9	50.1	67.2	74.8	82.3
5 FACTORS		38.7	60.8	81.7	90.9	100.0
NO.	NAME	COMMUNALITY				
1	AVINCOME	0.654		—0.518	—0.556	
2	FARMERS	0.906	0.750	—0.414		
3	UNDER1TH	0.833	0.853			
4	UNDER2TH	0.901	0.906			
5	UNDER3TH	0.932	0.917			
6	UNDER4TH	0.930	0.899			
7	UNDER5TH	0.924	0.879			
8	TOTFARMS	0.894	0.741	—0.442		

9	HRDCORE1	0.861	0.909					
10	SMALFRMS	0.834	0.879					
11	MACHINRY	0.480	—		0.620			
12	HRDCORE2	0.805	0.811					
13	INFANTMY	0.475				0.660		
14	NONFRMFA	0.917		—0.733	—0.499			
15	NFUNDER1	0.584		—0.752				
16	NFUNDER2	0.854		—0.845				
17	NFUNDER3	0.864		—0.829				
18	NFUNDER4	0.926		—0.869				
19	NFOVER5$	0.860		—0.654	—0.533			
20	VARSITY2	0.727						0.830
21	4THGRADE	0.724					0.735	
22	8THGRADE	0.813						—0.768
23	TOTHOMES	0.925	0.434	—0.470	—0.680			
24	FLTOILET	0.941			—0.769			
25	H+CWATER	0.946			—0.772			
26	FURNACE	0.902			—0.760			

Factor one in Table 3 associates all variables dealing with low farm incomes, small farms, large numbers of farmers, plus the two "hard core rural poverty" indexes constructed by the Canada Department of Agriculture. This is clearly a scale of *farm poverty*.

Similarly, factor two relates all non-farm low income data, and is a scale of *rural non-farm poverty*.

Note the implication: rural farm and rural non-farm poverty are distinct, independent dimensions. Note also that average incomes of farm operators are related to neither of these two dimensions. Instead, average income appears to be a variable in which two aggregate patterns of variation are merged. One of these, factor three, appears related to densities: where numbers of both farm and non-farm families are highest and the degree of mechanization of agriculture is least, incomes are highest and there are the greatest numbers of homes reporting household facilities. The second, factor four, states an inverse relationship between incomes and education, showing that where educational levels are lowest, so are average incomes, but infant mortality rates are highest. Finally, factor five shows an inverse relationship in the educational data between areas with the lowest and areas with the highest levels of education.

Percentage Municipality Data

Table 4 records results of factor analysis of 20 percentage-type variables. Factor one in this case reveals *relative rural farm poverty*: where the proportion of farm operatives with low incomes is greatest, average incomes of farm operatives are lowest, and there are low levels of household services. Factor two points out *relative rural non-farm poverty*, associating greater proportions of low income rural non-farm residents with low levels of educational attainment and low levels of household services. The third factor again relates to rural non-farm incomes, although from the factor loadings alone it is by no means clear how one should interpret what it means. Finally, the fourth factor points out areas of *relative social disadvantage* in which low educational attainment and high infant mortality rates are highly correlated.

TABLE 4

FACTOR LOADINGS FOR ANALYSIS OF UNTRANSFORMED PERCENTAGE DATA FOR MUNICIPALITIES

FACTOR NUMBER (BEFORE ROTATION)		1	2	3	4
SUM OF SQUARES		6.487	3.543	1.997	1.750
PER CENT 20 FACTORS		32.4	50.1	60.1	68.9
4 FACTORS		47.1	72.8	87.3	100.0

NO.	NAME	COMMUNALITY				
1	AVINCOME	0.484	—0.663	—		—
2	INFANTMY	0.326	—	—		0.558
3	4THGRADE	0.672	—	—		0.750
4	8THGRADE	0.746	—	—0.539		0.660
5	PC UNDER1TH	0.711	0.824			
6	PC UNDER2TH	0.847	0.901			
7	PC UNDER3TH	0.866	0.901			
8	PC UNDER4TH	0.848	0.897			
9	PC UNDER5TH	0.774	0.858			
10	PC HRD CORE1	0.589	0.676			
11	PC SMAL FRMS	0.641	0.789			
12	M+L/L+B	0.401	—	—0.533		
13	PC HRD CORE2	0.600	0.678	—		
14	PC NF UNDER1	0.990		—	0.995	
15	PC NF UNDER2	0.653		—0.791	—	
16	PC NF UNDER3	0.692		—0.814	—	
17	PC NF UNDER4	0.988		—	0.994	
18	PC VARSITY	0.478		0.552		—0.415
19	PC FL TOILET	0.712	—0.447	0.685		—
20	PC H+C WATER	0.760	—0.473	0.700		—

Table 5 shows that the factors are indeed orthonormal: means are zero, variances are unity, and the cross products are zero. Slight noise has been introduced because there were a few items of missing data which required approximations to factor scores to be made, but the important conclusion that the four factors described above are independent must be underscored.

Dimensional Analysis

Interpretation of the four factors shown by factor analysis to summarize the twenty percentage-type variables is facilitated by dimensional procedures. Table 6 lists the scores of each municipality on each of the four factors by analysis numbers 1-555, and then records the county and municipality identification of each.

Inspection of the scores for factor three shows that only one municipality (Freeman in Muskoka County) stand out, by virtue of a unique bimodal rural non-farm income distribution peaked in the lowest and highest classes. We believe this to be a result of sampling variability, and thus will disregard factor three in all that follows, although one suggestion has been that if the "wild-shot" is ignored, higher scores pick out areas with weaker bimodal income distributions caused by recent influx of middle-class commuters into very low income farming regions.

TABLE 5

DESCRIPTIVE STATISTICS FOR VECTORS OF FACTOR SCORES,
UNTRANSFORMED PERCENTAGE DATA ANALYSIS

FACTOR SCORE STATISTICS

	1	2	3	4
MEANS	—0.05	0.00	0.01	0.02
S.D.	1.01	0.99	1.00	1.03

CORRELATION COEFFICIENTS

	1	2	3	4
1	1.00			
2	—0.06	1.00		
3	—0.02	0.01	1.00	
4	—0.06	0.02	—0.08	1.00

To aid interpretation of the remaining three factors, maps have been prepared from the scores, with class intervals selected to provide extra differentiation at the end of the scales indicating poverty. However, because of the cartographic work involved, we have only mapped the southwestern and eastern Ontario municipalities (six maps rather than twelve), although inclusion of the scores in Table 6 should enable the reader to compare these maps with the northerly cases (we include base maps showing the municipalities for the northern balance of the province).

Figures 1 and 2 show the spatial pattern of scores on factor one, the scale measuring differences in relative farm poverty. Immediately evident is the contrast between Eastern and Southern Ontario. In Eastern Ontario (darker shades) relative farm poverty is much greater than in the south. Note how the darkest shades delineate the upland areas and poorer soils of the shield as it penetrates southwards along Frontenac axis, whereas the lightest shades are characteristic of the counties from Bruce to Brant and Waterloo to Essex. The overwhelming picture is one of variations in farm poverty as a correlate of variations in the resource endowment.

The "patchiness" of relative rural non-farm poverty in the next pair of maps is quite deceiving. Patterns on Figures 3 and 4 appear to be intermixed haphazardly. Yet this is far from the case. High scores, indicated by light shades and indicating prosperity, encircle the urban municipalities excluded from the analysis, embrace all municipalities containing the larger urban places that remained in the analysis, and extend in a loop around the edges of Algonquin Park in Eastern Ontario. The darker shades, indicative of relative rural non-farm poverty, follow the inter-urban peripheries. This may be seen more clearly in Figure 5, in which the zero contour has been interpolated by using centres of municipalities as control points. All areas with positive scores have been cross-hatched within the zero contour. These shaded areas are the ones with wealthier rural non-farm residents, and each centres upon an urban area of some size or represents the coalescence of zones focussing upon several urban centres. Dotted lines follow the lowest scores—the zones of rural non-farm poverty—and trace the watersheds between each urban "system". Evidently, rural non-farm poverty is related to the spatial organization of activities around the higher-order marketing centres, i.e., to the upper levels of the central place system.[28] Much of the pattern of prosperity must be related to commuting, so that the zones delineated should correspond to Ontario's labour sheds. The least accessible areas are those least able to take advantage of urban employment opportunities.[29] In addition, comparison of Figures 3, 4 and 5 with Figures 6 and 7 shows clearly enough that the zones of rural non-farm prosperity are the zones of recent population increase as Ontario continues to urbanize, whereas the inter-urban peripheries are the zones of greatest population decline.[30] Since some large share of this differential must be due to migration, the observation is consistent with our concepts of migration and economic opportunity. In Figures 6 and 7 the darkest shade indicates areas which experienced more than 13 per cent increase in population 1956-1961; the lighter shade indicates growth of less than 13 per cent; and the white areas lost population.

Figures 8 and 9 show areas of relative social disadvantage. The darkest shades identify municipalities in which the levels of education are lowest and infant mortality rates are the highest. This combination is, of course, symptomatic of a much larger syndrome. Perhaps the most noteworthy feature is the manner in which the zones of French occupancy stand out, shaded darkly, in Eastern Ontario. The reader will undoubtedly note other cases. For example, in the tobacco growing region and fruit farming areas of Simcoe and Elgin counties permanent farm labourers and migrant farm workers from Quebec, North Carolina and Virginia also give rise to a zone of social disadvantage.

Types and Regions.

Imagine a three-dimensional graph (scatter diagram) in which the 555 municipalities have been plotted as points using their scores on factors one, two and four. The differentiation according to factor one is based upon farm poverty and is most related to resource differentials. That according to factor two derives from rural non-farm poverty and is distributed spatially according to the pattern of urban organization and alignments of the inter-urban watersheds. Factor four differentials are those of social disadvantage, and appear to stem from cultural deprivation among the French Canadians. Each dimension is independent of the others; location of a particular municipality on one of the scales does not affect the probabilities associated with location of that municipality on either of the other two scales.

---

[28]For related contributions, see the kinds of documentation assembled in the following publications: Province of Saskatchewan, *Service Centers*, Regina, Queen's Printer, 1957; Borchert, J. R., *The Urbanization of the Upper Midwest 1930-1960*, Minneapolis, Upper Midwest Economic Study, University of Minnesota, 1963; Borchert and R. B. Adams, *Trade Centers and Tributary Areas of the Upper Midwest*, University of Minnesota, 1963; Adams, *Population Mobility in the Upper Midwest*, University of Minnesota, 1964; Borchert, T. L. Anding and M. G. Gildermeister, *Urban Dispersal in the Upper Midwest*, University of Minnesota, 1964. Also see Karl Fox's discourse on the functional economic area in W. R. Maki and B. J. L. Berry, *Strategy for Regional Growth*, Ames, Iowa State University Press, 1965.

[29]See in particular Adams, *op. cit.* and Reino Ajo, *Tampereen Liikennealue*, Helsinki, 1944; ————, "Liikenealueiden Kehittyminen Suomessa", *Fennia*, 69 (1946); ————, "An Approach to Demographical System Analysis", *Economic Geography*, 38 (1962), pp. 359-371.

[30]Borchert and Adams, *op. cit.*, Hodge, *op. cit.*

TABLE 6

FACTOR SCORES FOR MUNICIPALITIES BASED ON ANALYSIS OF UNTRANSFORMED PERCENTAGE DATA

OBSERVATION	FACTOR SCORES				COUNTY	MUNICIPALITY
	1	2	3	4		
1	0.28	0.58	—0.09	—0.14	ALGOMA 1	1
2	—0.38	2.21	—0.07	—0.53		2
3	1.31	0.89	—0.03	—1.18		3
4	2.14	—0.25	—0.11	0.37		4
5	0.33	—0.39	—0.11	—0.31		5
6	—0.29	—0.56	0.39	—0.14		7
7	0.45	—0.34	—0.06	—0.34		8
8	—0.29	2.28	—0.08	—0.42		9
9	0.46	0.07	—0.11	—0.87		10
10	1.47	1.84	0.02	0.54		11
11	0.55	—0.98	—0.03	—0.90		12
12	0.43	—0.51	—0.10	—0.25		13
13	—0.10	—1.84	0.37	—0.47		15
14	—1.04	—1.53	—0.09	1.04		16
15	—0.71	1.22	—0.01	0.14		17
16	—1.84	—0.32	0.06	5.11		18
17	—0.64	1.47	—0.06	—0.33	BRANT 2	1
18	—1.63	—0.01	0.01	0.69		2
19	—0.97	1.21	—0.01	—1.17		3
20	—1.19	1.43	—0.13	0.32		4
21	—0.68	0.62	—0.11	—0.39		5
22	0.67	—1.27	0.23	0.61		6
23	0.38	—0.90	—0.09	—0.43	BRUCE 3	1
24	0.13	—0.73	0.19	—0.18		2
25	—0.42	—0.19	—0.14	—0.03		3
26	—0.92	—0.18	—0.04	0.42		4
27	—0.54	—0.27	—0.01	—0.46		5
28	—1.19	—0.95	0.11	0.63		6
29	—0.85	—0.16	—0.01	—0.09		7
30	0.11	—1.50	0.07	—0.88		8
31	—0.82	—0.39	0.04	—0.54		9
32	—1.30	—1.11	0.10	0.27		10
33	—0.91	0.23	—0.07	—0.72		11
34	—1.04	—1.06	0.04	—0.61		12
35	—0.81	—1.51	—0.07	—0.38		13
36	0.38	—3.77	0.14	—1.05		14
37	—0.29	—1.40	—0.17	—0.20		15
38	—0.48	—0.09	—0.05	—0.55		16
39	—0.62	—0.01	0.03	—0.85	CARLETON 4	1
40	0.45	1.26	—0.15	—0.55		3
41	—0.21	1.28	—0.04	—1.75		4
42	0.44	0.96	—0.14	—0.80		5
43	—0.32	—0.23	0.08	—0.30		6
44	0.42	0.26	—0.11	—0.34		7
45	—0.18	0.89	—0.14	—0.59		9
46	—0.02	0.67	—0.18	0.04		10
47	0.54	0.81	—0.05	1.04	COCHRANE 5	1
48	0.21	1.27	—0.09	1.49		2
49	—0.05	1.03	—0.11	1.78		3
50	—0.03	0.01	—0.23	2.26		4
51	—2.14	0.95	—0.15	2.41		5
52	—1.14	1.60	—0.24	5.03		6

OBSERVATION	FACTOR SCORES				COUNTY	MUNICIPALITY
	1	2	3	4		
53	—0.04	0.98	—0.20	1.91		8
54	0.50	0.96	—0.12	1.86		9
55	0.07	1.39	—0.21	2.40		11
56	—0.68	—0.75	0.12	—0.31	DUFFERIN 6	1
57	—1.42	—0.41	—0.09	0.04		2
58	—0.78	0.51	0.05	—0.24		3
59	—0.62	—0.13	—0.09	0.29		4
60	0.06	0.56	—0.11	—0.18		5
61	—0.67	—0.40	0.07	0.04		6
62	—0.29	—1.16	0.09	0.33	DUNDAS 7	1
63	—0.65	—0.90	—0.08	—0.07		2
64	0.02	—0.56	—0.01	0.09		3
65	—0.85	—0.43	—0.11	0.05		4
66	—0.55	—0.32	0.07	—0.28	DURHAM 8	1
67	0.09	—0.10	0.05	—0.99		2
68	—0.43	0.54	—0.05	—0.29		3
69	—0.60	1.00	—0.07	0.12		4
70	0.13	0.49	—0.06	—0.24		5
71	0.04	—0.06	—0.01	0.33		6
72	—1.05	0.10	—0.04	—0.05	ELGIN 9	1
73	—1.87	0.11	0.01	0.61		2
74	—1.03	0.16	0.01	—1.23		3
75	—0.41	—0.55	—0.02	—1.25		4
76	—1.48	0.25	—0.01	—0.24		5
77	—0.70	0.57	0.01	—1.07		6
78	—0.76	1.31	—0.06	0.10		7
79	—0.23	1.44	—0.02	0.53	ESSEX 10	1
80	—0.60	0.37	—0.01	0.55		2
81	—1.30	0.45	0.03	—0.03		3
82	—0.72	0.98	—0.03	0.22		4
83	—0.76	1.13	—0.02	—0.27		5
84	—0.35	1.43	—0.05	0.07		6
85	—1.20	1.14	—0.05	—0.30		7
86	—0.91	0.88	—0.01	0.63		8
87	—0.88	0.26	—0.06	0.85		9
88	—1.16	0.34	—0.03	0.48		10
89	—1.09	0.42	—0.11	0.67		14
90	—0.59	0.63	—0.05	0.22		15
91	1.36	—0.65	0.13	0.13	FRONTENAC 11	1
92	1.09	—1.66	—0.08	—0.45		2
93	1.59	—1.01	0.04	—0.22		3
94	1.05	—0.83	—0.14	0.06		4
95	0.54	—0.15	0.79	—1.05		5
96	2.20	—1.06	0.12	0.07		6
97	0.54	1.91	—0.11	—1.12		7
98	0.34	—0.13	—0.02	—0.97		8
99	0.79	—1.42	0.06	0.52		9
100	0.74	—0.72	—0.03	—0.74		10
101	2.40	—0.57	0.13	—0.34		11
102	0.09	—0.46	0.04	—0.02		13
103	—0.13	—0.07	0.03	—0.69		14
104	—0.12	—1.04	—0.11	—0.92		15
105	0.07	0.27	0.03	0.69	GLENGARRY 12	1
106	0.52	—0.84	—0.01	1.06		2
107	0.06	—0.22	0.05	0.97		3
108	0.45	—0.99	0.08	1.33		4

OBSERVATION	FACTOR SCORES				COUNTY	MUNICIPALITY
	1	2	3	4		
109	0.75	0.67	—0.10	—1.58	GRENVILLE 13	1
110	0.09	—0.24	—0.09	—1.27		2
111	—0.17	—1.07	—0.17	—1.33		3
112	0.85	—0.51	0.01	—1.58		4
113	0.32	—0.34	—0.13	—1.59		5
114	0.29	—0.86	0.05	—1.39	GREY 14	1
115	—0.30	—1.30	0.16	—0.89		2
116	—0.01	0.31	—0.04	—1.48		3
117	—0.31	0.22	—0.01	—1.23		4
118	—0.43	0.10	—0.13	0.13		5
119	—0.73	—1.61	0.05	—1.22		6
120	0.45	—1.02	—0.12	—0.76		7
121	0.39	—0.72	—0.04	—1.17		8
122	—0.13	—0.92	—0.09	—1.15		9
123	—0.69	—0.74	—0.12	—0.08		10
124	—0.15	—1.11	—0.08	—1.08		11
125	0.08	—0.70	—0.07	—1.08		12
126	—0.53	0.03	—0.12	—0.82		13
127	—0.03	0.10	0.02	—1.29		14
128	—0.49	—1.80	0.13	—0.56		15
129	0.01	—0.23	—0.03	—1.03		16
130	0.26	0.90	—0.13	—0.80	HALDIMAN 15	1
131	—0.10	0.36	—0.07	—1.45		2
132	—0.30	0.20	—0.11	—0.43		3
133	—0.40	0.36	—0.11	—0.88		4
134	—0.06	—0.07	—0.11	—0.28		5
135	—1.33	0.36	0.05	—0.63		6
136	—0.40	—0.15	—0.07	—0.80		7
137	—0.37	0.90	—0.16	—0.35		8
138	0.86	0.65	—0.11	—0.13		9
139	—0.67	0.45	—0.13	—0.53		10
140	1.77	1.43	—0.08	0.12	HALIBURTON 16	1
141	—0.29	2.60	—0.10	—0.38		2
142	0.28	—0.33	—0.01	0.54		3
143	2.36	1.20	0.01	0.52		4
144	2.78	1.01	—0.02	0.34		5
145	1.72	—0.10	—0.08	—0.13		6
146	2.66	0.51	—0.05	0.47		7
147	—1.75	0.97	—0.16	0.98		8
148	0.54	—1.90	0.15	—0.30		9
149	1.20	0.66	—0.12	0.60		10
150	—0.54	1.10	—0.03	—0.81	HALTON 17	1
151	0.04	1.08	—0.17	—0.41		2
152	1.52	—1.06	0.19	0.48	HASTINGS 18	1
153	1.57	—0.87	—0.18	—0.61		2
154	0.89	—0.72	0.02	0.02		3
155	0.87	—1.69	0.10	—0.06		4
156	1.94	1.70	—0.10	0.18		5
157	1.92	—0.48	—0.08	0.05		6
158	0.18	—1.09	0.11	—0.68		7
159	0.48	—0.53	—0.17	—0.50		8
160	1.32	—0.54	—0.12	—0.17		9
161	—0.30	—1.68	0.07	—0.45		10
162	0.62	—1.19	—0.03	—0.83		11
163	1.42	—1.47	—0.16	0.08		12
164	1.52	—0.68	—0.12	0.63		13

OBSERVATION	FACTOR SCORES				COUNTY	MUNICIPALITY
	1	2	3	4		
165	—0.64	—1.32	0.02	—0.50		14
166	0.09	1.46	—0.12	—1.57		15
167	—0.41	0.55	—0.14	—0.43		16
168	1.73	—1.10	0.09	0.28		17
169	0.20	—1.12	0.01	—0.82		18
170	1.65	—0.81	—0.13	0.02		19
171	—0.91	—1.38	0.20	—0.97	HURON 19	1
172	—0.44	—0.05	0.03	—1.07		2
173	—0.46	0.24	0.09	—0.58		3
174	—1.18	—0.79	0.06	—0.76		4
175	—0.84	0.10	—0.10	—0.33		5
176	—1.25	—0.47	—0.07	—0.24		6
177	—1.10	—0.15	0.03	0.56		7
178	—1.83	—1.60	0.44	—0.76		8
179	—1.33	—1.41	0.17	—0.97		9
180	—0.80	—0.21	0.11	—2.08		10
181	—0.32	1.08	—0.01	—1.17		11
182	—0.79	1.31	—0.06	—0.90		12
183	—1.02	—1.79	0.07	—0.73		13
184	—1.58	—0.30	—0.06	—0.73		14
185	—1.02	—0.78	—0.05	—0.91		15
186	—0.79	—0.65	—0.12	—1.01		16
187	—1.14	0.47	—0.23	3.26	KENORA 20	1
188	—0.52	1.17	—0.20	0.96		2
189	0.17	—0.16	—0.23	1.37		3
190	—0.90	—0.08	—0.26	0.93		4
191	—0.69	2.18	—0.08	1.64	PATRICIA PORTION	1
192	—1.30	—0.33	—0.12	3.28		2
193	—0.63	—0.39	0.22	—2.47	KENT 21	1
194	—1.29	0.55	0.05	0.18		2
195	—1.43	0.20	0.02	0.46		3
196	—1.15	0.73	—0.06	—0.29		4
197	—1.41	—0.51	0.11	—0.59		5
198	—0.78	—0.02	—0.00	—0.51		6
199	—0.98	0.91	—0.00	—0.05		7
200	—1.15	0.42	—0.01	0.42		8
201	—1.37	0.62	—0.06	0.63		9
202	—0.67	0.53	—0.07	0.07		10
203	—0.71	0.18	—0.03	—0.46	LAMBTON 22	1
204	—0.76	—0.55	0.02	—0.51		2
205	—0.46	—1.21	—0.04	—0.58		3
206	—0.32	0.43	—0.14	—0.11		4
207	—0.26	—0.68	—0.06	—0.46		5
208	—0.07	1.27	—0.05	—0.63		6
209	—0.17	0.34	—0.03	—0.44		7
210	—0.32	1.20	—0.07	—0.10		8
211	0.17	0.60	0.06	0.17		9
212	—0.97	—0.34	—0.02	—0.42		10
213	0.53	—0.74	—0.16	—0.85	LANARK 23	1
214	0.75	0.09	—0.05	—0.79		2
215	0.75	—0.44	—0.18	—1.04		3
216	0.62	—2.01	0.33	—0.64		4
217	0.96	—2.62	0.06	3.74		5
218	—0.03	—0.65	0.07	—1.17		6
219	0.65	0.28	—0.16	—0.70		7
220	0.53	—0.74	—0.10	—0.82		8

OBSERVATION	FACTOR SCORES				COUNTY	MUNICIPALITY
	1	2	3	4		
221	0.60	—1.33	—0.12	0.69		9
222	0.87	0.70	—0.03	4.39		10
223	—0.10	—0.06	0.06	—0.83		11
224	—0.17	—0.42	0.00	—0.83		12
225	1.37	—0.86	—0.14	—0.50		13
226	0.14	—0.88	—0.07	—1.51	LEEDS 24	1
227	1.03	—0.30	0.04	—2.27		2
228	0.31	—0.96	—0.06	—1.65		3
229	0.11	0.43	—0.13	—0.44		4
230	0.85	0.82	—0.14	—1.68		5
231	0.73	—0.22	—0.05	—1.07		6
232	0.32	—0.59	—0.01	—1.05		7
233	0.25	—0.00	—0.06	—1.40		8
234	0.18	—0.68	—0.03	—1.48		9
235	0.63	—0.69	0.04	—0.14		10
236	0.15	—0.14	—0.19	—0.63		11
237	—0.17	—0.03	—0.14	—1.15	LENNOX 25	1
238	1.38	—1.09	—0.26	—2.40		2
239	0.49	—0.87	—0.00	—1.27		3
240	1.64	—0.79	—0.04	0.23		4
241	0.88	1.18	—0.12	—1.71		5
242	0.51	—0.44	—0.03	—1.16		6
243	—0.22	0.03	—0.15	—1.84		7
244	1.52	—1.59	—0.00	—0.83		8
245	—0.31	—0.80	—0.08	—1.27		9
246	0.08	—2.26	0.01	—1.52		10
247	—0.57	0.02	—0.01	0.18	LINCOLN 26	1
248	—0.02	1.54	—0.04	—0.96		2
249	—0.42	—0.17	—0.05	—0.17		3
250	0.50	2.36	—0.06	—1.85		4
251	—0.12	0.91	—0.07	—0.87		5
252	—0.83	1.39	—0.03	—1.13		6
253	—0.02	1.55	—0.07	—0.45		7
254	0.97	—0.26	—0.15	—1.05	MANITOULIN 27	1
255	—0.47	—0.34	0.81	—0.72		2
256	0.66	—0.19	—0.07	—0.24		3
257	0.28	—1.85	—0.15	0.36		4
258	0.82	—0.30	—0.10	—1.21		5
259	—1.82	—2.61	—0.16	2.99		6
260	0.36	1.26	—0.03	—1.49		7
261	1.16	0.02	—0.13	—0.25		8
262	—1.06	—0.28	—0.20	0.90		9
263	0.26	—1.57	—0.03	—1.06		10
264	1.04	—0.47	—0.07	—0.71		11
265	—1.26	0.39	—0.11	—0.14	MIDDLESEX 28	1
266	—0.59	0.42	—0.04	—0.81		2
267	—1.60	0.08	0.11	0.65		3
268	—0.37	1.61	—0.12	—0.75		4
269	—0.93	0.88	—0.08	—0.22		5
270	—0.82	—0.54	0.13	—0.46		6
271	—0.62	0.60	—0.05	—0.55		7
272	—0.95	—0.04	0.05	—0.48		9
273	—0.71	—0.59	—0.10	—0.36		10
274	—0.26	—0.27	—0.03	—0.39		11
275	—0.71	0.79	—0.04	—0.48		12
276	—0.85	—0.06	—0.20	—0.57		14

OBSERVATION	FACTOR SCORES				COUNTY	MUNICIPALITY
	1	2	3	4		
277	—0.50	0.09	—0.13	0.12		15
278	—0.20	—0.50	—0.06	0.04	MUSKOKA 29	1
279	—0.37	—3.15	—0.15	—0.97		2
280	0.05	0.58	—0.03	0.39		3
281	1.86	0.06	—0.04	0.52		4
282	0.17	0.50	—0.01	—0.37		5
283	—0.44	0.91	23.34	—1.75		6
284	—1.25	0.09	—0.04	0.21		7
285	1.11	0.19	—0.07	0.33		8
286	1.35	1.80	—0.04	—0.72		9
287	0.53	0.59	—0.05	—0.57		10
288	—1.00	—0.71	0.17	—0.80		11
289	0.31	0.07	0.08	0.91		12
290	0.68	0.46	—0.10	0.28		13
291	—1.98	—0.07	0.25	0.28		14
292	0.54	—0.85	—0.15	0.72		15
293	0.55	—0.55	—0.08	—0.35		16
294	0.80	—0.74	—0.07	0.12		17
295	0.54	—0.74	0.10	—0.24		18
296	0.49	—1.22	0.09	0.53	NIPISSING 30	1
297	—1.33	—0.52	0.27	1.31		2
298	0.85	—2.23	—0.01	0.72		3
299	0.10	—1.97	—0.08	1.20		4
300	0.52	—0.99	—0.12	1.15		5
301	1.69	0.83	—0.03	1.15		6
302	—2.27	0.49	—0.05	1.93		7
303	0.31	—0.63	0.07	1.62		8
304	4.25	—0.73	—0.10	1.26		9
305	0.41	—1.18	0.10	1.68		10
306	—0.15	—0.04	0.04	1.18		11
307	—0.33	1.84	—0.07	—0.20		12
308	—2.32	—0.18	—0.06	1.47	NORFOLK 31	1
309	—2.46	—0.44	0.02	1.93		2
310	—2.36	0.43	0.02	1.34		3
311	—0.79	0.40	—0.02	1.02		4
312	—2.91	—0.11	—0.06	1.35		5
313	—1.40	—0.24	—0.08	0.69		6
314	—2.35	0.35	0.02	1.36		7
315	—0.35	1.16	—0.10	0.01		8
316	0.04	—0.55	—0.09	1.38	NORTHUMBERLAND 32	1
317	—0.39	0.02	0.01	—0.07		2
318	0.06	0.42	—0.06	0.38		3
319	—0.10	0.44	—0.03	0.38		4
320	—0.20	1.22	—0.08	—0.47		5
321	—0.82	—0.60	—0.11	0.21		6
322	0.46	0.79	—0.07	0.16		7
323	0.05	—0.37	—0.13	—0.04		8
324	—0.48	—0.38	—0.04	0.31		9
325	—0.84	—0.39	—0.06	—0.63	ONTARIO 33	1
326	0.69	—0.02	—0.00	—0.65		2
327	0.42	—0.86	—0.08	—0.70		4
328	—0.55	—0.25	0.02	—0.77		5
329	—0.68	0.00	—0.01	—0.42		6
330	—0.52	0.18	—0.07	—0.68		7
331	0.19	—0.38	—0.10	—0.93		8
332	0.36	0.47	—0.05	—0.47		9

OBSERVATION	FACTOR SCORES				COUNTY	MUNICIPALITY
	1	2	3	4		
333	—0.14	1.72	—0.06	—0.74		10
334	—0.13	1.52	—0.09	—0.45		11
335	—1.48	—0.75	0.08	—0.36	OXFORD 34	1
336	—1.15	0.47	—0.05	—0.50		2
337	—1.23	0.39	—0.04	—0.78		3
338	—1.01	0.83	—0.11	—1.08		4
339	—1.22	0.50	—0.07	—0.56		5
340	—2.28	0.53	0.01	0.59		6
341	—0.83	0.93	—0.02	—0.79		7
342	—1.13	0.59	—0.09	—0.84		8
343	—1.47	0.54	—0.00	—0.33		9
344	—1.58	0.51	—0.01	1.04		10
345	—1.13	—0.29	—0.06	—1.14		11
346	1.15	0.73	—0.00	—0.05	PARRY SOUND 35	1
347	1.49	0.68	—0.14	0.92		2
348	1.46	0.31	—0.12	1.35		3
349	0.65	—1.29	—0.09	0.40		4
350	1.58	1.22	—0.12	0.87		5
351	1.28	—1.37	0.16	0.12		6
352	3.42	1.06	0.00	0.70		7
353	—0.13	0.16	—0.11	1.04		8
354	1.07	0.28	—0.09	—0.23		9
355	1.96	0.23	—0.08	0.32		10
356	0.14	0.91	—0.07	1.26		11
357	1.71	0.92	—0.14	—0.12		12
358	3.11	—0.22	0.01	0.55		13
359	1.68	—1.15	0.32	0.85		14
360	0.57	—0.48	—0.13	0.71		15
361	1.23	—0.23	0.02	0.56		16
362	1.64	0.44	—0.17	1.32		17
363	1.68	1.56	0.10	0.09		18
364	—0.17	1.12	—0.13	—1.03	PEEL 36	1
365	0.03	0.81	—0.05	—1.25		2
366	—1.21	1.40	—0.11	—0.71		3
367	—0.41	0.94	0.05	—1.10		5
368	—1.28	0.00	—0.08	—0.42	PERTH 37	1
369	—1.24	0.34	0.01	—0.15		2
370	—1.53	—0.32	—0.11	0.47		3
371	—1.32	—0.81	0.17	0.36		4
372	—0.99	0.27	—0.09	0.58		5
373	—1.68	—0.56	0.11	—0.05		6
374	—1.71	—0.71	—0.06	—0.12		7
375	—1.65	—0.78	—0.07	—0.17		8
376	—1.43	—0.15	—0.11	0.66		9
377	—1.59	—1.01	0.06	0.64		10
378	—1.25	—0.68	—0.05	0.00		11
379	—0.26	—0.59	0.12	—0.92	PETERBOROUGH 38	1
380	1.08	—0.71	0.06	—0.50		2
381	1.43	0.48	—0.04	—1.22		3
382	2.09	—1.05	—0.15	—0.16		4
383	0.89	0.86	—0.05	—1.34		5
384	0.69	—1.22	0.08	—0.34		6
385	0.98	0.35	—0.10	—1.37		7
386	1.26	—1.06	—0.10	—1.34		8
387	0.51	—0.61	—0.05	—0.68		9
388	—0.40	0.29	—0.01	—0.55		11

OBSERVATION	FACTOR SCORES				COUNTY	MUNICIPALITY
	1	2	3	4		
389	—0.41	0.28	—0.02	—1.22		12
390	0.19	—0.84	0.07	1.41	PRESCOTT 39	1
391	0.23	—1.75	—0.05	0.86		2
392	—0.09	—0.31	—0.02	0.83		3
393	0.54	0.74	—0.14	—0.06		4
394	0.58	0.30	—0.19	0.72		5
395	—0.05	0.18	—0.00	0.62		6
396	—1.06	—1.47	0.27	0.78		7
397	—0.49	0.42	—0.10	—1.13	PRINCE EDWARD 40	1
398	—0.38	—0.96	0.06	—0.96		2
399	—0.31	0.45	—0.08	—0.90		3
400	—0.82	—1.03	—0.16	—0.62		4
401	—0.24	—0.45	—0.17	—0.43		5
402	—0.33	—1.17	—0.14	—1.02		6
403	—0.29	—0.67	—0.12	—1.48		7
404	—0.26	—0.30	—0.15	1.00	RAINY RIVER 41	1
405	—0.94	2.02	—0.13	2.52		2
406	0.21	—0.02	—0.20	1.36		3
407	0.27	—0.44	0.73	1.75		4
408	1.05	—1.51	0.05	0.40		5
409	1.32	0.19	—0.21	1.29		6
410	0.50	—0.35	—0.07	—0.24		7
411	1.04	1.09	—0.19	0.73		8
412	0.13	—0.71	—0.24	0.77		9
413	0.41	—1.52	0.11	0.82		10
414	0.50	—1.66	—0.08	0.64		11
415	1.20	1.65	—0.15	1.51		12
416	0.57	—1.13	—0.06	0.25		13
417	0.43	0.05	—0.12	0.58	RENFREW 42	1
418	1.48	—0.45	0.10	0.66		2
419	1.62	—2.24	—0.11	1.12		3
420	1.43	0.71	—0.13	1.45		4
421	1.01	—0.50	0.17	0.18		5
422	—0.21	—0.32	—0.15	0.01		6
423	1.48	—1.20	—0.02	—0.19		7
424	2.91	—1.62	0.12	1.47		8
425	1.49	—1.13	—0.04	0.52		9
426	2.07	—0.79	—0.11	0.36		10
427	2.85	—0.30	0.15	0.99		11
428	0.86	—0.77	—0.16	1.43		12
429	0.91	0.64	—0.14	0.41		13
430	0.23	0.36	—0.06	0.21		14
431	—0.62	0.84	—0.11	0.15		15
432	1.40	2.51	—0.06	—0.80		16
433	2.70	0.20	—0.08	0.13		17
434	2.96	0.60	—0.07	1.64		18
435	1.71	1.98	—0.14	0.35		19
436	—0.01	0.17	0.08	—0.39		20
437	1.66	1.46	—0.13	—1.00		21
438	3.49	—0.74	0.29	2.70		22
439	—0.20	0.07	—0.00	0.87		23
440	—0.26	—0.32	0.05	0.19		24
441	1.15	—0.96	0.09	0.85		25
442	—0.75	—1.37	0.09	0.81	RUSSELL 43	1
443	—0.08	0.15	—0.05	0.75		2
444	—0.12	0.51	—0.05	0.54		3

OBSERVATION	FACTOR SCORES				COUNTY	MUNICIPALITY
	1	2	3	4		
445	—0.19	—0.26	—0.09	—0.12		4
446	—0.03	0.25	—0.12	0.21	SIMCOE 44	1
447	—0.15	1.81	—0.03	—0.67		2
448	—0.23	0.02	—0.03	—0.08		3
449	—0.59	0.58	0.01	0.72		4
450	—0.26	0.60	—0.05	0.00		5
451	1.04	—1.35	0.29	0.48		6
452	0.30	—0.18	—0.06	0.31		7
453	—0.37	0.07	0.06	—0.07		8
454	0.01	0.93	—0.02	2.96		9
455	—0.18	1.03	—0.11	0.33		10
456	—0.37	0.59	—0.07	0.46		11
457	0.27	0.45	0.03	0.47		12
458	—0.51	0.73	—0.06	0.26		13
459	0.00	0.55	—0.00	1.74		14
460	—0.43	1.26	—0.15	0.70		15
461	—0.74	0.73	—0.09	0.45		16
462	0.73	0.70	0.06	—0.12	STORMONT 45	1
463	—0.89	—1.08	—0.04	—0.50		2
464	0.12	—0.15	—0.04	—0.85		3
465	0.02	—1.10	0.17	—0.02		4
466	0.60	1.63	—0.17	1.11	SUDBURY 46	1
467	—0.58	0.82	—0.03	1.13		2
468	—0.49	1.37	0.02	0.38		4
469	—0.14	—0.40	—0.04	1.44		5
470	0.66	—0.62	0.12	1.22		7
471	0.46	1.35	—0.16	0.71		8
472	1.56	1.68	—0.14	0.66		9
473	—0.78	1.65	—0.12	0.41		10
474	0.45	0.49	—0.29	1.87		11
475	1.18	0.99	—0.05	—0.53		12
476	—0.08	1.59	—0.11	0.96		13
477	—2.11	0.05	—0.23	2.02		14
478	0.25	3.01	—0.11	—2.47		16
479	—0.33	—0.30	0.10	0.77		17
480	—0.76	1.35	—0.11	0.53		19
481	0.01	—1.28	0.07	0.63		20
482	—0.57	1.21	—0.16	—0.16	THUNDER BAY 47	1
483	0.01	—1.16	—0.17	0.57		2
484	—0.23	—0.69	—0.20	0.71		3
485	—0.64	—1.80	—0.06	0.40		4
486	—1.05	0.57	0.87	0.69		5
487	—0.51	2.23	—0.11	0.31		6
488	—0.74	1.18	—0.13	0.67		8
489	0.04	0.87	—0.09	0.81		9
490	0.28	1.94	—0.11	1.48		10
491	—0.12	—1.15	—0.12	—0.98		11
492	—0.64	—0.21	—0.11	0.43		12
493	—0.52	0.48	—0.04	0.69		13
494	—0.71	0.93	—0.14	0.67		14
495	0.16	0.67	—0.11	0.57		16
496	—1.00	1.23	—0.06	1.28		17
497	—0.59	0.65	—0.06	0.86	TIMISKAMING 48	1
498	0.43	—0.79	—0.10	2.70		2
499	—0.15	—0.36	0.06	0.99		3
500	—0.29	—1.02	—0.03	1.72		4

OBSERVATION	FACTOR SCORES				COUNTY	MUNICIPALITY
	1	2	3	4		
501	1.06	—2.07	—0.03	0.85		5
502	—2.39	—0.71	—0.07	2.54		6
503	0.37	—1.74	—0.09	—0.11		7
504	—0.30	0.51	—0.13	1.26		8
505	0.63	0.41	—0.17	1.14		9
506	—0.44	2.00	—0.19	1.27		10
507	0.93	—1.06	—0.22	1.09		11
508	0.21	0.76	—0.20	0.73		12
509	0.62	—0.27	—0.21	1.57		13
510	—0.65	0.11	—0.16	1.78		14
511	—1.45	—0.40	—0.14	1.29		15
512	—0.26	—1.27	—0.08	1.14		16
513	—1.73	—1.94	—0.17	3.74		17
514	—1.11	1.18	—0.01	2.47		18
515	—0.93	1.77	—0.07	2.12		19
516	—1.15	1.01	—0.00	2.67		20
517	—0.75	1.38	0.05	0.54		21
518	2.47	0.14	0.05	—0.59	VICTORIA 49	1
519	0.25	—1.57	—0.06	—0.95		2
520	1.31	0.59	—0.21	—0.35		3
521	0.28	—0.53	—0.11	—0.80		4
522	0.11	—0.30	—0.08	—0.65		5
523	0.24	—0.19	—0.12	—0.99		6
524	0.51	—1.81	0.12	—1.08		7
525	—0.41	—0.77	0.10	—0.19		8
526	—0.19	—0.11	—0.09	—0.75		9
527	0.34	—0.43	—0.09	—0.85		10
528	—0.10	—1.14	0.09	—1.11		11
529	—1.71	—0.72	—0.06	0.77	WATERLOO 50	3
530	—1.55	0.20	—0.03	0.16		4
531	—2.01	—0.09	—0.08	0.64		5
532	0.49	1.92	—0.01	—1.41	WELLAND 51	1
533	—0.16	0.97	—0.06	—0.09		2
534	0.10	1.68	—0.06	—0.29		3
535	0.19	1.74	—0.05	—0.94		4
536	—0.10	1.45	0.01	—0.54		6
537	—0.21	0.48	—0.09	—0.20		7
538	0.36	1.78	—0.06	—1.19		8
539	—0.99	—1.82	—0.01	0.12	WELLINGTON 52	1
540	—0.72	1.06	—0.12	—0.03		2
541	—0.51	0.13	—0.03	—0.27		3
542	—0.94	0.84	—0.11	—0.29		4
543	—0.30	2.36	—0.12	—0.83		5
544	—1.23	—1.54	—0.03	0.34		6
545	—1.37	—0.68	—0.11	0.25		7
546	—1.05	0.05	—0.13	0.54		8
547	—0.43	0.79	—0.06	—0.15		9
548	—1.72	—0.73	—0.14	0.95		10
549	—1.53	—0.71	—0.04	—0.07		11
550	—0.26	1.26	—0.14	—0.32		12
					(WENTWORTH 53)	
551	—0.67	—0.33	0.01	—0.76	YORK 54	2
552	—0.14	1.00	—0.04	—0.34		3
553	—0.36	0.50	—0.02	—0.67		4
554	—0.47	1.55	—0.08	—0.04		5
555	0.02	1.02	0.06	—1.03		9

How do the municipalities cluster in this graph? Those located close to each other are quite similar; the greater the separation, the greater the dissimilarity. Do clusters of municipalities in the graph also cluster spatially, thus forming uniform regions? Or do members of clusters scatter widely, showing instead that poverty is distributed as a spatial type?[31]

The Eastern Ontario example may be examined in some detail as these questions are explored. One hundred and fifty-eight municipalities were located first in a two-dimensional scatter diagram based on factors one and four and then in the three-dimensional space created by addition of factor two.[32] In each case two analyses were undertaken, the first developing the complete unconstrained linkage tree and the second the linkage system constrained by contiguity. The objective function minimized was total within-group squared distance.[33] Figure 12 shows the linkage tree for the 158 observations, and the accumulative criterion value at each step. This diagram is not, of course, the more familiar "dendrite" form of linkage tree. Instead, a column of "X's" descends from the point of linkage to the base, so that "valleys" of white space indicate principal breaks between classes. Figures 13 and 14 present the typology of areas and the contiguous regionalization in the two factor (1, 4) case, and Figures 15 and 16 the same for the three factor (1, 2 and 4) case. The main and sub-regionalizations of Figure 14 may be checked against the arrows indicating the levels of regionalization selected from the linkages in Figure 12.[34] In Figures 13, 14, 15 and 16 the four-group and four-region solutions are presented. Figure 14 shows, in addition, the subdivisions of the four principal regions of the two-variable (1 - 4) case into seventeen sub-regions.

---

[31]We distinguish uniform *regions* — clusters of contiguous areas which are very much alike, and *types* — such as type of farming areas in which the elements are similar but not located in contiguity.

[32]Refer to Table 6. The 158 observations are, in order, the municipalities listed in Counties 4, 7, 11, 12, 13, 16, 18, 23, 24, 25, 32, 38, 39, 42, 43, and 45. We do not present the scatter diagrams here, in the interests of conserving on illustrations. However, for similar graphics, see the Ray-Berry study of Ontario and Quebec, *op. cit.*

[33] See the discussion of mathematical procedures above. The program for grouping with or without contiguity written by Peter M. Neely was used. A linkage tree shows the successive clustering of the 158 observations initially treated as one-member groups into 157, 156, 155, . . ., 7, 6, 5, 4, 3, 2, and 1 groups in a total of 157 steps. From this tree it is possible to select the number of groups or regions most appropriate to the problem in hand. Sharp breaks in the accumulative objective function may also indicate critical regional boundaries. In what follows we select the four-type and four-region solutions for consistency.

[34] We chose Eastern Ontario as the case for further study because of the debate concerning regionalization of the area reported in Ray and Berry, *op. cit.*, and because of the stimulating series of insights into the area's problems presented by Barbara Moon in her series of articles on "Ontario's Rural Slum" published in the *Toronto Globe and Mail* from 11 January 1965 to 15 January 1965, followed by the 16 January editorial on "The Hopelessness and Hope of the Eastern Counties". Barbara Moon records the "extreme poverty" and "extreme conditions of social and economic disadvantage" of the eleven counties of Eastern Ontario. For example, she notes "up on the Shield there is a sub-region stretching across Lanark, Renfrew and Frontenac that is informally known as the Ozarks of Ontario. A few thousand backward, under-educated, reclusive people scratch out a living on bush clearings or on high rocky pastures, but the land is so bad that between 1951 and 1961 nearly 2,000 farms had to close down." However, she says little of the rural non-farm or of cultural patterns of deprivation and disadvantage that we have shown to be of equal importance.

Compare first Figures 13 and 14. The unconstrained grouping of Figure 13 isolates three main regions, one for each of the three main types: rural poverty of the Shield in Renfrew and Frontenac, Lennox and Haliburton (C); the easternmost "tip" of Glengarry, Prescott, Russell and Stormont, the main region of social disadvantage (B); and the relatively prosperous balance of Carleton and Leeds; Hastings and Prescott (A). In addition, however, municipalities of both A and B types (the prosperous and the socially deprived) scatter outside their main regions, and an additional type (D) occupies western Renfrew and scatters elsewhere. By constraining the results to require contiguity, the three main regions and types (C, Shield; B, East; and A, "rest") remain, but a fourth region (D) of *eastern* Renfrew is created; see Figure 14. The breakdown of the four major regions into seventeen sub-regions re-emphasizes the internal differences of the main regions resulting from the scatter of the more homogeneous types identified in Figure 13. Both the typology and the regionalization agree completely on two groups of disadvantaged municipalities however: that of intense farm poverty (C)[35] and that of the most intense social deprivation (B).[36] Disagreements are essentially on how the "rest" should be classified and regionalized, and on isloated examples of farm poverty and social deprivation that lie beyond the main regions.

Addition of factor two as an extra dimension of classification does not shift the essential results, as Figures 15 and 16 indicate clearly enough. Both maps show again the main regions of farm poverty and social disadvantage. The additional scattering in the typology of Figure 15 is a result of differentials in rural non-farm poverty as they snake across the province following the inter-urban peripheries. The final three-variable four-region solution emphasizes the farm poverty of the Shield (C), a more northerly zone of rural farm poverty in which there is, by contrast, rural non-farm prosperity (D), the lakeshore counties, which fare relatively well on all three factors (A), and the zone of social disadvantage (B), extended along the Ottawa Valley by incorporating the contiguous zone of relative rural non-farm prosperity that surrounds Ottawa.

A sub-regionalization would subdivide each of these main regions: the zone of farm poverty on the Shield into segments in which non-farm incomes are high by virtue of recreational and other developments and those inaccessible backwaters in which non-farm incomes are also low; the eastern zone surrounding Ottawa into a relatively prosperous commuting and urbanized zone, and the easterly region in which a French Canadian population dominates; and a variety of others. Each has a highly distinctive combination of relative prosperity and disadvantage, and the occurrence of disadvantage of one kind does not necessarily lead to disadvantage of another because different processes appear to be at work.

The regionalization of farm poverty, whatever the intervening historical conditions and processes of natural selection that may have operated upon the residents, ultimately stems from major differences in resource endowment. Rural non-farm poverty is clearly distributed in ways resulting from the urban-orientation of much of our life, and the decline in employment opportunities with increasing distance from urban centres. Thus, it concentrates in the least accessible portions of the area, along the inter-urban peripheries. Social disadvantage is a cultural phenomenon, related to differences in the background, standards, mores, and aspira-

---

35 See Moon, *op. cit.*
36 Refer to Ray and Berry, *op. cit.*

tions of population groups. Thus, in Eastern Ontario the most marked social deprivation is associated with the French Canadians, whereas in Southern Ontario (Simcoe) it is related to large pools of agricultural labourers, many of whom are migrants.

How are these problems of economic and social disadvantage to be remedied? We are not sure, for we do not have good models which enable us to assess the direct effects and feedbacks of alternative strategies, and the interplay among combinations of strategies. What is clear from the foregoing, however, is that different public policies will be needed to attack several distinct poverty syndromes.

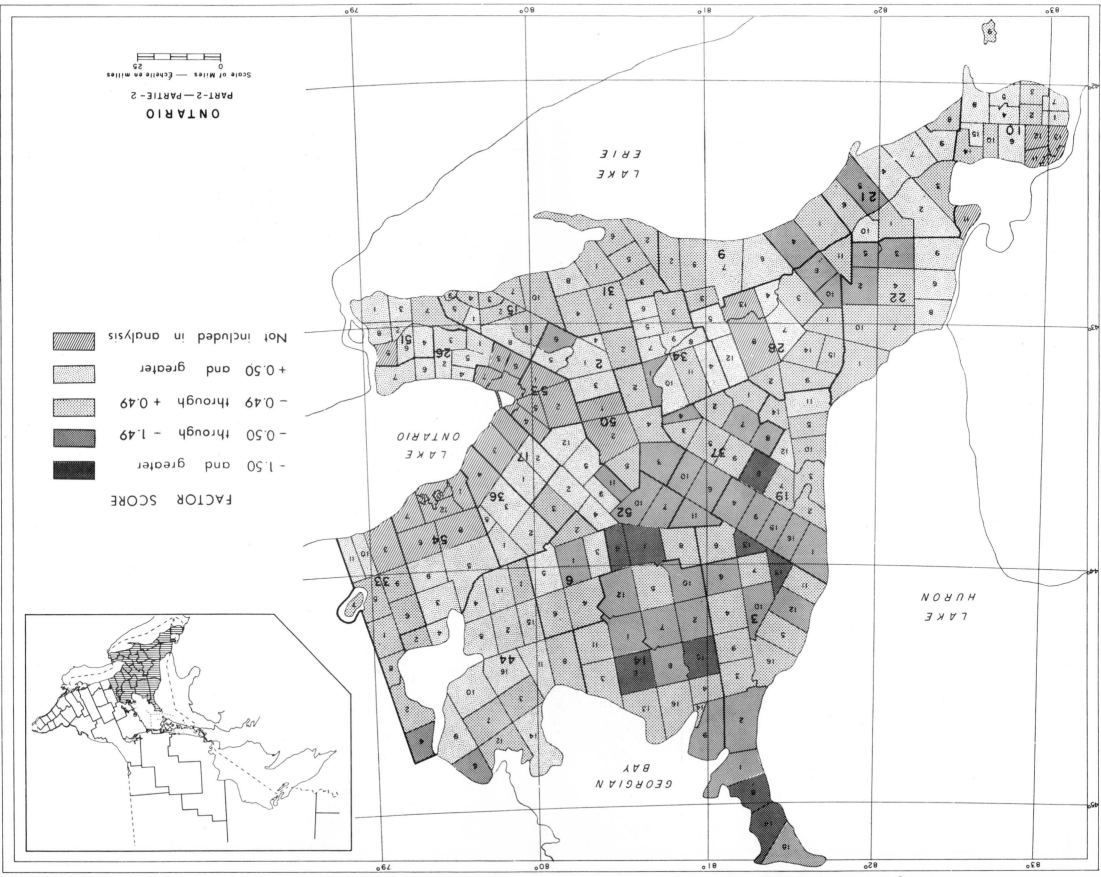

ONTARIO

PART-2 — PARTIE-2

Scale of Miles — Echelle en milles

0   25

FACTOR SCORE

- 1.50   and   greater

- 0.50   through   - 1.49

- 0.49   +   through   + 0.49

+ 0.50   and   greater

Not   included   in   analysis

LAKE   ERIE

LAKE   ONTARIO

LAKE   HURON

GEORGIAN   BAY

Factor 2

Fig. 4.—Factor two—Southern Ontario.

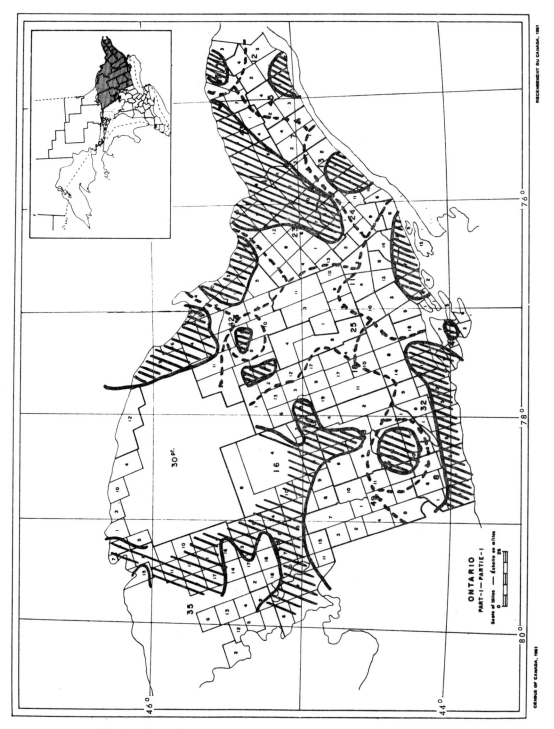

Fig. 5.—Generalization of the factor two pattern for Eastern Ontario.

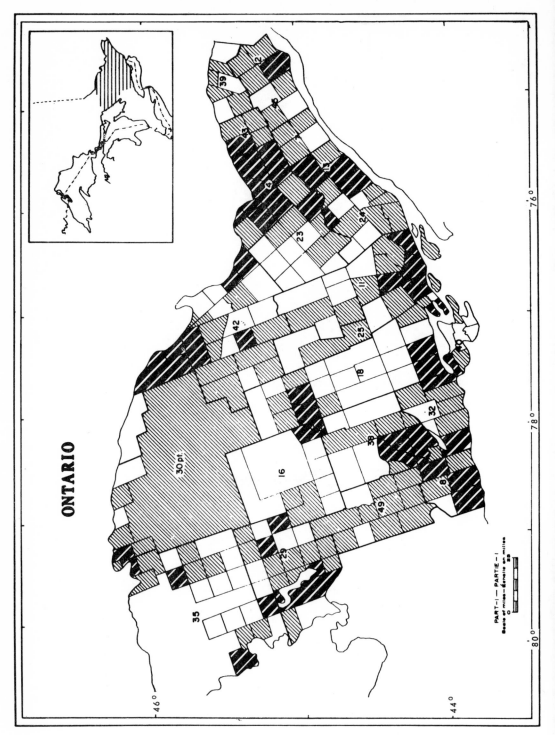

Fig. 6.—Population change—Eastern Ontario.

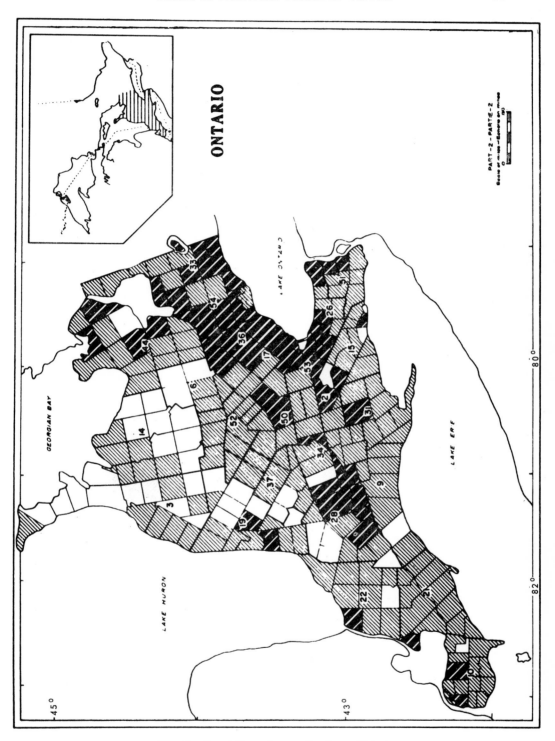

Fig. 7.—Population change—Southern Ontario.

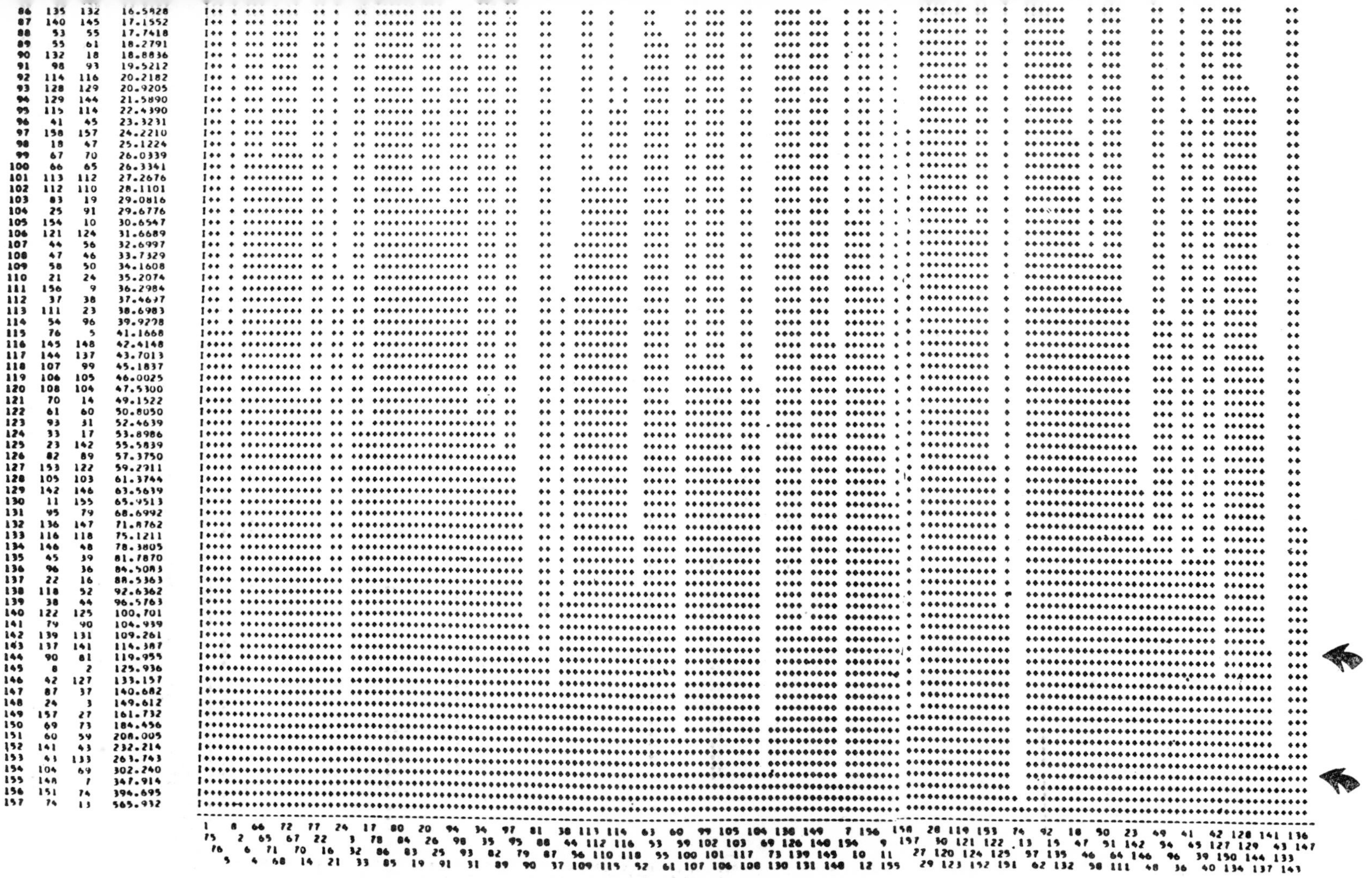

Fig. 12.—Linkage Tree for 158 Eastern Ontario Municipalities. Two factor space (1 and 4) with contiguity constraint.

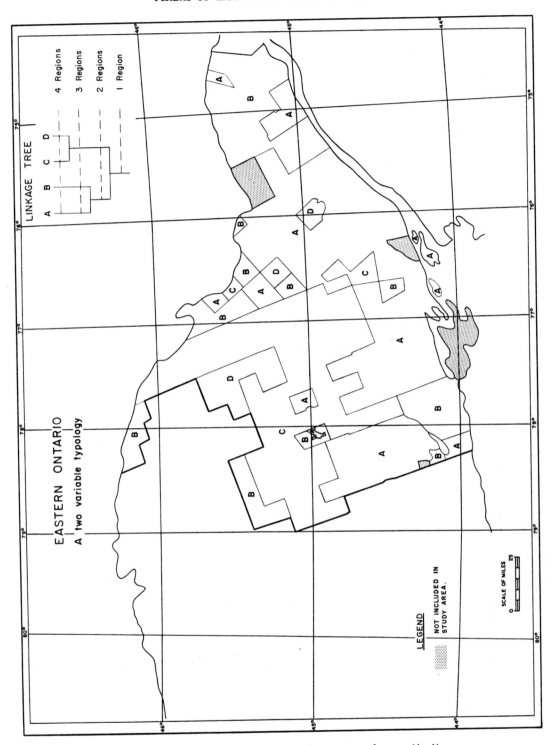

Fig. 13.—Four Group Typology based upon two factors (1, 4).

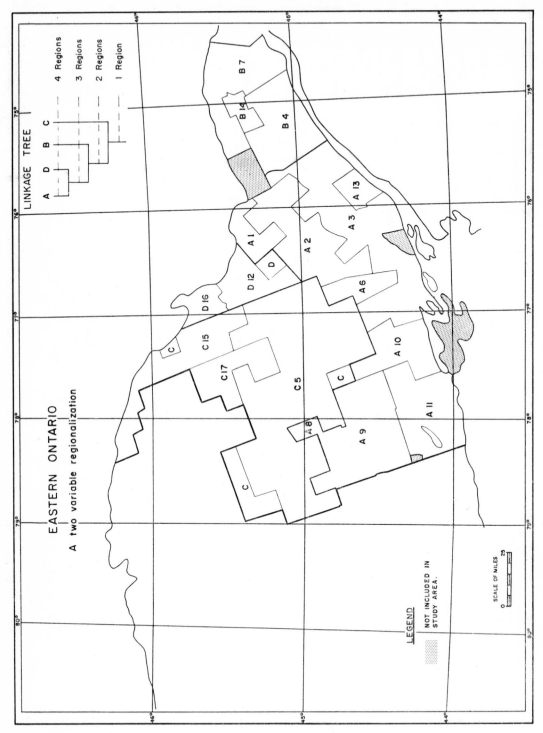

Fig. 14.—Four and Seventeen Group Regionalizations based upon two factors (1, 4).

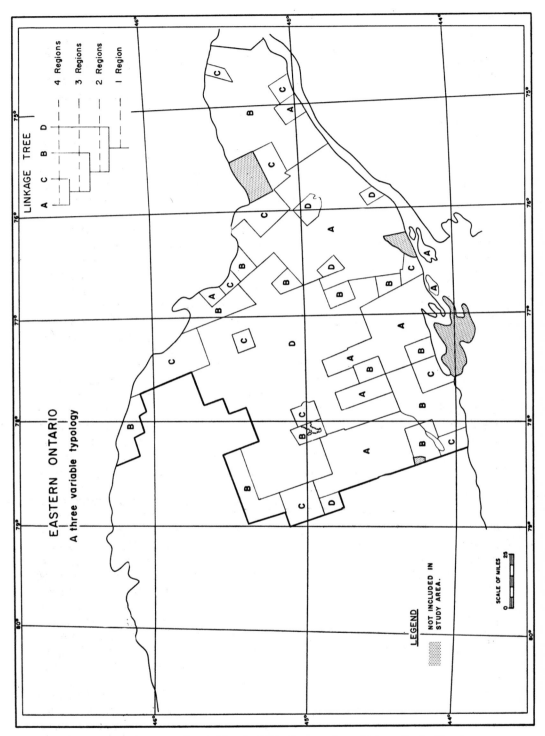

Fig. 15.—Four Group Typology based upon three factors (1, 2, 4).

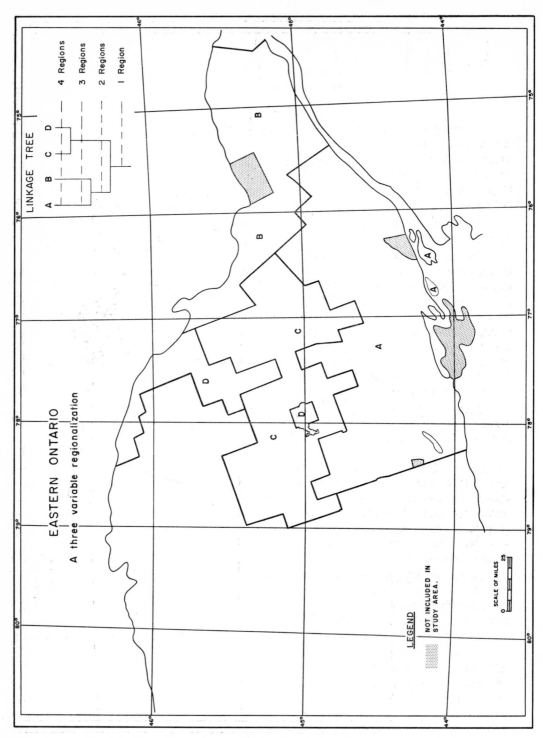

Fig. 16.—Four Group Regionalization based upon three factors (1, 2, 4).

COMMENTS

DR. PIERRE CAMU,
Vice-President,
St. Lawrence Seaway Authority.

Professor Berry is a modest man. In summarizing briefly his paper, he did not elaborate on the type and scope of research that he put into it. He rightly presented its conclusion and explained in passing a few ideas and techniques. Because of the length of the paper and the lack of time to study it, and also to give proper credit to the author, a few words about the context appear indispensable.

There are three distinct parts which could be labelled as the method, the case and the conclusion.

The author explains the method of measuring the dimensions of economic distress and their regional differentiation by the use of elaborate formulae. Three examples are then studied to demonstrate the application of the method: — a) the first example shows what can be done when one compares 95 countries using 43 indexes — this is an example taken at the international level; b) the second example deals with economic health in New York State with a replica for Ontario based on 54 counties and 16 variables — an example at the provincial or state level; c) the third example relates to the prediction of trade centre viability in Saskatchewan (a paper by G. Hodge) based this time on 473 trade centres, using 35 variables and 6 components — an illustration at the local level.

Pursuing the explanation of his method, the author elaborates on spatial variation and regionalization, and in so doing introduces another example, based this time on 120 census counties of Quebec and Ontario in terms of 88 variables. (It is at that point of the study that Professor Berry introduces the "linkage tree" technique.) Three basic dimensions were found: — 1) differences between French and English counties, 2) variations on an urban-rural scale, 3) contrasts between shield and southerly lowlands. These basic dimensions reached by the use of techniques, methods, computers, tools and formulae which belong to mathematical geography were also arrived at by the classical investigation (inventories, field work and questionnaires) used in our recent study *Economic Geography of Canada*, Macmillan, Toronto, 1964.

In the second part, the author explores the "dimensionality of rural poverty in Ontario", and finds a clear zone of rural poverty sweeping Eastern Ontario along the Frontenac axis. Such a zone includes the counties of Frontenac, Lennox, Haliburton, Hastings, Renfrew, Nipissing and Parry Sound which are predominantly rural non-farm counties.

In its conclusion, Professor Berry notices, as the most basic trend, the increasing nodality or urbanization and the shrinking of rural areas engulfed more and more by the spread of cities. Where do we go from there? There seems to be two avenues, the first one is to accelerate the process and plan accordingly, the second avenue is to tackle particular problems in particular places. In the first instance we are talking about a new organization of space, while in the second instance, it is a case of fighting the problem where it is.

The distribution and dimensions of rural poverty, as it applies to Ontario, are based on factors, components and variables which are all represented by numbers. One weakness to such a study is the absence of factors that cannot be numbered, and they are very important when dealing with rural regions. For instance, the factors of relief, hills, valleys, mountains, of poor drainage, of climatic conditions such as rainfall, snow cover, length of vegetation season, the soil conditions, the "vital top six inches", the depth and intensity of the forest cover — in other words, the physical factors taken separately or as a whole.

The same remark could apply to the human factors such as the ways of life of the inhabitants of these regions, their conception of a standard of living, their local history, the landmarks, the "cultural landscape" (Sauer) in which they live, the "icones" of Gottmann, their folklore, briefly the soul or the personality of regions. These factors cannot be measured, but they often provide the answers to the problems investigated. Do we not move to this conclusion that the greatest number of variables or components must be used, selected, sorted and analysed and the results described and explained; but beyond that point, as an indispensable complement, the qualitative approach is necessary. That is the point where geography ceases to be a science and becomes an art. We could not venture to reach similar conclusions for other social sciences. Following the above approach and using as many techniques and statistical refinements as possible, as well as weighing carefully the physical and human factors, would it be possible to make a case for a study of regions of abundance or regions of economic wealth, so that in finding the causes of their existence, one might get some ideas about what the regions of economic stress are lacking and why did they not succeed in getting wealthy.

I wish to stress the fact that the imponderable factor in Part 2 of this study is, what does rural poverty mean to farmers? At what point do they, themselves, think they are rich, wealthy or very poor? One might come out with 15 counties of economic stress in Ontario based on a given scientific method, but it is also important to discover from the inhabitants of these 15 counties what their conception of poverty is, and what are the means, if any, they are using to cure it. This might be the clue to the answer to some regional problems of relocation or new land use. Professor Berry's study taken as such, is a very reliable piece of research. If I isolate Part 2, Rural Poverty in Ontario, as an example, I find that this part satisfies me in describing and explaining the dimensions of rural poverty, but it stops where many of us would like to start, i.e. how to solve it, what are the solutions to the problems?

Again, if tools, techniques, methods of measurements lead to problems and answers, then the tools have merit and should be used.

In reading this paper and Professor Graham's paper, may I suggest to this group an area where studies should also be undertaken. In talking about areas of economic stress, one has mentioned a large area — the Atlantic Provinces. Could we also look at the wards and districts of some Canadian cities where thousands of our people live in deplorable conditions, very close to wards or districts of immense wealth. It is not only slum clearance that we should look at, but also rehabilitation and the search for a better urban way of life.

COMMENTS

PROFESSOR DONALD KERR,
Department of Geography,
University of Toronto.

Of the various statistical methods and techniques which have come into prominence in the last few decades, that of factor analysis has had the greatest appeal to regional geographers. It seems increasingly that problems of identifying and analyzing regions of distress may find their solutions in regional geography and it is indeed understandable that factor analysis to use Professor Berry's own phrase ". . . appears to be a useful methodology for measuring the dimensions of economic distress and their regional differentiation". Undoubtedly, the great strength of Berry's paper lies in the use of this technique in the tasks of identification and description of areas of rural poverty in Ontario; the only serious weakness is that it assumes to do more.

In the long run, the success of any statistical manipulation, sophisticated or otherwise, depends on the selection of data. In this study, Professor Berry has chosen 31 variables which had been made available to him by the Federal Department of Agriculture. They can be grouped under the following broad headings: income, value of buildings (machinery, land, livestock, etc.), educational levels, mortality rates, amenities? (plumbing, heating, etc.). Without question the fact that all these data were provided on the basis of a relatively small unit, the municipality, made it possible for the author to study the geography of rural poverty much more intensively than heretofore. Those of us who have been frustrated by the lack of township data in making similar studies in the past warmly welcome this change in policy.

Now the question must be asked, are these 31 variables (increased to 47 by a process called transgeneration) necessarily the most appropriate to use in dealing with the problem at hand? The answer may be an unqualified yes, but surely the reader is entitled to some discussion of their respective advantages and disadvantages beyond the statement that they correspond closely to those used by ARDA in a folder of maps of Economic and Social Disadvantage in Canada. I must be brief and will therefore raise only one question. Why in dealing with rural poverty should 3 variables pertaining to university education be selected and none for high school?

The procedures of factor analysis leading ultimately to four factors (on the basis of percentage type variables) are reviewed by Professor Berry and the factor scores for each of the 555 municipalities in Ontario are listed. Unless I have misinterpreted this study, quite possible because my knowledge of factor analysis is as yet incomplete, the real substance of the paper is to be found in these factor scores. It is therefore a pity that the author did not have time to map the results for this conference.[1] In a cursory examination of the extreme values, the author confirms some of the fundamental patterns in the geography of Ontario such as the prosperous farm belt in the southwest. The most important contribution (to be read from the maps at a later date) however will be the discovery of individual and/or groups of poverty-stricken townships. Equally significant will be the identification of "pockets of affluence" in poor areas. The suggestion that rural non-farm "prosperity" is scattered in parts of the Shield invites attention.

I am somewhat disturbed by the author's frequent references, in discussing broad patterns, to the "French-English differential", "the Shield-Lowland contrasts", etc. (introduced first in an earlier paper in collaboration with Ray). Can one make such assumptions with only patterns of associations as ammunition? Would it not be better to leave all labels off until substantial research has answered at least in part some of the whys and hows of various spatial patterns. Clearly, factor analysis is a very important tool in identifying characteristics of local areas and depicting broad patterns but it is simply a prerequisite for explanatory analysis and not a part of explanation *per se*.

There is little question that Professor Berry has made a splendid contribution to this conference by focusing on multivariate analysis. I wish to emphasize however that the task of proper identification may be accomplished only if we build into such research programs both reconnaissance and detailed field studies. Let subjectivity creep in, for it is a fact that the human aspects of distress do not yield to quantification as readily as the economic. I would then argue that from properly integrated statistical and field studies, a typology of non-metropolitan poverty should emerge having broad regional application across Canada. This in turn could be the basis of selection of case studies which would lay bare the rationale of the economic and social structure of specific areas. It would be hoped that broad generalizations would come from a number of local studies. May I urge that such studies should have a strong historical orientation for it is true that most inhabitants of distressed areas have a deep attachment to the land on which they live and are in fact able to claim family ownership for several generations.

To recapitulate, the difficult problem of identification can be solved in part by the application of sophisticated statistical techniques to judiciously chosen variables within the confines of small areal units. Full solution can be achieved by employing traditional field methods to complement the type of multivariate analysis which Professor Berry has expounded here today.

---

[1] Editorial footnote: However, the maps were received after the conference (Figs. 1 - 16 in Berry's paper).

PART II

THE BASIC PROBLEMS — TREATMENT

- Policy for Declining Regions: A Theoretical Approach

  Professor A. D. Scott,
  Department of Economics,
  University of British Columbia,
  (1964-65, University of Chicago).

  Discussants:

  Professor Clarence L. Barber,
  Department of Economics,
  University of Manitoba,
  (1964-65, McGill University).

  Professor K. G. Crawford,
  Department of Political Studies,
  Queen's University.

- Growth and the Canadian Economy: The Problem of Regional Disparities

  Professor T. N. Brewis,
  Department of Economics,
  Carleton University.

  Discussants:

  Professor Yves Dubé,
  Faculté des Sciences Sociales,
  Université Laval.

  Dr. W. R. Dymond,
  Assistant Deputy Minister,
  Department of Labour, Ottawa.

POLICY FOR DECLINING REGIONS: A THEORETICAL APPROACH

A. D. SCOTT,
Department of Economics,
University of British Columbia,
(1964-65, University of Chicago).

PART I. INTRODUCTION*

This paper is written in response to a request to present an exposition of the theory of regional economic development, and its implications for the choice of policy for regions with less than the national standard of growth and income.

In Part II, the relevant bodies of theory are introduced. It is found that trade and location theory are suggestive, but not really helpful, for their conclusions usually depend on the assumption that factor inputs (the various kinds of labour, capital and enterprise) are not mobile among regions. A version of the staple theory is found to be more useful, and is developed for its implications, especially for declining regions.

Part III depends directly on Part II. It is devoted to examining the staple theory for its policy implications for the aid of those living in declining regions. The discussion is classified according to the *aims* of the various types of policy, not of the policies themselves.

Readers who are antipathetic to economic theory are advised to begin with the discussion of the staple approach in II (c). The earlier sections are devoted to eliminating other types of theory as unhelpful in leading to policy conclusions. Readers who wish to avoid all of Part II should realize that a crucial element in this paper's policy argument is that regions that are in some sense "less-developed" are here regarded as "declining". Furthermore, declining regions are defined as those with low incomes per person, not those with low or declining populations.

PART II. CLASSIFICATION OF SOME THEORETICAL APPROACHES TO THE REGIONAL ECONOMY

(a) *Trade Theory*—Although trade theory was developed to deal with the movement of goods and money between nations, most of it applies to movement between regions of the same nation. We shall note its lessons and limitations.

Many Canadians, in thinking about inter-regional and international trade, and especially about the tariff and similar obstacles to inter-regional trade, implicitly apply so-called "classical" or Ricardian trade theory. It produces conclusions in terms of a region's "comparative advantage" in specializing in certain activities. For example, in considering the trade between eastern and western provinces in food and manufactures, it might begin with the proposition that the given resources of labour, capital and land in the east could produce both food and manufactures at lower unit costs than could the resources of the west. Nevertheless, the theory continues, it pays the east to concentrate its activities on one of these two products, consuming and exporting it and consuming imports of the other (say, food) imported from the west. Both regions could get more of both products this way. Superior versions of the theory then proceed to discuss

---

* Professor H. G. Johnson has kindly made suggestions for revision, but is not responsible for the views advanced.

the process by which this specialization becomes profitable to workers and capitalists in both regions, and thus lead to a prediction that trade, rather than regional self-sufficiency, will be observable. It also leads to a prediction that the east, the region with the absolute advantage in both processes, will have higher incomes or standards of living.

This theory has many advantages, but it has been supplanted. As I have mentioned, it does seem to account for the movement of goods and services, and for regional richness or poverty. It has been supplanted chiefly because of two omissions from its elegant structure. First, it fails to explain for what reasons the eastern region has a comparative advantage in specializing in one type of product. A related difficulty is that it must be seriously modified (though not rejected) in order to explain why we can observe both regions making some of *both* products. Second, because it originated from *international* commerce, it ignores the movements of labour and capital between the regions, in addition to the trade in goods.

The first of these omissions, the reasons for specialization, is remedied in a body of theory usually associated with the name of Ohlin. In its basic version, this theory, like the classical theory above, continues the assumption that each region has a *given* resource "endowment" of land, labour and capital. It also is able to proceed on the very restrictive assumption that methods of production are fundamentally similar in all regions.

Time and space do not allow me to explain this assumption fully, nor the reasons for its being made. But because its implications are important, the following properties of the assumption are worth listing. (a) If two regions had equal amounts of land, labour and capital as inputs in some process, they would produce identical amounts of the final good. (b) Among other things, this implies that the technical knowledge, managerial abilities, labour skills, equipment qualities and natural resources are either identical in both regions, or that deficiencies in some are balanced by superiorities in others. In fact, the first implication is assumed at the outset: inputs are homogeneous and identical in both regions. It is also implied that it is possible to include all "natural" production conditions such as climate, soil and location among the identical and homogeneous inputs. No production condition is left unaccounted for. (c) A third property of the assumption of similar production conditions is that there are no advantages in large-scale production. The per-unit costs of each good do not alter if the scale of a factory, or an industry, is doubled.

The consequence of this assumption and some of its properties is that it is possible to explain, and so to predict, the specialization pattern in each region. From the assumption, it follows that certain products will everywhere require large inputs of capital; others will be labour-intensive; and still others will everywhere be heavy users of the conglomerate properties of "land". The theory proceeds rigorously to show that regions will concentrate upon, and export, those things whose production requires relatively large amounts of the kind of input with which it is well-endowed. A capital-rich country will produce and export goods that require (no matter where they are produced) large amounts of capital. Similarly, regions will import goods made primarily from those inputs which they lack.

The theory can be generalized to admit more regions than two regions, and more than two products; and to subdivide the inputs into more clearly-identifiable types of labour, capital and natural resource.

The theory is satisfactory in that, like its predecessor, it accounts for the observed trade among regions. It also goes farther: it explains or predicts which goods are traded by observing the endowments of each region, and the productive processes that are universally available to fully employ each region's endowment.

The attractiveness of the Ohlin theory, however, as it has been augmented by Lerner, Samuelson and others, is that it leads to another prediction. It follows from the assumptions that a region must either specialize so much in those products that require much of the factors with which it is well-endowed that it produces none at all of other products, or else, obviously, must produce at least small amounts of most products. Theorists have shown that if it has enough of every factor to allow it to produce some of every product[1] (even if it must import most of its consumption of that product), then there will be a tendency for factor-prices to be the same in that region as in other regions with which it trades. If some products have been dropped, as is likely to be the case (so that there is "complete specialization" in the other products), then the tendency for factor-prices to be the same in both regions will be unfulfilled. Nevertheless, the tendency will be there: even with complete specialization, there will be a *tendency* for wages, the yield on investment in capital, and the rents of natural resources to be the same in all regions.

This does not, of course, mean that *average* incomes will be the same in all regions, for average incomes depend not only on the amount of each kind of income but also on the number of each kind of income-source. The higher the rent is in all regions, then the higher will be the average income in regions where there are many units of land in relation to numbers of workers and units of capital. Thus the Ohlin theory has the capacity to explain the differences in the average incomes of regions on the basis of different endowments of factors.

But it is able to explain wage rates that differ among the regions (in excess of the difference that would be expected from such factors as education differences and freight costs) only by saying that either the assumption of identical production conditions is not satisfied, or that certain regions must have specialized in some products so completely that the wage-equilization mechanism has not been able to work.

Now, as between regions in a country like Canada, we do observe differences in wage rates from region to region. Workers doing the same things appear to be ill-paid in some places relative to what they could earn in other regions. The Ohlin theory is deficient in that it offers more than one explanation of this difference: specialization, different production conditions, transport costs, and education. Furthermore, our observation may be incompatible with the theory because the equalization of wage rates and other incomes may be coming about, but will take a generation or two to emerge. Finally, we come to the second of the two omissions in the "classical" theory, that factor-inputs are mobile among the regions: this observed fact suggests that the Ohlin theory, so often used for explanations of what is observable between nations, does not take into account all the forces that are at work within a country.

There are two branches of the type of theory that deal with the movement of factors among regions. One deals with the choice of industrial location. The other deals with the decisions of workers to migrate to, and of investors to invest

---

[1] Rigorously stated, to produce as many products as it has types of factors.

in, different regions. Obviously, the two overlap, although the first tends to be used chiefly for movements within a country, while the second is used chiefly for international factor movements. For brevity, I will keep them together under the heading of "location theory".

(b) *Location Theory*— Can the economist explain the locations of industries? He has been most successful explaining the rings and zones of trade, industry and agriculture around large cities. He has also devised increasingly complex models that, by consideration of transport and labour costs, weight-loss in manufacturing, and size of establishment, suggest where particular premises of particular firms can best add to that firm's profits. In turn, much of this has been generalized into broad theories of industrial location that promise, with the aid of geographers, sociologists and demographers to become a new discipline: "regional science".

In this view, distances, resources and size gradually attract various densities of population and industry, until a final stable regional system emerges: an unchanging map of people and production. The equilibrium which emerges depends upon migration of labour and capital from region to region, by trial and error.

But at any given time, the map of population and production is fixed. Theories can tell us the abstract characteristics of the world toward which that map is gradually tending, but depending as they do upon the attractive force of random urban groupings, tell us little about the *process* which reshapes the economic map. Thus we are unable to deduce, from location theory, whether recent trends and migrations will be continued, or must be reversed. Furthermore, while the map is temporarily fixed, the business incentives to produce, sell and trade continue to exert forces toward new, temporary, regional specializations, and factor-price patterns. We may well imagine that this production and trading will alter the equilibrium map toward which the entire country is moving. Similar changes of path toward the final equilibrium will result from changes in the technical processes used by the various industries, and from changes in taste and fashion.

We are forced therefore to rely upon theories that are little more than *ad hoc* hypotheses, their assumptions tailored to the situations observed in particular regions. Such a procedure is, of course, scientifically respectable and productive; but it makes it difficult to survey "the" theory that is applicable.

We may first inquire why factors move from region to region. Here it must be confessed that we have very few strong generalizations. Canadians are aware for example, that it is possible for politicians, lobbyists, university presidents, trade unions and local chambers of commerce to make assertions about migration to the United States that imply a view about why people move, without fear of successful contradiction. Few comprehensive studies have been made. Even in the United States, where statistics of arrivals and departures from state to state are far superior to the records of Canadian immigration and emigration, there are few widely-explored theories about the motives, timing and extent of migrations.[2] I need only cite the uninformative state of the debate about the "Brain Drain" from Canada to illustrate the lack of consensus about human migration.

---

[2] See Sjaastad, L.A., "The Costs and Returns of Human Migration", *J. P. E.*, 70, October 1962, Part 2, pp. 80-93.

For the motives behind capital migration, there is perhaps too strong a consensus. Economists at least are convinced that the owners of wealth, whether they be persons holding liquid securities and equities or firms holding plant and equipment, are quite ruthless in shifting wherever their net return, after taxes and risk have been allowed for, is the greatest. And experience has shown that this hypothesis can give good predictions, although rates of return to investors do not necessarily reflect the regional differences in the social productivity of capital, but merely the strength of the local consumers' desire to borrow. For example, capital moves to municipal borrowers in all parts of the country, and the higher rates of return may well be paid by the municipalities in the poorest regions. Again, migrating workers and families bring liquid funds with them; the investment of these funds in local assets then reflects the forces which led to the migration of people, not the local productivity of capital.

We have little information on the regional movement of capital, and it is difficult to frame hypotheses that would cast light on the various forces causing it to move. There are more data on human migration.

Unsystematic observation, introspection and a leavening of documentation, however, suggest that there is also little uniformity behind migration statistics. We may picture the migrants ranged between two extreme types. At one extreme are those near-destitute people who have exhausted all local opportunities and decided to look farther afield, perhaps in the wake of relatives or friends. Many of them are unskilled, the manifestation of "baby booms" and "rapid recruitment to the labour force" in rural areas and regions of slow industrial growth. With them are former employees of declining industries or of industries whose labour requirements have declined, such as mining, farming, fishing, logging, construction, or transportation. These people have skills and trades of a sort, but they are not transferable locally, and may be obsolete.

At the other extreme are employed, well-paid workers and managers who are tempted or lured by better pay, working conditions, environment or promotion-opportunities in similar industries elsewhere.

Ranged between these extremes are persons and families wtih a large number of combinations of these individual circumstances. There is a great need for studies of Canadian migration, so that we may discover which migration-inducing forces are the most powerful, statistically speaking. Furthermore, studies are required to discover *when* they operate. For example, it is clear that when employment is high everywhere (by the various local standards of high employment), mobility in search of jobs or better pay is greater than when business is poor everywhere, even though the differences between pay levels or unemployment rates would appear to become wider in depressions. Thus, in depressions people move "back" into areas of net emigration, and "back" into contracting industries such as logging, fisheries and farming.

One generalization is possible, however. Just as in the theories of trade surveyed earlier in this paper, theories of location and migration must focus attention on factor endowments (the amounts of labour, capital and resources available in each region) and on the productive techniques used by the various industries.

Beyond this, the theory must take account of new variables. It can no longer be assumed that there is a given demand for each kind of good—instead it must be recognized that growing populations, higher standards of living, changing technology and tastes lead to changing demands for each commodity or raw material. Second, it must be recognized that at least one of the inputs—capital—is in the long run almost completely mobile and responsive to profit opportunities, especially changing market demands. Third, migration theory, in North America at least, must take account of the changing "land" endowment: not only do new resource discoveries, transportation and agricultural techniques rapidly endow some regions, but depletion, logging, and over-cropping impoverish others. Finally, it must be recognized that each region's population is not only mobile in response to opportunities elsewhere, but is growing from the pressure of natural increase. Furthermore, it is broadly true, both in Canada and the United States, that natural increase is highest in low-wage regions. It is at least a plausible hypothesis that large families are typical of low-income people, the employees of low-wage industries, which are often the major industries of low-wage regions: thus high natural increase, low wages, unemployment, and eventual net emigration may once again be traced back to each region's mix of inputs and industries.

Thus it can be seen that a general theory of regional fortunes must take into account not only the three elements: factors, techniques, and demand, but also their growth over time, as in population growth, innovation, and opulence, and further, their change through space, as in labour and capital migration, the diffusion of new techniques, and the opening of new regional markets.

To take all of these factors into account, however, creates a model of such generality as to be uninformative. From the general model must be compressed, or distilled, a partial view that stresses the role of certain critical elements, rates of growth, and migrations, to the virtual exclusion of others. One such theory, familiar to Canadians, is the export or staple model.[3] It can be profitably examined (for testable hypotheses) not only with respect to the form and rate of regional growth, but also, as we shall see, with respect to the explanation of regional decline.

(c) *The Export, or Staple-Commodity Approach*—The theory is most frequently applied to the occupation and settlement of an undeveloped region. Innis, for example, applied his version to the fur trade, the early cod fisheries, and the mining camps, and his associates examined the forest frontier and the wheat economy. It is not usually realized, however, that the mere posing of the question, "How did this unsettled region begin to grow" is bound to be answered by a description of the export commodity or staple.

That this is so can be seen by eliminating the only other contender as a theory of growth: the series of stages described by European (chiefly German) economic historians. Reconstructing their own development, they concluded that the earliest inhabitants must have begun with agricultural self-sufficiency; then in later stages developed some local division of labour; then, with some changes in the political structure permitting improvements in transportation, sold excess produce to neighbouring regions until agricultural specialization emerged; finally, pressure on the land, accumulation of capital, and the induced discovery of manufacturing techniques led to industrialization and international specialization.

Doubtless there are new-world settlements that developed as the "stages" theory would predict, especially if it were altered slightly to take account of the technology and literacy of the seventeenth, eighteenth and nineteenth centuries.

---

[3] For a good review, see Mackintosh, W. A., "Innis on Canadian Economic Development", *J.P.E.*, 61, June 1953, pp. 185-194.

But most migration and settlement was, and is, a response to what Innis called commercialism or capitalism. The former, represented by the Hudson's Bay Company and the cod fisheries, were trading ventures for scarce, high value, natural products. The latter, represented by mining, lumbering, and steel, involved heavy investment in fixed capital. Settlement and growth could not begin until techniques, transport and markets existed for particular raw materials, *because labour and capital could not be attracted otherwise*. The "stages" theory cannot be applied to areas of new settlement because it cannot explain this factor migration.

Indeed, the essence of the "stages" theory is spreading-out from self-sufficiency. It is implied that immigration of labour and investment of capital in quantities large enough to explain growth, were initially attracted to self-sufficient farming colonies. Such a theory obviously cannot have wide application. As we have seen, workers usually leave regions in search of higher returns, or greater advancement, not for the opportunity of repeating in the new world the up-from-the-soil drama of prehistoric Europe. And self-sufficiency cannot bring high returns, save in areas of very exceptional fertility, or to factors of production that were previously so poorly rewarded that they will accept any improvement, howsoever small.

The staple or export-community approach, on the other hand, offers an explanation both of regional growth and of decline, chiefly in terms of factor migration. In outlining this approach, four aspects must be discussed:

1. Factor accumulation;
2. Factor migration and regional growth;
3. Regional decline;
4. Regional contribution to national growth.

1. The theory does not rely on regional savings or natural increase of population to explain growth. It relies on migration. It is assumed that population growth continues everywhere: abroad as well as in neighbouring regions; and that saving and investible funds will be chiefly generated outside the region. This assumption, essential for explaining the initial occupation of vacant lands, continues in modified form after the region has become developed. Obviously, however, in later periods the theory must now explain how the region holds people and capital, including people born locally and capital generated in local industry. In general, the view is that the factor endowment can be better explained by examining factor migration than by examining the pace of local factor generation.

2. Factors come in response to the high returns offered by a staple export. The problem for theory is to explain the timing of the commencement of growth. (We cannot use the attractive term "take-off", because Rostow has appropriated it for one of his "stages".)

Typically, labour and capital are available in other regions, at going wages and rates of return. There is no sudden cheapening of these inputs. Hence, the growth must commence either when productive technology makes it possible to supply a natural product, or when the demand price rises. Examples of the former include new modes of access; new techniques of winning or reducing ores; new types of farming; and resource discoveries themselves. Examples of the latter include improvements in inter-regional transportation; new tastes for certain final products; and new industrial demands for raw materials, probably stemming from technical discoveries of substitution possibilities. In either case, the potential value added by using local resources is now enough to cover the going factor costs, including the private and social costs of migration itself. (At least, it is thought to be. The Klondike gold rush showed that the resource was not adequate to sustain all the factors that rushed to exploit the region; and there is some doubt that the social costs of providing transportation and other services are ultimately covered by the value added in the new region. See point 4, below.)

It can be seen, therefore, why historians in the "staple tradition" have found it so necessary to document changes in technology and demand. They have not been social historians in the English or American sense, paying little attention either to the fortunes of the various social classes (which is relevant to explaining the supply of investible funds) or to living conditions (which explain in part the rate of natural increase). A staple theory of regional growth, by focussing attention on factor immigration, can treat indigenous factor accumulation as of secondary importance.

How great is the geographical extent of the region affected by a given staple? Such a question obviously cannot be answered *a priori* except to echo Innis' insistence that much depends upon the land-using characteristics of the staple. Furs and wheat, being area-intensive (many acres per dollar of product; using land *extensively*) affected enormous regions. An important mining development, on the other hand, may directly involve very little land though Innis tried to show that even this industry can have a profound effect on a large surrounding area.

The question of the extent of the region can be examined from another direction. If the region whose growth or decline is to be explained is small in extent, and homogeneous in resources, a staple industry of a given size is obviously much more important than if the average income or growth in a vast heterogeneous region (such as Quebec or Ontario) must be explained. The few Canadian studies of regionalism have suffered from the absence of statistics of such small regions or districts. In this respect, the larger number of American states, for each of which data are collected and assembled, has provided superior material for the study of regional growth. In any case, in what follows it must be assumed that the "region" discussed is one small enough for all its parts to be in social and economic contact with one another.

For some staples, regions may obviously be small in population, income, and wealth, even though large in area. In this type of region, the impact of central government activities may in effect resemble private staple industries. Indeed, in some parts of Canada, the provision of space and facilities for defence establishments is the chief activity, and has most of the consequences noted in the next paragraph. But, of course, the economic behaviour that led to the selection of these regions may be different from that of industry. In addition to finding good sites, and transportation, the national government may also stress the equitable division of defense spending on property among provinces, and indeed the favourable effects on "residentiary" activities that are discussed immediately below.

Private or public, the sustained growth of a staple provides a "base" for local growth. In attracting workers and their families, it is soon surrounded by a cluster of manufactures, trades and services, and by a network of organizations providing social capital. It also provides a market for specialized inputs. The providers of all these market-oriented products are residentiary industries, depending on the staple export "base". The latter appear slowly, because the original entrepreneurs in the staple industry could not commence until they could rely on profitable operation without local suppliers (apart from suppliers of the basic raw material) depending instead on imported machinery, equipment, fuel, etc. In time, the export base may become a minor employer, compared to the labour force and investment in the dependent industries. Furthermore, the residentiary industries may not only impart the air of being independent of the base, but may, through the development of internal and external economies, become exporters themselves. Should this happen, and should the region have grown to sufficient size, the area may now take off into self-sustained growth, in the Rostow sense.

3. Whether or not a region's growth is self-sustaining can only be ascertained when the staple industry's growth falters or ceases. For reasons explained in Keynesian income and employment theory, we should, of course, expect an initial decline in the export sector to produce a larger decline in regional domestic product. But this decline should be limited, and temporary in any case, for trade theory leads us to expect that in the long run the regional factors will recombine in other domestic industries. Hence if the region no longer depends upon a staple export base, the crumbling of that base should result in a period of reallocation of inputs among industries, accompanied by unemployment, a repricing of labour and capital services, all eventually followed by a resumption of growth with full employment. This would be self-sustained regional growth.

But the staple theory would lead us to expect different results: the crumbling of the export base will, given time, lead to the emigration of its labour and capital, the decline of the residentiary industries, and the eventual reversal of the region's growth rate.

Before examining the process of regional decline, however, it is worth digressing to examine the decline in the staple industry. It was shown that the staple industry became established when the gap between demand price and the price to be paid for the inputs to be imported from other regions was wide enough and certain enough to promise a profit: the prospective value added would cover factor prices. In technical jargon, factor supplies were elastic, in that in other regions large amounts of labour and capital services are sold at given and constant prices.

After the staple is established, this outside situation continues. There is still a market for labour and capital that can absorb workers and investible funds at given and constant prices. In technical jargon, the outside demand for factors is elastic.

Thus, if the demand price for the staple falls relative to the regional (and national) prices of factors, the pay that can be offered these factors will be insufficient to hold them in the industry or the region. They will move out, in response to the elastic demand for factors in other regions. The demand price for the staple may fall for reasons that are either the reverse of the reasons for its previous rise (tastes change, consumer incomes fall, transport connections deteriorate, consuming industries substitute a new raw material), or reflect a new, superior source of the same staple in another region (one with better transportation connections, lower factor prices, or superior natural resources). Furthermore, of course, the natural resource itself may be commercially exhausted. In all these situations the staple export industry is no longer able to offer the going rates to its labour and capital.

To return to the region's reaction to the decline of the staple industry, it is necessary to notice first that the reaction will be slow. There is now an established, and aging, labour force less inclined to mobility than those who originally moved in. It may accept a pay cut (or forego a national pay rise) rather than migrate. Evidence is scanty, but it may be presumed that the wider the gap below outside levels, the larger the percentage of the remaining labour force that will move, at least until the remaining labour force consists of people who are employable elsewhere only at below-average wages or who remain for reasons unconnected with their pay. Thus emigration may match or be slower than the decline in the scale of the export industry.

Fixed capital, too, will remain. Plant, of course, cannot move at all, and its owners can only transfer their wealth to other industries or regions by prolonging the life of the industry as long as it has a net cash inflow. Machinery is physically mobile, and if returns fall enough it may pay to literally move the contents of mills and factories to new regions. But, on the whole, the emigration of capital to new regions will be more rapid than that of labour. Savings generated will be invested outside; there will be little or no renewal of old plant.

Those factors released (or not newly employed) by the staple industry can either migrate or search for local employment. If they migrate, they reduce the size of the local market for the residentiary industries, so that rates of pay and return in such industries can be maintained only by a similar migration (probably involving at least as many units of labour and of capital again). If such augmented migration does not take place, wages and capital returns must fall. If the former employees of the staple industry do not migrate, they will enter the residentiary-industry labour market, once again causing a fall in local wages, and a slightly smaller fall in the return on capital.

What happens next depends upon the appearance of other staple exports. (a) The area may continue depressed, the tendency of wages and rates of return to fall being offset by continuous factor emigration. If, however, the previous staple industry were, or if the surviving residentiary industries are, agriculture, the region may stabilize into self-sufficient farming, with a low-income "staple" providing a little cash. In such circumstances, the rate of emigration may be balanced by the natural increase common in poor farming regions.

Because the local rates of return will now be relatively low, the regional stock will remain stable or decline, so that capital per worker may fall continuously. Hence, real income per worker will fall continuously. Now local real incomes will no longer depend on the price of an export staple in relation to outside price of labour and capital, but, basically, upon the local birth rate. Apart from the opportunity to emigrate setting a floor below these incomes, the region's economy is in effect cut off from the outside economy. This is a regional manifestation of the international "backwash" of growth in the more prosperous regions, that has been stressed by Gunnar Myrdal. Just as Myrdal advocates massive aid to reverse this deterioration in the poorer nations, Buchanan (and many others) advocate special capital assistance to the poorer American states, successive Royal Commissions have recommended aid to the retarded Canadian regions; and Great Britain, France and other European countries have created fiscal incentives to industry to locate in "development areas" that were formerly dominated by staples like coal-mining and cotton textiles.

(b) A new staple may come along. Mackintosh and Innis have stressed that Canadian development may be characterized by a sequence of staple booms, the period between being depressed. However, these writers were discussing Canada as a whole. It is presumably less likely that new staple production will be located

Please change my address effective
Veuillez changer mon adresse à compter du.. 19.........

Name
Nom...
(Block Letters — Lettres moulées)

From
De...
(No. and St., P.O. Box or R.R. No. — N° et rue, case postale ou route rurale)

....
(P.O. — Bureau de poste)   (Zone)   (Province)

To
En...
(No. and St., P.O. Box or R.R. No. — N° et rue, case postale ou route rurale)

....
(P.O. — Bureau de poste)   (Zone)   (Province)

Reference No...
(Account, Subscription, etc.)

Référence...
(N° du compte, de l'abonnement, etc.)   SIGNATURE

POSTES CANADA POST

CHANGE OF ADDRESS ANNOUNCEMENT
ANNONCE DE CHANGEMENT D'ADRESSE

IMPORTANT

To expedite delivery of your mail and to help the post office to maintain efficient service, please take note of the change of address given on the reverse side of this card.

Afin de hâter la livraison du courrier et d'aider les Postes à assurer un bon service, veuillez prendre note du changement d'adresse indiqué au verso.

Postmaster - Le Maître de poste

86B-(8/64)

Postage free
to
Canada-U.S.A.-Mexico
To other Countries 3¢

Canada-É.-U.-Mexique
en franchise
autres pays : 3¢

To
A ....
                    (Name — Nom)

....
(No. and St., P.O. Box or R.R. No. — N° et rue, case postale ou route rurale)

....
(City — Ville)   (Zone)   (Province)

in the same regions as the old. Thus continued Canadian economic progress leaves in its wake a series of depressed regions whose populations, and governments, are immobile. However, it is not unknown for regions to revive. Sometimes, substantially the same staple may yield "another crop", as it were, as in the southern pine forests and the northern Ontario mining camps. Sometimes the local resources may yield another staple, as in Alberta's transition from farming to oil and gas. The theory of trade tells us that an export commodity is bound to appear if incomes fall enough; what is of interest is whether it will yield incomes high enough to prevent net migration of factors.

These possibilities, interesting in themselves, should help to establish the main proposition that the decline of a region can be ascribed to the decline of a staple. Unless the export base of a region contains other staples that can pay capital and labour, the returns available in other regions, both production and the input endowment will shrink to a low level whose characteristics depend on the mobility of the remaining population in response to outside opportunities and on its rate of natural increase.

Before turning to the fourth point, it should be mentioned that statistical verification of the processes summarized so far can be very difficult. Chief among the difficulties[4] is that the agricultural incomes are, on the average, lower than urban incomes in all regions. Part of this deficiency is, of course, explainable by the fact that many farm incomes are augmented by income in kind and psychic income. Another part of the deficiency may be accounted for by the fact that the distribution of farm incomes is skewed, so that the average does not reflect the high cash incomes of a few efficient farmers. But these two explanations leave much to be accounted for. If farm families were a separate input, and were not mobile out of agriculture, the remaining deficiency could be accounted for on the basis of trade theory: that factor prices had been equalized and all farmers got the same low incomes everywhere. But this explanation does not square with the facts: there is mobility out of agriculture, and farm incomes are lower in some places than others, even when the same enterprise (such as dairying) is carried on. The basic explanation seems to be a compound of two tendencies: a continent-wide contraction in the labour requirements of food production (coupled with a rather slower growth for demand for food than for other goods) and a high rate of natural increase among farm families, and in rural regions generally.

These two tendencies prevent a steady rise in farm incomes, and force a steady migration to the cities and to other industries. Hence in every region there will be *two* general income levels for labour, and the simple mechanism of inter-regional migration in search of higher factor incomes used in the preceding analysis of the staple theory is complicated by movements from country to city, and by the general minimization of inter-regional movements of factors within agriculture such as the simple theory would predict.

This difficulty of statistical verification, of course, parallels the real difficulty of adjustment in declining regions whose staple product is, and continues to

---

[4] For examples, see Howland, Robert, *Regional Aspects of Canadian Economic Development,* a study for the Royal Commission on Canada's Economic Prospects, Ottawa, 1956; Borts, G. H. and Jerome L. Stein, *Economic Growth in a Free Society,* New York, Columbia University Press, 1964; and numerous papers by Easterlin, Smolensky, Hanna, Perloff and associates, and Tiebout. For a collection, with comments, see Hanna, F. A., ed., *Regional Income,* Studies in Income and Wealth 21, Princeton, 1952.

be, agricultural. Indeed, the statistical and adjustment problems, while serious in their separate ways, are perhaps even more dangerous for the confusion they create in the planning of long-run policy. They both suggest that certain industries, like fishing, agriculture, small-scale forestry and personal services are "bound" to offer low incomes anywhere. That this need not be so can be proved by pointing to areas where labour scarcity and efficient management enable such industries to pay incomes as high as in manufacturing industry in that region. This paper cannot expand on the point, but it must be pointed out that the staple-and-mobility approach indicates that there are *no* "inferior" industries (unless there are inferior people). Local industries that appear to be inferior in their income-opportunities are that way only because labour is locally in relatively excessive supply; thus it pays employers to use much labour and little capital, imagination or organizational ability; thus, to the layman, it appears that the industry "cannot" pay higher wages. Higher wages, indeed, would necessitate local contraction, the abandonment of marginal resources, and some labour migration. But the extent of the contraction by each industry, in response to higher wage-costs, would be determined by the resources and the markets, not by some eternal "inferiority" of the industry. To conclude, it is putting the cart before the horse to say that because a region has low-paying industries, it must have a low-income population. The causation, amenable to policy manipulation, is the other way around.

4. Regional development of staple industries is usually assumed to be the mechanism of national economic growth. This will obviously be true if the national population and stock of capital is closed to international migration. Under such circumstances, the staple theory will provide the mechanism by which the national endowment is allocated and reallocated among industries, in response to changing domestic and international demands. The crucial point is that such reallocation requires the abandoning of some types of resource and location, and the development of others—a point often neglected in trade theory, which assumes that resources are homogeneous within each nation. Assuming that labour-and-capital productivity is improved by technology faster than these factors accumulate, and/or that there is a rising international demand for the products in which the nation has a comparative advantage, the staple theory also describes the mechanism of economic growth in the narrow sense: rising income per person.

But when the economy is open, as is Canada's, to international migration, it no longer follows that the staple-theory mechanism produces higher incomes nationally. The immigrant labour (and capital) may be attracted to regions where staple-industry incomes, while higher than those abroad, are lower than those earned in other regions of the new country. Thus a new staple may initially lower the national average standard of living. Even if the new immigrants, learning that their new incomes are not the highest to be earned in the new country, now continue their migrations to the better paying regions, the average income will remain lower than it might have been because they have "diluted" the national labour market. Furthermore, they may be replaced by new immigrants from abroad, whose presence will continue to inhibit the rate of income growth, per person, of the entire economy. Finally, the effort of the old regions to establish the staple industries in the new regions may in itself produce a costly loss of capital for the old regions.

It should be stressed that all this is not to assert that encouraging international immigration is always a mistake for those already employed. The new staple in the new region may yield higher returns than incomes in the old regions. Furthermore, the new immigrants may bring capital, skill, technology and enterprise which more than compensate for the new region's inferiority had it been exploited by those who were already in the country.[5]

(d) *Summary of Regional Approaches*—To summarize thus far, it has been argued that trade theory provides a good explanation of factor income and regional industrialization to the extent that labour and capital are not mobile. Unfortunately for users of the theory, however, factors are mobile, so that recourse must be had to what has been called location theory. But this too is unsatisfactory because, in its present state, it is essentially static, neglecting not only nationally and regionally growing supplies of labour and capital but also changing techniques and demands.

The remaining approach is a model based on the staple theory which focuses attention on four elements: factor mobility, export price, resource availability, and technology. It is shown that this model not only provides an explanation for regional growth with mobile factors of which the competing "stages" growth theory is incapable, but also can account for declines in regions in which the export base has become a small part of the local economy. The main lesson from the model is almost a truism: regional incomes need not decline below the national average if labour is at least as mobile as capital, and if both inputs emigrate at the rate dictated by the rate of decline of the staple industry's market (while it pays national wage and interest rates) *and* by the associated decline of the residentiary industries.

For the more footloose manufacturing industries, of course, this model needs some modification. (It has already accounted for resource-oriented industries and market-oriented residentiary industries.) If industries are truly footloose, which one may doubt, then there is really no accounting for their location by this or any other theory. Having once become established in a region, they may prefer to stay while the region declines, thus taking advantage of lower wage rates. But it may be doubted that the category includes many important industries. Certainly most manufacturing industries are resource-oriented, if the world resource is defined to include natural advantages in transportation, cheap access to raw materials, and so forth. It must be admitted that the sheer size of industries such as steel and automobile manufacturing does create a considerable inertia in the mechanism of resource and market-orientation. But recent changes in the location of new plants in these two industries suggest that their inertia is less than infinite, even after tariff and political incentives have been allowed for.

PART III. GOVERNMENT POLICIES

(a) *The Aims of Effective Policy*—In the analysis of Part II, factor migration was assumed to be a fact of economic life. Even when it is admitted that emigration is less rapid than immigration, that labour is less mobile than capital, that some persons are not mobile at all, this assumption in itself leads to two propositions. First, a truism: when an industry and its region begin to decline relatively to the whole nation, the more mobile people leave first. Second, more substantially: the people who leave first impose a greater loss than those who are

---

[5] Some of the points in this section have been suggested by an unpublished paper by Professor Donald Gordon of the University of Washington.

squeezed out later. This second proposition actually stems from a recognition that labour is not a homogeneous stock, but is composed of persons of different ages, strengths, marital and family states, skills, training, risk-taking propensities, and propensities to participate in local institutions and governments. Of these, some characteristics are valuable both to employers and to the local community; furthermore, it may be suggested, they are highly valuable to employers in other regions. Thus people with these valuable characteristics are likely to be the first lured away when local opportunities falter, and their departure is likely to impose the greatest per capita loss.

Thus a community which has been declining for a few years is usually observed to have more than the national percentage of older, married, unskilled, uneducated and risk-averse people, conservative and individualistic with respect to the proposal or support of community "booster" projects. Obviously, this composition of the labour force is going to reinforce the tendency of the local population to specialize in activities connected with the old staple and in agriculture. Furthermore, it will make them disinclined to remould the structure of regional government and its services to accord with the new circumstances.

This line of argument leads to two conclusions: first, because of the strong incentives for the mobility of those who first leave, little that government can do (if it would) can prevent the initial, the most serious stages of the regional decline; second, the inclination of local government to take whatever action seems indicated, at the *local* level, will be weakened by the disinclination of the remaining local people to abandon local institutions. Instead, they will appeal to the central government for help in the form of tariffs, public works, tax subsidies, and low-interest loans.

This personal conservatism is fortified by the apparent absence in most constitutions of provision for the dismantling of local, county or provincial governments. It might be objected this lack reflects the absence of any observed need ever to wipe out municipalities or provinces. But this objection involves a circular argument.

It is circular because it relies on the observation that depopulated provinces and regions, and "ghost towns" always have *some* population, *some* business, and therefore *some* functions to perform. Business decline does not result in total abandonment. But it neglects to inquire whether the residual factor of immobility is the cause, or the result, of the agonized survival of government units. Thus the objection can be countered by the argument that unless local government is dismantled, final evacuation of the area by the people that it is serving, and by their descendents, will never take place.

More positively, we may postulate that local and regional government, though set up to serve people and business, is defined by an area (not a group of people, each of whom is mobile), and is given some jurisdiction over the land. For example, this postulate underlies the frequent defense of land (property) taxation as a source of local revenue: land is all the local government really "has". Those connected with or participating in this government therefore usually have duties connected with land (registration, property protection, zoning, transportation, drainage, flood protection, water services) that are almost independent of the number of citizens involved, except that they depend upon local tax revenues for their performance. Thus, when a population exodus commences, the impact on local government is less in the number of services to be performed than in the tax revenue produced. Its reaction follows logically: instead of reducing the number and standard of services, preliminary to shutting up shop, or amalgamating with a larger government capable of performing the services, it attempts to prevent the decline in tax revenue. To avoid confusion with the various meanings of "regional", this preoccupation with the geographical area may be described as "regionary".[6]

This is equivalent to saying that it attempts to find devices and gimmicks that will hold and attract business, although the local individual interest might best be served by a swift decision to dissolve, first providing such services and incentives as would expedite the complete evacuation of their declining area.

Based on the analysis so far, therefore, our policy conclusion must be that because it is impossible for government to do much about the complete emigration of capital, and impossible for it to prevent the emigration of the most valuable part of the regional labour force, it might better concern itself with minimizing its problems by promoting emigration (down to a level where a more "modest" staple can pay the national rates of return on labour and capital) than with trying to halt or reverse the flow.

A second conclusion depends upon the proposition that because the inertia of the last-remaining people and units of capital is fortified by the survival of inappropriate units of government, dismantling the regional economy to a level appropriate to the industries that it can now sustain requires the re-apportioning of regional governmental functions.

These two policy conclusions reflect the hard-boiled implications of the staple approach. When a region's export base has dwindled, its superstructure of population, investment and government must also dwindle, in order that the national level of income and growth can be recovered. Any policy that impedes this dismantling, raising the hopes and apparent prospects of the residual factors, merely postpones the day of regional *per capita* recovery. Unless policy succeeds in finding a new regional staple, it is profitless to attempt to attain the earlier relative size and *total* income of the region.

Policies that might establish a new export base are examined below. First, however, we examine a few government actions for illustrations of the wrong, implicit, policy.

(b) *Unhelpful Policies*—A helpful policy is, of course, one that leads to incomes that equal the national level, not one that merely leads to more industry or more employment at lower standards, nor to a slowing of the appropriate rate of regional decline.

The discussion is helped by dividing "policies" into that group that is apparently intended to be helpful to special regions, and that group that has an unintended regional impact.

Among the well-intended group are to be found policies that attempt to remedy the transportation difficulties of declining export industries. These include not only lavish spending on such public works as port and highway facilities, but also subsidies to land, sea and air carriers. Occasionally these aids succeed in building an industry up to a scale where it can cover its own transport costs. But more typically there is an annual cost.

---

[6] Although it appears to be coined from the combination of *region* and *reactionary, regionary* is actually an old form of *regional*. In its various senses it is both adjective and noun.

It is worth stressing that this annual cost never ends. A highway, for example, when completed might seem to be costless thereafter (apart from maintenance). But in fact its construction deprives other regions of the same expenditure on highways, other works, or private goods. Formally, there is a perpetual loss on the outlay measured by the extent that its rate of return to the nation is less than elsewhere. It is more obvious that subsidies to carriers never end, and are a perpetual drain on the incomes of other regions.

Unrelated to transportation problems, but just as costly to the nation as a whole, is that class of "development assistance" that is earmarked for declining communities. The provisions vary, but examples include special income-tax deductions for industries in specified locations, assistance in supporting the renewal of social capital such as housing, hospitals and schools, and the deliberate siting of provincial and federal installations in areas of low income or employment, without regard to their extra expense.

Third, the nation as a whole, or the province, may be persuaded to acquiesce in tariffs, discriminating purchase policies, quotas, or protection concealed in quality or content requirements. It is well-known that such measures, although not subsidies from government, impose similar burdens on consumers. Canada seems to have progressed less than other countries, however, in investigating the regional distribution of the protection these measures offer. In the United States, for example, it has been found that certain tariff and "Buy-American" provisions, though costly to the nation as a whole, work to the advantage of industries in a very few isolated regions. (And, it might be remarked, this discovery has led to suggestions of more effective and less costly methods of aiding the same group of persons.)

All these costs of regional protection are distributed unsystematically over the nation as a whole. They have not only the direct effect of diffusing the low incomes received in the declining region, but also the indirect effect of reducing the gap between real incomes in that region and others, thus reducing the incentive to the mobility that can only ultimately remedy the regional decline.

Costs that are born locally, of course, take real income out of one pocket and put it into another. For example, the remission of local taxes on certain industries, provision of utility services at prices less than would otherwise be charged, and the acceptance of local industrial nuisances like air and water pollution, all may help to maintain local employment at the price of lower real incomes after taxes. For the most part, this price is paid by the same persons whose employment is maintained. But it also reduces the real incomes of persons employed in other local industries, and thus, paradoxically, may promote the emigration of the wrong people or capital.

In American discussions of regional problems, it is usual to see national minimum-wage legislation cited as one cause of regional decline. The argument is that the necessity of paying effective minimum wages makes certain staple industries unprofitable, puts them out of business, and thus leads to greater regional depression. Although, because national minimum wages are paid in very few industries in Canada (owing to the fewness of industries coming under federal jurisdiction, and of industries for which nation-wide collective bargaining is customary), this argument has little application in Canada. It may be remarked that its general drift runs counter to the approach suggested in this paper. Leaving aside the obvious difficulty that minimum wages may be set too high, so that they can be attained only by monopolistically restricting entry to certain industries, or by general inflation of wages and prices, minima have the desirable result of discouraging or preventing labour from working at wages below those received elsewhere. They thus encourage labour migration (parallel to the capital migration that reflects the "minimum yield" behaviour of investors), until the region's resources and sites can support a reduced number of employers and factors at national living standards.

Finally, we may examine the ideas implicit in the recent efforts to formulate regional plans. Foremost among these are the studies made in the northern territories, Saskatchewan, Manitoba, Quebec and the Atlantic Provinces, and to them may be added the tax studies and local-purchase policies in Ontario. These studies are to be encouraged to the extent that they increase knowledge of the regional economy, and admired for their courage in forecasting on the basis of Canada's negligible store of regional data. But their aims are greatly to be feared, for not only do their predictions largely neglect the possibility of any migration except the investment of funds from "abroad", but also their format suggests a regionary preoccupation.

These studies commence with a population forecast based primarily on regional rates of natural increase. It is then shown that, on certain assumptions about the growth of residentiary and staple industries (the latter, because of their discrete nature, are almost impossible to predict), local job opportunities will fail to keep up with the size of the labour force. The studies then trail off into voluminous appendices and commissioned reports on the means by which the government, in cooperation with local industry, can encourage or subsidize the growth of local opportunities to soak up the new supply of workers. That I have yet to see a study that goes beyond the regretful observation that "some emigration is likely", is not surprising, for one may summarize the implicit aim of these studies as the maximization of employment within the region, subject to a given minimum of labour emigration. Thus the researchers may well be reproached for seeking a certain type of regionary success, not high average incomes for the present residents and their children, wherever they choose to live. Similarly, the government programs endorsed are deficient in that they usually contain many more provisions for the attraction and holding of industry than for the embodiment in the labour force not only of skills and abilities, but also of an adaptability, a capacity to adjust to the techniques, languages, customs or laws of other regions.

(c) *Qualifications*—This point of view may seem unreasonably harsh. The poorer and more deprived people in the country are concentrated in certain regions, so that the criticism in the previous section seems to amount to an inhumane advocacy of the withdrawal of assistance to them.

But this would be a misinterpretation. The target of the criticisms was the preoccupation with regions rather than with people. The point of view can be restated thus: regions with unemployment and low incomes should be studied. Study will show that some people are deprived of a national standard of income because they are ill-educated, unadaptable or indeed unemployable. Others are simply in the wrong region. Let us examine the two groups.

No one can object to remedying deficiencies in human capital. Both a generous concern for those with low income and a selfish concern for the national product indicate that nothing but gain can result from policies that inculcate skill, training and experience into that human capital. It is inexcusable that people and their employers in Canada are burdened by the low level of training that is typical of the country. Many American studies, and a few Canadian guesses, have in-dicated that the rates of return on *all* costs of education are extremely high, often as much as 20 per cent per year for life. If raising the standards of people in any region, whether it is rich or poor, requires more assistance to education, few people can object. If, in addition, this aid to education (and to other methods of investing in the capacity of human capital) requires direct subsidies to the gov-ernments of the retarded regions, the complications of this method must be accepted.[7]

Furthermore, it must be conceded that in many poor regions there are people whose age precludes the possibility of much profitable investment in their training or adaptability. Humane policy suggests that they should be helped wherever they live. But the same indifference to training and location should not apply to their children.

The policy criticisms above are directed at policies intended to remedy the plight of the second group of people. To reiterate briefly, these criticisms are that such a policy is, in the first place, biased by the regionary preoccupation of maintaining local employment and activity and, in the second place, distorted by those actions of higher levels of government that reduce instead of increasing positive incentives toward labour mobility.

Thus, instead of the lack of education of the local population being taken as an excuse for disregarding the long-run advisability of labour migration, and concentrating instead on bringing funds to the people, the staple approach indi-cates that education should be regarded only as the first step, preparing most of the regional population for migration, taking people to the resources and capital.[8]

Professional economists will wish for reassurance on the "welfare econom-ics" of these condemnations of unhelpful policies. They will be aware that a policy of strengthening the strong regions, and of abandoning policies such as tariffs that perpetuate the declining regions can be defended technically only by invoking the Kaldor approach to potential compensation. They will know that the ethical acceptabilities of this principle are usually regarded as weak unless full compensation is actually paid, in which case the Kaldor approach is not needed. Tariffs, regional subsidies, fiscal equalization and the like may be regarded as compensation, and thus as a sort of conscience-money paid by a growing econo-my for the havoc its growth creates among the regions that are unable to stand the pace.

It should be clear that I reject both the analogy with compensation and the implied growth theory. To take the latter first, the theory of growth outlined here does not depend on a set of regions, with given populations and different growth rates, successively taking-off by clambering over the people of regions that have failed to grow. Instead, it depends on a group of factors moving from region to region as export advantage dictates. Just as the recreation of a group of grow-

---

[7] The problems that transfers from one region to another, whatever their motives, create for regional mobility have been surveyed many times. See for example J. F. Graham's *Fiscal Adjustment and Economic Development,* Toronto, 1963, for an examination of transfers within a province. My own paper contains an extensive bibliography: Scott, Anthony, "The Goals of Federal Finance", *Public Finance,* Vol. 19, 1964, pp. 241-292.

[8] The debate on this subject between James Buchanan and myself has been reprinted in Benson, C. S., ed., *Perspectives on the Economics of Education,* 1963; surveyed by J. F. Graham in the book mentioned above; and extended to apply to other goals than growth and efficiency in the *Public Finance* articles mentioned in the previous footnote.

ing children requires first nurseries, then gardens, playgrounds, pools, gymnasia, golf courses and so forth, so a country growing by grasping the opportunities to produce those export staples that promise the highest incomes must migrate from one region to another. Of course, there can be more than one staple; there is more than one kind of person; and the migration cannot be apprehended or performed overnight. But these qualifications do not suggest that the abandoned region, any more than the abandoned nursery, should be "compensated".

My rejection of the analogy with the compensation principle follows from these remarks about growth. The failure of a region to grow is reflected by a gradual reversal of a growth path. If it is gradual enough, and if there is no government to offer comfort to those who will not observe the unmistakable signals, all those who are in danger of losing by the reversal can take their productive capacities elsewhere, except the owners of land. They, and their local government, will naturally have a regionary bias. But even their loss will be small if the decline is recognized and is slow.

If migration begins early, no one needs to be compensated. Early migration of people means that the subsequent decline will be slow; indeed if those who can gain will only migrate as soon as possible, it is likely that regional incomes per person will never decline. Just as a worker who is promoted need not be compensated for the "loss" of his previous position, so a population that steadily moves off to jobs elsewhere need not be compensated for the inferior positions left behind.

Economists will recall that the compensation controversy arose from study of the gains and losses from the repeal of the Corn Laws. Losses were anticipated by land-holders, the only class whose earning capacity was not versatile or geographically mobile. This reflection may suggest that the maintenance of a versatile and mobile economy among regions might be expedited if land were leased rather than bought by its users from the government.

(d) *A New Export Base*—The above approach to theory and policy is less applicable to regions whose labour is, as a matter of fact, permanently immobile. Thus the approach to policy does not work as between Quebec and the rest of the world, if migration into and out of that province is only effective at the margin. Similar reservations about its applicability might be made by those concerned about the Eskimos, the northern Indians and a few other groups. However, the argument obviously applies *within* French Canada as a whole, as recent patterns of internal migration will testify.

Furthermore, the approach is inapplicable if provincial and lower levels of government persist in their regionary bias. As a matter of policy, one might urge them to contemplate the economic abandonment of their regions—but as a matter of fact, they may reject the advice.

The dilemma of the small country, or the province whose labour is immobile, is that such regions cannot stop migration completely. Capital continues to flow in search of a high return; if the local staple promises a low return, capital will leave. Or, if capital can be held only by a drastic decline in the wages of labour, then labour will tend to migrate, or will revolt.

If capital is not willing to remain, the policy of the government must be to find some substitute for private investment in the old staples.

First, it can try to increase the local rate of saving. Because private saving, embodied in securities, will emigrate when possible, it follows that the capital goods, and the profits to them, must be owned by the province. This may account for Quebec's wave of nationalization.

Second, it can attempt to attract private capital on new terms. As we have seen, these terms can only involve a cost to someone. If it is to the taxpayer, then the real income of the population will be reduced as surely as if wages had fallen sufficiently to attract the capital.

Third, it can try to increase the resource base. This is a route that Canadian provinces have tended to ignore. Geological surveys, forest products research, agricultural research and fisheries' investigations have been left, thankfully, to the federal government and to the interested companies. But the federal government has no regionary bias, and so does not focus its efforts on increasing the known wealth of a particular region: it is as happy to find marble near Churchill as it is to find copper near Moncton. And the private companies are rarely biased toward making discoveries in particular regions. Thus the burden of increasing its regionary wealth must eventually be born by the region itself.

Thus the initial burden of finding a new natural staple must usually be born by the region itself, or if it is born nationally, must be oriented toward the declining region.

This is the most attractive way out, for if a new staple is found, it will last, whereas new sources of capital either depend on the maintenance of helpful policies by the central government or (in the absence of complete nationalization at the regional level) tend to drift away. It follows that the pay-off period for regionary expenditure in investigation of mineral wealth, forest-product conversion, and other natural-resource opportunities will be longer than the period of benefit from other types of developmental expenditure.

(e) *Conclusions on Policy*—It may be helpful to gather together the policy conclusions developed in this Part.

First, it was stressed that regions decline because their staple industries decline and motivate factor emigration. Governments, especially local governments, have a "regionary" bias that tends to arrest this migration and aggravate local conditions.

Second, it was suggested that government policy should be reversed; it should be biased toward promoting migration. Incidentally, it should aid in the dismantling of governments that are, by their responsibilities, forced to display a regionary bias.

Third, it was shown that one mode of assistance would be to promote education in skills useful elsewhere, and in attitudes productive of mobility and versatility.

Finally, it was argued that where mobility of labour was impossible, it was necessary to attract and hold capital in order to develop a new high level regional staple apart from generating and holding capital through nationalization (publicly-owned enterprise); this can only be done by obtaining grants or tariffs and subsidies from the national government. A more productive route to recovery is the discovery of a new regional staple, in the discovery of which the regional government should invest.

The general theme of this paper is that factor mobility is a fact of economic life in Canada. The aim of policy should be to assist this mobility, thus raising the incomes of all factor owners. It should not be "regionary": we owe nothing to the resources themselves, and can gain little, in the long run, by "aiding regions" now destitute of a high-income staple. To make policy of this type humane, it must be applied slowly. But too often the humane modifications tend to overpower the policy itself.

COMMENTS

PROFESSOR CLARENCE L. BARBER,
Department of Economics,
University of Manitoba,
(1964-65, McGill University).

Scott builds his analysis around the staple thesis which argues that the growth or decline of a particular region depends on the growth or decline of the region's export staple. Essentially this is an application of the local or geographic multiplier with the term staple interpreted widely to cover any export product. Pushed to its logical conclusion this thesis would imply that the growth or decline of Canada as a whole depends on the prosperity of its export industries. One weakness of the staple or export model is that it breaks down when we apply it to the world as a whole. More generally its validity declines as the size of area to which it is applied increases. If we divide the world into ten major regions, we can say for each region that its growth and prosperity depends on its exports to the remaining nine. Yet if we consolidate all ten into a single region we have nothing left to explain what determines the growth of the area as a whole.

Although he does not make it fully explicit, Scott appears to recognize this. Growth in the world as a whole depends on the growth of population, the accumulation of capital, the development of new techniques and the establishment of new productive enterprises to employ the growing supply of labour and capital and to exploit the new techniques. The particular goods produced reflect the pattern of demand. The areas in which they will be produced must be explained in terms of location theory as modified by tariffs and other forms of government intervention. Now it is evident from the way in which the world has grown over the past few centuries that there is nothing automatic about growth or predestined about the location of particular activities. Some parts of the world have had strong, even spectacular, growth. Other regions and countries have stagnated. In some degree this is also true of areas within particular countries. And while the work in growth theory of the past few years has given us some insights into why these differences exist we are still far from a fully satisfactory explanation.

While the location of some industries can be explained quite simply in terms of their resource orientation there are other industries whose location is partly due to the chance of history. Watches in Switzerland, diamond cutting in Amsterdam, optical equipment in Germany, are examples that come to mind. That both footloose and market-oriented industries are located where they are today, is the outcome of a long series of interacting decisions made in the past.

It is clear, of course, that the staple thesis has a great deal of validity as an explanation of the growth of an isolated local area dependent on a particular resource. The growth of Thompson, Manitoba or Kitimat, British Columbia, is almost entirely dependent on a single resource based industry. And if such an industry loses its economic rationale the wisest economic policy may be that which Scott recommends, to encourage a movement of labour and capital out of the area. But when we are concerned with the future of a much larger area whose original development took place on the basis of several industries a much wider range of considerations becomes relevant.

Yet Scott does not appear prepared to make any distinction here. Whether we are dealing with Springhill, Nova Scotia, the Atlantic Provinces as a whole or perhaps even Canada as a nation he takes a slightly modified laissez-faire position. Our objective, he argues, should be the maximization of the per capita income of Canadians, with allowances one presumes for the non-pecuniary advantages of different locations, although this latter qualification is not explicitly made. Thus, in areas that are declining or are growing too slowly to provide employment for their native born labour force, the government should restrict its policy measures to encouraging the surplus labour force to move to other areas.

It is an implication of Scott's position that the decisions of private business firms with respect to the location of industry will promote a maximum real per capita income for Canadians and that any attempt to interfere with or redirect these decisions will involve some loss. Yet in reaching this conclusion Scott makes no reference to the possibility that there may be substantial divergences between the private costs and gains as they appear to individual business firms and the social costs and benefits that accrue to the economy as a whole. His silence on this point suggests that Scott thinks the difference that may exist here is unimportant. I wonder if we have any evidence to support such a conclusion.

Nor is any allowance made for the fact that the structure of Canadian manufacturing industry departs widely from the perfectly competitive model. Yet monopoly pricing practices, such as the basing point system that often exists for heavy raw materials, may exert significant effects on the location of industry.

Then, too, one wonders if Professor Scott has considered all the implications of the disequilibrium model advanced by Gunnar Myrdal. It is Myrdal's contention that economic forces far from being always equilibrating are often disequilibrating. Thus, if an area's major industry suffers a serious setback, a sequence of events may begin which leads to a progressive deterioration in the area's economic position. Capital and skilled labour may begin to move out. Unemployed workers who stay on will find their skills and employability deteriorating. This in turn will make new firms more reluctant to come into the region. Some existing firms may reduce the scale of their operations. With lower income levels educational facilities may deteriorate and this will further reduce the chances for further growth. Yet all this need not prove that a viable and growing economy could not exist in the region. It may be that an infusion of new capital and enterprise could reinvigorate the whole area and thus reverse the disequilibrating movement.

It seems to me that what is needed in the case of each declining area is an honest appraisal of the future economic prospects of the area as a whole. Only then can we decide whether some new transfusion is required or whether we should set underway steps leading to a winding up of the whole enterprise.

Scott has expressed concern about the preoccupation with regional growth that has developed in different provinces across Canada. Personally I think this interest is desirable and potentially useful. That there are dangers I would be the first to agree. Local protective devices can be just as harmful to economic efficiency as national tariffs; and in markets that even for Canada as a whole are often too small to achieve all the economies of large scale production, measures that further subdivide these markets are greatly to be deplored. But I think most provinces are aware of these dangers. Moreover, there may be a good deal that a province can do to promote regional development that is not inconsistent with or harmful to the growth of other areas.

Consider, for example, the province of Manitoba, the region with which I am most familiar. By Scott's standards this is a declining area for its rate of growth in terms of employment and income over the past decade has been below the national average. Moreover, current prospects are that without some acceleration in the area's growth a significant movement of labour out of the area will be required. If I understand Scott correctly he would argue that the provincial government should do little or nothing to encourage the province's growth and if unemployment develops labour should be encouraged to move elsewhere.

In fact, as many of you know, some four years ago, the provincial government in cooperation with local industry undertook to sponsor a comprehensive survey of Manitoba's future economic prospects and the government is now implementing some of the recommendations that were an outgrowth of that survey. As a result of this study many business firms and other local citizens began for the first time to give some serious thought to the question of just what did determine whether the province grew or developed. It soon became apparent that Manitoba in general and Winnipeg in particular had developed to a large degree as a transportation, financing and trading centre for the prairie grain economy. As long as prairie agriculture was expanding, Winnipeg and Manitoba shared in that growth. But prairie agriculture is no longer a growth industry and as a result Manitoba has had to turn to other industries to support its continued growth. The so-called COMEF report represents a serious attempt to appraise in some detail the prospective growth of the province. In the main its recommendations are for government encouragement of economic developments which are sound and viable.

Economists are fond of operating with economic models in which knowledge is perfect and an all-wise group of private business firms make economically sound decisions. Yet we know in fact that in almost any industry levels of operating efficiency vary widely among different firms. Again as between different countries levels of efficiency may vary widely in similar industries. If it is considered appropriate in underdeveloped countries for governments to assume an active role in attempting to accelerate the rate of economic growth why should we deny a similar role to provincial governments.

Still, I do not wish to overemphasize my disagreement with Scott's position. Governments may often be under pressure to prop up and support industries and areas which have little economic future. There seems to be little economic rationale to recent federal legislation which discriminates uniformly in favour of areas of slower growth irrespective of their economic prospects.

Moreover, there is merit in Scott's stress on the need for mobility. For there is reason to believe that much more mobility of labour will be required in Canada during the next few years than has been true in the past. During the first decade after the war when the rate of growth in the native-born Canadian labour force was slow and when net immigration into Canada was heavy, the need for mobility within Canada was minimized. The more rapidly growing areas—Alberta, British Columbia and Ontario—could attract the new immigrants whereas areas where growth was slower could fill all or most of their labour requirements from their own natural increase. But now that we face the prospect of having a much larger proportion of new entrants to the labour force come from the native-born, a regional growth pattern similar to that which has prevailed over the past decade or more will require a much larger movement of labour within Canada. Unless this movement occurs easily, Canada may find it has to tolerate a significantly higher unemployment level as the price of avoiding a given amount of inflation. But given the fact that more mobility is desirable how can this best be attained?

Several proposals suggest themselves. Every person who has been unemployed for more than some specified period, say six months, should be given free transportation to areas where jobs are more plentiful. If he finds work elsewhere the actual cost of moving his family should be heavily subsidized. The cost should be borne by the federal government and the policy should be made in general in its application. If this were done no particular area should feel that it was being singled out for invidious treatment. The details of such a policy could easily be worked out. But I see no reason why such a policy cannot exist side by side with provincial government policies designed to encourage the growth and development of provinces as a whole or of declining areas within a province.

COMMENTS

PROFESSOR K. G. CRAWFORD,
Department of Political Studies,
Queen's University.

To the layman the term "declining" implies something that is on the way down or at least that is not going up. "Declining regions" by the definition in Prof. Scott's paper includes those that are in some sense "less developed" and those with low incomes per person, not those with a low or declining population. This practice of re-writing the language makes it confusing for the reader, especially when it comes to considering matters of policy. The major proposals are (1) to raise the skills of the people through education, (2) to attempt to develop a new high level regional staple, and (3) the heroic policy of promoting migration from the declining regions. With the first two there can be little quarrel but I would like to touch on the third.

I do not question the policy proposals as an exercise in theory, given the original assumption of the primary aim. While it would be desirable that all persons should receive the national level of income, it should be kept in mind that "man does not live by bread alone". For some the price of attaining that level of income may be more than they want to pay. As the Gordon Commission noted in discussing the Atlantic region, "Many people in the Atlantic region would not exchange on any terms their more peaceful way of life and the comparative ease and quiet that goes with it for the noise and bustle and tenseness which one associates with living in large Metropolitan areas like Montreal, Toronto and Vancouver".

This does not mean that we can cheerfully accept the fact that many people have a lower standard of living in declining areas, as defined, on the assumption that they are content as evidenced by the fact that they stay there. It does suggest, however, that there are certainly some who prefer a lower standard but with other compensations. Surely this explains at least in part why all the Canadians who are neither communists nor possessed of a criminal record have not migrated to the United States.

In discussing the desirability of encouraging population migration from declining areas the paper suggests that government policy should aid in the dismantling of governments that are, by their responsibilities, forced to display a regionary basis. This presumably means the dismantling of provincial and municipal governments. It seems to me to be pointless and unrealistic to expect to eliminate such governments in a country such as Canada. Surely in a federation this is just one of the facts of life that has to be lived with.

As long as we have provinces and local governments their policies are going to be regionary — and rightly so under our system of government. No Nova Scotia government is going to promote policies designed to encourage people to emigrate to Ontario to take advantage of better economic opportunities. At least if it does so, its not going to admit it. No municipal council is going to urge its people to go elsewhere to better themselves. In both cases the policy makers are put in office to promote the interests of their region, be it province or municipality, to do otherwise would be political suicide. Local and provincial governments exist to fulfill many functions; the promotion of the economic welfare of the inhabitants is only one. To eliminate these governments for the purpose of eliminating regional bias in dealing with the problems of declining regions would be to throw out the baby with the bath water.

It is suggested in the paper that at the onset of decline in a region the more progressive and highly skilled in the population emigrate. This leaves a community composed of the older, married, less educated, less skilled, more conservative types and it is argued from this that they are disinclined to remould the structure of regional governments. What is suggested with respect to the composition of the remaining population seems reasonable. It is questionable, however, whether or not this has much to do with the disinclination to remould the governmental structure. If there is one issue that seems to meet with universal resistance, whether in communities with a soaring economy or communities in declining regions, it is a proposal to remould their structure of government, and particularly local government. If this residual population is disinclined to change, the difference would appear to be merely a matter of degree and, on the basis of experience, not many degrees.

Professor Scott suggests that this personal conservatism "is fortified by the apparent absence in most constitutions of provision for the dismantling of local, county, or provincial governments". It is true that there is no provision for dismantling provincial governments but at least five provinces make provision for reducing the status, dissolving or, as unhappily expressed in one province, disorganizing local governments.

He raises the question as to whether the residual factor of immobility is the cause or the result of the "agonized survival of government units", and implies that unless local government is dismantled, final evacuation of a declining area by the people it is serving and their descendants will never take place. This implication follows from a misunderstanding of the basic purpose of municipal or local governments. It exists to serve people, to do for its people those things they want done, in the way they want them done, and which they can do jointly through the medium of a local government more effectively and economically than if they did them as individuals. On what basis then can you justify dismantling the local government as long as the inhabitants are prepared to meet their share of the cost. Assuming, as the paper does, that it may be desirable to attain complete evacuation of an area, the dismantling of local government gives no assurance of this result as is suggested by the many population clusters in unorganized territory in several of the provinces.

The speaker in discussing policy stated that "A helpful policy is, of course, one that leads to incomes that equal the national level, not one that merely leads to more industry or more employment at lower standards, nor to the slowing of the appropriate rate of regional decline". Such a statement may be correct in theory, again given the primary assumption but it is difficult to accept from a practical point of view. I suspect that there are many declining regions where policies which led to more industry and more employment, even at lower than the national level of incomes, would be enthusiastically received. In cases where policies resulted in the slowing down of the so-called "appropriate" rate of regional decline it would seem that the opportunity for a less abrupt readjustment would entitle such a policy to be classed as "helpful" rather than "unhelpful", at least by those immediately affected.

It is all very well to take the position that the government knows best and should apply those policies which in the long run they believe to be in the best interests of all, however much those most affected may dislike them. However, there is the possibility that the government does not know best what is good for its people. It should be kept in mind also that our system of government is based on the idea that if the people prefer the second best, they are entitled to have it. The policies which governments have to find, with respect to declining regions as in other matters, are not the theoretically ideal solutions but those which are as near to the ideal as can be sold to those of the community who are involved.

THE PROBLEM OF REGIONAL DISPARITIES

PROFESSOR T. N. BREWIS,
Department of Economics,
Carleton University.

In Canada, as elsewhere, economic growth follows an irregular pattern over time. Growth has been much more rapid in some decades than others and shorter run periods have been dominated by the fluctuations of the business cycle. Not only has the pace of development varied over time, but it has been unevenly distributed over the country as a whole, with the result that income and employment opportunities differ markedly from one part of the country to another. In certain cases, as in the recent development of oil and gas resources, the expansion of a particular area has been at the direct expense of others.

This uneven spatial development, inherent in technological change and the growth process, gives rise to a variety of problems with social, economic and political implications. The strains to which uneven distribution of income and employment opportunity can give rise require no elaboration in a country such as Canada where national unity is a constant political preoccupation.

The matter is one which has been receiving increasing attention in Canada in recent years and the federal government has been assuming a more specific role in influencing the course of what is generally described as regional or area economic development. This paper looks at some of the considerations underlying federal action, questions objectives and contains certain recommendations with regard to policy.

There are several strands to the discussion. Prominent among the economic considerations are the following:

(a) Concern over the relatively high unemployment levels, and low labour force participation rates prevailing in certain areas of the country, with the attendant loss of production.

(b) The instability of employment or income due to heavy dependence on some particular industry or form of activity.

(c) The uneven distribution of income across the country.

(d) The depopulation of certain areas and fears of overcrowding in others.

As will be seen from Table A on the following page, personal income per capita in Newfoundland has been typically around half that in British Columbia or Ontario, and in some years it has been significantly less even than this. Incomes in the Prairies have varied around the mean for the country as a whole, but, as will be noted, incomes in Saskatchewan specifically have been very erratic. They were as low as 47 per cent of the national average in 1933 and as high as 106 per cent in 1944. In 1961, they were 77 per cent and in 1962, 102 per cent. No other province shows anything like this degree of instability. The explanation lies, of course, in Saskatchewan's heavy dependence on wheat production and exports.

As for employment, it will be seen from Table B that, here too, there have been substantial differences across the country. The Atlantic Provinces have clearly suffered from much heavier unemployment than the country as a whole, unemployment reaching a peak of 12.5 per cent in 1958, and an average not far short of 10 per cent for the quinquennium 1956-1960. The quinquennium figure in Ontario, by contrast, was little more than 4 per cent. As for the Prairies, unemployment there has been less than anywhere else in the country.

TABLE A

Personal Income* — Per Capita — Canadian Provinces
Expressed as a Per Cent of the Canadian Average
1926—1962

	1926	1929	1933	1935	1939	1944	1946	1950	1955	1958	1959	1960	1961	1962
Newfoundland								52	54	54	55	58	59	59
Prince Edward Island	57	60	51	56	53	53	58	58	55	59	60	64	62	61
Nova Scotia	67	72	77	77	76	79	86	75	73	74	75	76	77	75
New Brunswick	64	65	66	64	65	65	75	66	66	65	65	69	69	67
Quebec	85	92	94	91	88	80	82	85	85	86	85	85	87	86
Ontario	114	122	129	127	124	119	115	121	120	119	119	117	119	117
Manitoba	109	98	93	90	90	92	103	101	95	100	100	100	96	102
Saskatchewan	102	67	47	63	77	106	97	91	93	86	87	95	77	102
Alberta	113	92	74	79	87	97	108	103	103	106	104	102	103	102
British Columbia	121	128	132	128	125	111	114	118	122	117	117	117	118	114

*Personal income includes all transfer payments and imputed net-income of farmers.
Source: D.B.S.

TABLE B

Estimated Unemployment as a Per Cent of Labour Force — Canadian Regions
1946 — 1963

	Atlantic	Quebec	Ontario	Prairies	British Columbia	Canada
1946	5.5	4.0	2.8	2.2	3.9	3.4
1947	4.7	2.5	1.8	1.4	2.8	2.2
1948	4.4	2.4	1.7	1.5	3.4	2.3
	5.5	3.3	2.2	1.9	3.6	2.9
1949	5.3	3.4	2.3	1.9	3.4	2.9
1950	7.8	4.4	2.4	2.3	4.4	3.6
1951	4.3	2.9	1.7	1.6	3.4	2.4
1952	4.6	3.7	2.2	1.9	3.8	2.9
1953	5.5	3.8	2.1	1.9	4.0	3.0
	5.5	4.5	2.4	2.2	4.0	3.5
1954	6.6	5.9	3.8	2.5	5.2	4.6
1955	6.4	6.2	3.2	3.1	3.8	4.4
1956	6.0	5.0	2.4	2.2	2.8	3.4
1957	8.3	6.0	3.4	2.7	5.0	4.6
1958	12.5	8.8	5.4	4.1	8.5	7.1
	9.6	7.4	4.2	3.3	6.3	5.6
1959	10.8	7.9	4.4	3.3	6.4	6.0
1960	10.6	9.1	5.4	4.2	8.7	7.0
1961	11.1	9.3	5.5	4.6	8.5	7.2
1962	10.7	7.5	4.3	3.9	6.7	5.9
1963	9.6	7.5	3.8	3.7	6.3	5.6

Source: D.B.S.

Such figures, it will be realized, mask large differences in unemployment rates which exist within the provincial boundaries and the averaging of unemployment rates for the Atlantic Provinces together conceals the fact that unemployment in Newfoundland frequently exceeds 18 per cent of the labour force. This 18 per cent, it should be emphasized, constitutes not just a seasonal peak, but an annual average. In spite of improvements, Newfoundland remains a depressed area.

The relationship between income and employment, which is very close in some parts of the country, is much less so in the Prairies and this is as we might expect. Incomes from farming fluctuate much more than labour input.

There is another aspect of these figures, however, which deserves particular note. Levels of unemployment show a high degree of correlation across the country. Typically, when unemployment rises and falls in Ontario, it rises and falls in the Atlantic Provinces too. From 1946-1963, yearly changes are in the same direction in every year except 1952-1953 and 1959-1960. In like manner, Ontario and Quebec move together. Only in two years, 1952-1953 and 1954-1955, were the trends in opposite directions, and the difference was marginal in 1952-1953. Similarly, the Prairies and Ontario move together and so does British Columbia, though the relationship is not quite so strong in the case of British Columbia. Clearly there are forces at work which tend to influence all regions in the same direction, but, and what is no less striking, is that the impact of changes in the general level of activity are very unevenly distributed.

Just what the functional relationship is between levels of unemployment in the Atlantic Provinces and other parts of the country is a moot point, but it is striking that once unemployment in Ontario exceeds 4 per cent, the position in the Atlantic Provinces, which suffers from consistently higher unemployment, becomes very much more serious. Thus, in 1958, when unemployment in Ontario increased by 2 per cent from 3.4 to 5.4 per cent, it increased from 8.3 per cent to 12.5 per cent in the Atlantic Provinces. Moreover, as long as unemployment in Ontario remained above 4 per cent, it never dropped below 10 per cent in the Atlantic Provinces.

It is apparent from past experience that, if there is a general slack in demand, the Atlantic Provinces suffer much more than the rest of the country. Policies designed to maintain aggregate demand can thus claim a high priority in our measures to reduce the ills which face the Atlantic Provinces specifically. A high level of aggregate demand will not only stimulate growth in the economy as a whole, it will also do much to reduce the problems of the less favoured regions.

In Newfoundland, as mentioned above, unemployment is especially heavy; in many years it has totalled between 20,000 - 25,000 of a labour force of approximately 120,000. Had it been possible over the past decade to reduce unemployment in Newfoundland and the Maritime Provinces to around 3 - 4 per cent, there would have been an increase of some 40,000 in the employed labour force contributing a potential $100 million a year to the Gross National Product for labour income alone. Increased rewards to other factors of production would have raised the figure further. In other words, if we assume that unemployment could have reached an attainable minimum around 3 - 4 per cent, unemployment in the Atlantic Provinces in excess of this appears to have cost the country something like a billion dollars during the last seven or eight years. This figure may appear to overstate the loss of production but it may not be far off the mark when it is remembered that labour force participation rates are significantly lower in the Atlantic Provinces than in other parts of the country, a difference attributable in large measure to lack of employment opportunity.

There is the further consideration that high levels of unemployment are likely to slow down the rate of capital accumulation. The reduction in the upward pressure on wages attendant upon heavy unemployment can be expected to reduce the rate of installation of cost-saving techniques of production.

The chronic persistence of lower incomes and higher unemployment in some areas of the country is in itself a phenomenon which calls for explanation. With freedom of movement, and given higher rewards to labour and capital in the Central than in the Atlantic Provinces, one would assume that labour and capital would be attracted to the former from the latter, contributing thereby to a more uniform level of income and to a reduction in unemployment. On the face of it, such a transfer of resources conforming with the principles of a simplified equilibrium analysis would contribute to efficient resource use. In fact, notwithstanding substantial migration from the Atlantic Provinces, marked differences in employment opportunity and incomes continue to persist. At the first Canadian decennial census in 1871, over 20 per cent of the Canadian population lived in the three Maritime Provinces of Nova Scotia, New Brunswick, and Prince Edward Island. By 1961, that percentage had dropped to less than eight per cent. Between 1881 and 1931 net out-migration from the Maritime Provinces is estimated to have averaged some 90,000 per decade and, as shown in Table C below, this movement has continued since. If we include Newfoundland the number increases for the decade 1951-1961 to almost 100,000 out of a total population in the Atlantic Provinces of currently rather less than 2 million. In spite of this migration and relative decline in population, per capita income in the Atlantic Provinces remains a third below that of the rest of the country, and unemployment remains very much higher.

TABLE C
Changes in Population due to Net Migration —
Canada and the Provinces
1931 - 1961
(thousands of persons)

	1931 to 1941	1941 to 1951	1951 to 1961
Newfoundland	NA	NA	— 14.6
Prince Edward Island	— 2.7	— 12.4	— 11.4
Nova Scotia	+ 8.0	— 38.9	— 33.9
New Brunswick	— 10.0	— 41.6	— 37.2
Maritime Provinces	— 4.7	— 92.9	— 82.5
Quebec	+ 6.6	— 12.3	+ 205.2
Ontario	+ 77.6	+ 304.9	+ 685.1
Manitoba	— 48.1	— 60.7	— 4.5
Saskatchewan	— 157.7	— 199.4	— 78.9
Alberta	— 42.4	— 7.0	+ 127.2
Prairie Provinces	— 248.2	— 267.1	+ 43.8
British Columbia & Yukon N.W.T.	+ 82.2	+ 236.3	+ 243.6
Canada	— 86.3	+ 169.0	+1080.6

Source: D.B.S. and Citizenship and Immigration.

It may be wondered why relative declines in the Maritime population have not improved more substantially the economic situation of those who remain. A possible explanation is that the migration has not gone far enough. Given the fact, for example, that per capita incomes in Newfoundland are 40 per cent below those in the rest of the country, it could be argued that, if something like one third of the population were to leave that province, the per capita incomes of the remainder would rise fairly close to the national average. I can see how one might argue such a case but I have certain reservations about it. Even if such a migration could be induced over say, the next decade, by various forms of encouragement, I suspect that a substantial income gap would still remain. For one thing, certain overhead costs would have to be borne by a smaller population and, for another, the decline in population would reduce still further the incentives to produce for a local market. To the extent, moreover, that the migrants consisted largely of young adults, as seems likely, the age distribution of the remaining labour force would be less favourable than it is at the present time. Some migration is to be expected and should be facilitated, for market forces alone operate too slowly and painfully, but the net gains from such movement are unlikely to be such as to make other action to raise output appear less urgent.

The above may appear to be taking a rather pessimistic view of the potential gains from migration, and I am not unmindful that there are important offsetting considerations to be taken into account. Thus in the matter of overhead costs, it should be possible with a declining population to effect economies in educational expenditures by closing down some of the smaller schools and such action would have the additional merit of contributing to a rise in educational standards. There is the further consideration that with the passage of time, the number of older people will also diminish. The point I wish to stress is that we need to bear the limitations in mind in advocating the merits of migration; otherwise we shall expect too much of it.

Birth rates in the Atlantic Provinces are much the same as in the country as a whole with the exception of Newfoundland where they are almost 50 per cent higher. As a result, the population of Newfoundland is rising more rapidly than elsewhere in the Maritimes. It may be noted too that the economic situation in that province is the most adverse. The fact, indeed, that incomes are so low in Newfoundland may account in part for the high birth rate. The relation between income and birthrates is an issue with which the demographers are still wrestling. The problem of a high birth rate is the more pressing in Newfoundland since the technological changes conducive to improved economies of operation in the fishing industry are likely to entail still further reductions in needed manpower. It may be noted that, according to the 1961 Census, the percentage of population in the 0-14 age group was 41.8 per cent in Newfoundland, compared with the 32.20 in Ontario and 33.95 per cent in Canada as a whole.

In so far as migration out of the Atlantic Provinces does raise the per capita incomes of those who remain — and to *some* extent it seems likely to do so — it suggests that such migration should be encouraged. This raises the question of the ultimate objective of policy. Is it *total* income we are interested in — in this case the income of a particular area — or is it per capita income in that area? Is migration out of the Atlantic Provinces to be one of the objectives of a policy of development?

This choice between gross and per capita income presents itself in a variety of ways. Thus, in the matter of the ARDA program, there have been sharp conflicts of opinion as to what precisely is meant by development. The only promising way to raise per capita income in a rural community which is farming poor land, and where other employment is limited, might be to encourage the consolidation of farms, take the poorest land out of cultivation entirely, improve technology, and induce less able farmers to migrate. Under such a program, the total income of the community might very well decline, but per capita incomes of those remaining rise. Local unemployment might also rise, in the sense that people who were under-employed before will now become manifestly unemployed.

Whatever the view of others on the subject, however, it is clear that this is not what many advocates of development understand by the term. By develop-ment they mean an increase, not only in per capita income, but also in the aggre-gate income of the area as defined plus increased employment opportunities for the local labour force. A mere increase in per capita or family income is not regarded as an adequate criterion for policy; indeed, in many cases, increases in per capita income are the subject of less concern than the growth of population and aggregate income within the community or area as defined. Political and religious leaders, not to mention economic historians, are prone to identify development with growth in population, hence the repeated assertion that such and such a community or area must find sufficient jobs to absorb the expected increase in its numbers. Migration out of the area is interpreted not as an indicator of a trend which could raise the per capita income of those remaining, but as the failure of government to implement effective policies to stimulate local development. Local religious leaders have been more concerned at times over the potential loss of their flock than with an ambition to raise the per capita income of those who remain, though there is a greater readiness on their part to accept migration from rural areas than there used to be.

In general, the larger the region or area under consideration the easier it will be to side-step the awkward political questions raised by migration and the easier it will be to create employment opportunities. In so far, for example, as the Atlantic Provinces are treated as a whole for purposes of development policy, then any migration that takes place within them entails no necessary conflict of objectives. Assistance can be concentrated where it shows greatest promise. If we are faced, however, with provincial boundaries and we try to raise employment opportunities within each province individually, the task immediately becomes more complex. Not only do we have to worry about interprovincial migration but we run the risk of less efficient resource allocation in terms of the country as a whole. If we narrow the boundaries still further — say to a county level or National Employ-ment Service area — then room to manoeuvre decreases sharply. At the town-ship level, room to manoeuvre disappears almost entirely and we are left with the task of finding employment for workers in areas which show no prospect whatever of developing without continued and heavy subvention. There is the further and very sensitive consideration that any assistance which is given may have to be concentrated in effect on individual firms. Questions of equity would become that much more acute.

The problems involved are not confined to *industrial* development. Similar issues are entailed in the objectives of the ARDA program. Thus, among other things, the ARDA program is designed to help farmers raise incomes and efficiency by improving land. But land which may be regarded as worth improvement in one province may be considered as sub-marginal in a neighbouring province more richly endowed with good agricultural land. The latter province may indeed plan to take land out of cultivation superior to that which the first province plans to develop. There is no reason to suppose that such a course, which may commend itself to either province in isolation, is necessarily in the interests of both considered together, of the persons directly concerned or of the country considered as a whole. Latterly, and which is likely to add to the problem, the provinces have been pressing for a greater degree of autonomy in the designation of areas which will qualify for assistance under the ARDA program.

The matter of designation of areas which are to qualify for assistance brings us back to a discussion of basic policy objectives. What primarily are we trying to achieve? Is our prime concern that of creating jobs for the local unemployed? Are we concerned with raising per capita incomes in an area or the total incomes of that area? Is the distribution of population across the country an end in itself or is it not? Is our prime concern one of social welfare? Is it a matter of redistributing income? Or it is one of economic growth, and if so, are we primarily thinking of growth at the national or subnational level?

The designation of areas, as well as the criteria for assistance, will depend ultimately on the priorities which are accorded to these various objectives. If we are concerned with growth rather than welfare, larger areas will normally appear more appropriate, and those offering greater scope for expansion will be preferred to those which offer less. If it is local welfare in which we are primarily interested, then smaller areas will tend to be selected and the measure of their distress rather than their potentiality for growth will assume importance. It is quite fruitless to seek a concept of designation which will be appropriate for all the objectives which we may have in mind. There may be occasions when a very depressed locality offers the greatest scope for long run development, and from the standpoint of designating an area this is an ideal combination, but it is not one which is likely to arise frequently. We are faced with the fact that, as a broad generalization, those areas which are most depressed are likely to be precisely those with the poorest growth prospects.

The cost of assisting such areas, it should be noted, cannot be measured just in terms of financial outlay. The cost in real terms is the loss of potential production resulting from the use of resources in one direction rather than another, the alternative or opportunity costs in the terminology of the economist. Given a sufficient capital input, employment could be found for every potential worker in Newfoundland but the net rate of return on that investment would almost certainly be less than that involved in a similar volume of investment elsewhere. In estimating whether such is the case or not, it is essential, however, to use social accounting concepts rather than private. The increased output resulting from increased employment may not accrue to the private investor but it represents a real gain to society. If the alternative to government aid is no output at all — where the alternative in other words is not employment elsewhere but unemployment — the "real" cost of spending nothing may be much higher than any subventions which the government might be called upon to make to ensure that work is made available. In the deciding of such issues, or whether one type of project is to be preferred to another, cost benefit studies have a useful role to play. In their absence, policy is apt to depend on hunches and political expediency.

As for the direction of assistance to ensure effective development, it may be helpful to draw attention to a discussion which has occupied a prominent place in the literature on regional development, the discussion of external economies.

Essentially, the argument runs as follows. There may be little incentive for any one industry to become established to supply a local market in an area where incomes are low, because the local market is too small. If, however, investment were undertaken over a wide field it would become profitable, for each development would provide a market for the other, as well as make services available to the other. From a production standpoint, firms do not like to be isolated from each other; they depend on each other's services. Isolation adds to inconvenience and to cost. Not only are specialist services less readily available in less developed areas, but the facilities of technical schools and a trained labour force are likely to be deficient. Were a combination of firms to be induced to establish in a particular area, such deficiencies might be overcome. The particular combination would depend on the nature of the interrelationships which appeared most likely to offer the maximum external economies. The choice of such a combination calls for technical studies of the types undertaken by Isard and others in their examination of the Puerto Rican economy. Given particular factor inputs and prices, what initial type of development offers the greatest promise of success and how will that development induce and react on others, so that each step, in effect, will induce the next in a chain of mutual interaction?

Related to this type of approach, and bearing on the magnitude of the assistance that may be required, is the notion that a big push may succeed when a little one will fail. A big push, it is argued, will make possible external economies that will greatly enhance the prospects of success of the whole venture.

Admittedly there are limits to this type of argument. Firms may, for example, compete for limited labour supplies or other resources but there is certainly something in the view that a major effort may succeed when a smaller one will fail. Growth tends to feed on itself. On a modest scale, there is sufficient empirical evidence of the success of trading parks or estates to indicate the advantages of a location where the costs of services can be shared among many firms rather than a few. As for large industrial centres, the very fact that they do exert such a powerful pull on new industry constitutes in some ways the essence of the problem for other areas.

In considering the type of development which may be encouraged, the implications for inter-regional trade and balance of payments deserve consideration. Imports into the region have to be paid for and the growth of a region is likely to depend primarily on the capacity to export. Typically, indeed, a region's growth is related to its capacity to produce goods for export outside the region or to provide services as in the case of tourism. Export markets are thus considered the prime mover of the local economy.

Studies of the interrelationship of different regions of Canada is currently being undertaken by several economists in Canada, among them Professor Green at Queen's and Professor Kari Levitt at McGill. Input-output studies can provide valuable statistical insights for the policy maker concerned with regional development.

No less important is an awareness of the ever changing patterns of industrial location and the reasons underlying them. The relative price of factor inputs and the determinants of optimum location are rarely constant for long. Changes in technology, the size of the market, transport power and labour costs give rise to a never ending adjustment in industrial location. This is the province of the economic geographer and it is a source of regret that much more work has not been done on this aspect of the Canadian economy. The extent of the change in industrial location is particularly marked in certain industries and a discussion of regional development which lacks an awareness of the significant trends is certain to be incomplete.

The economist can, and does, develop theories of location but, without empirical evidence of particular movements and their determinants, the discussion is apt to appear sterile. Mere description of change, on the other hand, or a catalogue of underlying forces, leaves us without understanding.

In the "Resources for Tomorrow" Conference held in Montreal in October 1961, there were a number of papers on regional issues which contributed useful background to the Canadian scene, among them, Professor Slater's discussion of Trends in Industrial Locations in Canada. Professor Slater, you may remember, drew attention to the important regional implications of the great changes which have been taking place in the structure of Canada's resource industries, and he also commented on the far reaching effects of improvements in medium distance communications on locational choices. Commenting on the factors which influence locational decisions, he suggested that the reason why more decentralization of manufacturing has not taken place may well lie in the uncertainty of a dynamic world. The larger industrial centres provide greater scope for coping with risk and uncertainty. Locational analyses, in short, cannot be conducted in a static context. This combination of analysis and description is urgently needed by government officials entrusted with the problems of influencing locational decisions.

In similar vein, mention might also be made of Professors Kerr's and Spelt's discussion of the reasons which prompt manufacturers to choose some localities in Southern Ontario and not others. Writing in the *Canadian Geographer* in 1960, they draw attention to a lengthy list of economic and non-economic considerations as well as to the specific requirements of individual firms and then underline the importance of prevailing attitudes of the public towards industry. They observe, in this last connection, that some towns actively solicit and encourage new industry whereas others do not, and add, "Undoubtedly an intelligent and enthusiastic industrial commissioner greatly aids a community in its quest for industry". But of particular importance and, in their view, perhaps the main reason in explaining why existing industrial concentrations continue to expand and weakly industrialized communities to stagnate, is the tendency of businessmen to follow the leader. The presence and success of other industries is reassuring.

In many cases, however, the forces making for specific location cannot be very strong, for Professors Kerr and Spelt express the belief that a very large segment of industry is footloose over most of Southern Ontario and they contend that a much greater dispersal of industry is possible than has been the case heretofore. This discovery, they add, should be of great interest from the point of view of regional planning and development.

Their study will, I hope, encourage others to foster further enquiry. I think it would be worth a great deal of effort to try to narrow down the area of uncertainty regarding locational decisions. In a matter of such great importance as the location of industry, it is extraordinary that we should know so little. Economic geography is an area of study which has been seriously neglected in Canada in academic as well as government circles. Far more resources have been devoted to physical geography than to the geographical aspects of industrial location and urban development.

For my own part, I find it difficult to escape the impression that many of the poorer and more remote communities, angling hopefully for new enterprises, have little conception of the underlying economic forces which are constantly at work influencing industrial location and are too easily persuaded that, if the government just does this or just does that, or they can get a good public relations man, then new firms will come their way.

This brings me, then, to the final part of my discussion, the subject of federal policy specifically.

POLICY

At the outset, it may be worth emphasizing that there are a great variety of federal policies bearing on the subject of regional economic development, though such bearing may be only fortuitous. Agricultural support programs, federal provincial financial transfers, freight rate subventions, allocation of defence contracts, the tariff on imports all influence the distribution of income and employment opportunity across the country. What the net effect of all these influences may be is a matter for conjecture. My expectation would be, however, that in the aggregate they tend to favour the wealthier and more industrialized provinces, largely because of the dominating effect of the tariff.

My concern, however, is largely confined to certain policies specifically designed to influence the location of industry and, particularly, to the objectives and programs of the Area Development Agency in the new Department of Industry. In concentrating on the latter I realize that I am only looking at part of the picture. The Department of Labour, ARDA and the Atlantic Development Board, also have important roles to play and these roles bear on the operations of the Area Development Agency itself.

The functions of that Agency, as announced in one of its brochures, follows:—
"to plan within designated areas, the replacement of those industrial activities dislodged by advances in technology, resource depletion, or changes in world markets;

to provide incentives for the establishment of industry;

to evaluate and publicize the potential of each area in terms of unused human skills, resources and power, and such natural or social advantages as it may possess;

to seek out potential new industries or new products for each area and facilitate their introduction;

to promote the development and improvement of existing industries.

These functions are to be carried out in collaboration and, in some instances, in accordance with formal agreements with other federal, provincial and municipal agencies, industrial associations, research foundations, and other interested organizations."

Each Area Development Officer — and there are 14 of them — will be required to develop a thorough economic appreciation of assigned areas, including: natural resources, primary and secondary industry, the business and financial community, services, transportation resources, distribution of labour and age groupings. Through direct studies, and with the assistance of local and provincial authorities and other specialists, it will be his responsibility to coordinate the preparation of the overall development plan for each area and the proposed program elements within it. Upon approval of the plan, he will have the task of coordinating its implementation by the responsible government and industrial authorities.

Area Development Officers are obviously going to earn their pay! To plan within designated areas the expansion of its industry is no mean task. It will call for quite exceptional talents, and one may wonder with what powers of influence, cajolery and persuasion the Agency will need to be equipped to fulfill its task.

Part II of the Act, establishing the Area Development Agency, includes among the powers and duties of the Minister the following:

"the preparing and carrying out of such programs and projects to improve the economic development of designated areas as may be appropriate to the purposes of this Part and that cannot suitably be undertaken by other departments, branches or agencies of the Government of Canada."

Paragraph 11 of the Act empowers the Governor in Council, subject to any existing statutory provision, to authorize and direct departments, branches and agencies of the Government of Canada to undertake in the execution of their respective duties and functions such special measures as may be appropriate to facilitate the economic development of any designated area or the adjustment of industry in that area.

The legislation, in short, provides extensive powers to facilitate economic development. So far, in fact, little use has been made of those powers. For the time being, at least, the Government is proceeding with great caution, gingerly feeling its way.

Some of the official statements on the subject made prior to the 1963 legislation display a vigour which has been lacking since. Thus, in November 1961, one Cabinet Minister, addressing an Industrial Development Conference, in Alberta, observed:

"The industrial program, which you are carrying out, is an example to the many other regions of Canada where production is still concentrated mainly in primary industries. The drought last summer gave us a far too vivid example of how variations in the weather can seriously affect the incomes of large numbers of Canadians who rely on the production of one or a few primary products for their livelihood.

"We must develop secondary manufacturing in all parts of Canada to process to final form the raw materials we produce in such abundance, so that the economies of these regions may become diversified, and not reliant solely on the production of one or a few crops or primary products." He wound up his remarks by saying, "I sincererly hope all regions of Canada will show the same initiative which you are doing, and work with us to establish secondary industry in all parts of this country."

The official in question was the Honourable George Hees, Minister of Trade and Commerce.

Similar ambitions were expressed by the Polish delegate to the European Congress of Regional Scientists in The Hague in 1961. "Industrialization", he said, "is the main tool for creating a socialist society, therefore, the introduction of industry to every part of the country is of vital economic, social and political importance. Socialist society is an equalitarian one, therefore everybody, wherever he lives, should have the same opportunity for work, good living conditions and social advancement." Even socialists have their problems, however, and he added that, "Although on the whole the plan was successful in diminishing the differences in development levels between regions, it is generally felt that in this direction it has somewhat missed its very ambitious aims." The Area Development Agency in Ottawa can take heart in the knowledge that it is not alone in its trials.

How far it is the ambition of the present administration to encourage second-ary industry all across the country is doubtful. Ministerial statements have to be taken with a pinch of salt, but in 1963 a list was announced of 35 designated areas across Canada (now reduced to 32) which would qualify for special measures of federal assistance for economic or industrial development. The criteria were to be high levels of unemployment and slow rates of growth. Thirteen of these areas were in the Atlantic Provinces, 13 were in Quebec, 8 in Ontario and 1 in Alberta. The special measures included a three-year income tax exemption for new enter-prise, plus accelerated capital cost allowances for buildings, machinery and equip-ment, whether involving new or old industries.

In announcing the policy, the Ministers of Industry and Labour did not raise the question of objectives beyond stating that, according to the definition, selected certain areas qualified and others did not. The criterion in fact was limited essen-tially to levels of unemployment and levels of income were ignored. In other words, the fact that people had low incomes in a particular area was irrelevant so far as aid was concerned. Except in so far as slow growth was implicit in the percentages of unemployment, the question of growth was ignored too. Unemploy-ment stood alone. To have incorporated a concept of growth and a measure of income would, of course, have complicated the problem of defining areas and have introduced an added element of uncertainty and subjectivity with all the political implications this would entail. Anxious to get something moving it is not difficult to understand the preference for a relatively simple, ascertainable measure of unemployment. But, in selecting such a measure, the crucial issues involved in a development policy were in effect side-stepped. Implicit in such a selection is a downgrading of the growth objective, for the areas suffering from heaviest un-employment may be precisely those with the least growth potential. Indeed, the formula for designation makes this highly probable, for unless the unemployment was of a chronic nature, the areas did not qualify for designation. Nor is this all.

Measures to increase per capita income and output per worker, if this is how we are to interpret growth, are likely, in certain cases, to involve an increase rather than a reduction in unemployment. Extensive mechanization of farming, fishing, lumbering and manufacturing in an attempt to raise per capita output will not necessarily lead to increased local employment, especially if the equipment is obtained from outside the designated region. On the contrary, it is likely to lead to a reduction. Demand may rise with a fall in production costs but not necessarily by enough to absorb a concomitant decline in labour input per unit of output. A choice must then be made between raising levels of local employment and raising incomes.

The smaller the region designated, the more likely it is that some of the gains of local expansion will accrue to others. The same effects can be seen even in the case of quite large areas. Thus, typically, machinery is produced in the central rather than the Atlantic Provinces and the gains which result from increased utilization of machinery by the latter will increase incomes in Central Canada too. Ontario may reap much of what the Atlantic Provinces, with the help of the federal government, have sown in the way of capital cost incentives. This is not, I suspect, an unlikely possibility. While I do not wish to imply that such a possibility is necessarily to be regretted, the likelihood that the local employment multiplier effects of certain types of development may be small needs to be borne in mind.

Apart from machinery, it is likely that the income elasticity of demand for imports of consumer durables generally into the Atlantic Provinces is quite high.

If this is true, such a situation might stimulate a desire to reduce the dependence of the Atlantic Provinces on regional imports. Were such a course pursued, and there is evidence of this type of attitude in various parts of Canada, we may find ourselves involved in a slower rate of national growth. It is not an uncommon practice at the present time for provincial governments and municipalities to favour local suppliers, and there are campaigns like the Ontario Trade Crusade. Though the volume of goods affected thereby is presumably very small in comparison with total inter-provincial trade, the attitude underlying such practices carries with it obvious dangers.

So far as the federal government is concerned, if its actions appear to be having the effect of reducing regional unemployment by reducing dependence on regional imports as by, for example, encouraging local production in competition, then it can be expected to have to run into opposition from regional exporters. In short, its policies will only be acceptable to the extent that they accomplish little. It is likely that the Government of Ontario will support federal programs of regional development only so long as they have no significant effect either in attracting industry from Ontario to other parts of the country, or in reducing the demand for Ontario produced products.

So far as the employment criterion for the designation of areas is concerned, it seems that, by concentrating on the creation of employment opportunities within designated areas, we are getting ourselves into a box. Such a policy is justified only in so far as the creation of local employment is an end in itself. There will be occasions when such may indeed be the case, but surely they are the exceptions.

Our ultimate objective, presumably, is an increase in output per man hour at the national level. At one extreme, the achievement of this objective will entail migration of labour out of certain areas which have lost their economic base. As Brinley Thomas observed in his book, *The Welsh Economy* — "There is no sense in giving artificial respiration to economic dinosaurs." At the other end of the scale, extensive inducements of various kinds may be necessary to hasten the pace of development and thereby provide opportunities for incoming migrants. In this connection, there is room for more than one type of designation.

There are some areas which are not worth developing which might qualify for what in effect amounts to welfare assistance; there are others which might need temporary support to help them through a crisis of transition; and there are still others which may need extensive and prolonged aid to achieve their potential. We need to separate these out.

It is, I think, very important in this regard to be honest about the apparent economic potentials of particular areas, and not encourage hopes which will almost certainly be disappointed.

It should not be beyond our competence to assemble data on past and present trends in particular areas of the country, to form some impression of the potentialities of growth and the lines along which it might be encouraged, as well as of the costs and benefits of such encouragement. There will be cases where a high degree of uncertainty prevails but the evolving pattern should be fairly clear in others. Feasibility, economic base and cost-benefit studies are well established techniques of enquiry. The sensible course at this stage is surely to concentrate attention on those areas whose potentiality for development is least in doubt, those at both ends of the scale.

We need, in my view, not a blanket form of assistance to all areas suffering from chronically high unemployment — which is what we have at the moment —

but rather a program of assistance based on the specific needs and potentialities of individual areas. This will entail a substantial element of discretion on the part of the policy administrator but such discretion in my view is indispensable if we are not to misallocate resources. Not all depressed areas are alike. There is no point in treating them as though they were.

Not only are all depressed areas not alike, but the inducements necessary to attract industry into them vary with the nature of the industry. Cheap power may be the essential element in one case, an increased supply of trained labour in another, improved transport in a third and so on. A blanket tax concession based on capital expenditures, such as we have at the moment, is too crude an incentive. We need to give some thought to the types of industry which are to be encouraged, and to their specific potentials and needs. Whether the civil servant is the right person to be making these assessments, I leave you to decide. Of one thing I am quite sure, assessments should not be left to local pressure groups.

As for the geographical designation of areas which are to qualify for special assistance, there are administrative advantages in the present system of utilizing National Employment Service areas,[1] but it is to be hoped that extensive use will be made of the provision which permits consideration to be given to contiguous localities, and, under exceptional circumstances, a strong case can be argued for the designation of an entire province. Such circumstances would include cases where individual and contiguous National Employment Service areas were seriously lacking in potential for development, and abnormally high levels of unemployment or low income prevailed in the province as a whole. Newfoundland affords an excellent illustration.

Before leaving the subject of policy, there are two further issues which call for comment: federal-provincial relations and population movements. To a greater or less extent, all provincial governments are committed to policies of economic development within their boundaries. It would be totally unrealistic, therefore, to assume that the initiative for area development will be left with Ottawa, or that the views of the federal government as to what is appropriate in the way of policy will necessarily conform with the views of provincial administrations. Indeed, the contrary will sometimes be the case.

One of the potential sources of disagreement arises out of population movement. It is unlikely that provincial governments would ever attempt deliberately to discourage migration as by, for example, limiting the portability of benefits under various social service programs. But it is likely that they would view with suspicion federal measures designed specifically to encourage migration from one part of the country to another. In neither its efforts to encourage the movement of people, nor its efforts to influence the location of industry, is Ottawa likely to be given a free hand.

In the former connection, it has sometimes been suggested that federal measures designed to equalize incomes across the country will inhibit movement indirectly by reducing the incentive to move. This is a possibility. Federal transfer payments of one sort and another constitute the bulk of the income of an important segment of the Newfoundland population. On the other hand, it can be argued that the raising of incomes in Newfoundland, and some of the poorer communities

---

[1] It should be emphasized, however, that the present National Employment Service Areas were never delineated with the objective of providing focal points for economic development and in some ways are quite unsuitable for such a purpose.

elsewhere, may enable more people to migrate and thereby induce movement. It is questionable which is the more likely. What does seem clear is that migration is easiest during the upswing of the business cycle, when economic opportunities generally are increasing, and that this is the most promising time to foster it.

Whatever our views on the desirability of inter-provincial migration specifically, we cannot escape the implications of industrial development on population movement. Whether such is our intention or not, once we embark on regional development policies we are, in effect, committing ourselves to actions which will influence the distribution of population. At the outset, therefore, it is worth giving some thought to the sort of population distribution that we want. This is the more important since, to some extent, population movement can be an alternative to the movement of industry. We are deluding ourselves if we believe that we can have an industrial development policy which is not in some sense a population policy too. It would help to clarify thought if this were recognized explicitly by the federal government in its area development programs.

In summary, then, I would recommend the abandonment of reliance on unemployment levels as a sole criterion for designating an area and would include income and an evaluation of growth potential; secondly, I would recommend a substantial measure of flexibility to permit aid to be tailored to individual needs and not be just uniform across the country; thirdly, I would advocate where it seemed appropriate, not only a combination of National Employment Service areas, but the designation of a whole province; and, finally, I would urge that the federal government give more thought specifically to the question of population distribution and furnish some indication of its objectives in this regard.

COMMENTS

PROFESSOR YVES DUBÉ,
Faculté des Sciences Sociales,
Université Laval.

Mr. Brewis' paper is a most stimulating one to read. His presentation of the most recent views concerning regional economic growth is both thorough and lucid. The complexities of the problem are not shied away from and the policies advocated well thought out.

My own approach will perhaps be a little different in that I am going to follow a more traditional way of reasoning. In so doing, I am not going to differ markedly from the author but I hope that I can focus attention on some of the implications of national economic growth on the regions rather than concentrating on the regions themselves.

Regional economic growth is to me a by-product of well-designed policies designed to promote national economic growth. In turn, maximum national economic growth cannot be achieved without a maximum degree of mobility of resources, of goods, capital and labour, between regions. Mr. Brewis has emphasized the same point when he talked about the effects of the cyclical fluctuations on the regions. But he stopped there. I want to elaborate somewhat.

Let us discuss first the problem of mobility. We are all agreed that labour is not perfectly mobile and that there are great difficulties in trying to achieve mobility through persuasion, incentives or compulsion. There is the sociological and psychological problems of leaving behind a familiar environment and the economic problems associated with moving, risk of loss on property and real expenses of transportation and establishment in a new location. But there are some hopes that in the long run one will be better off. The real economic — and political — difficulty is with those who stay. With a declining population they will have to bear more and more of the overhead costs and their incentive to produce for a local market will be reduced. There is some truth in this but it is not the full story. A good many of the migrations that are taking place in this country are a result of technological changes which make it possible for a smaller population in a given area to be provided at about the same opportunity cost with the same or better social services as previously. The consolidation of farms, for instance, is the result of better farm machinery which makes it possible for a farmer to exploit much more land with less hired labour. The consolidation of farms leads in turn to the consolidation of school districts or of municipal territories. With the automobile, the farmer is not further from the big school, as far as time is concerned, than he was previously from the small school. Of course, there are some indivisibilities here too. These have to be taken into account when the decision to move or not to move is taken. On the second point, we have again a feature of technological progress. Markets are getting bigger and production is centralized in focal points. Imports replace local production. Those who stay have to compete with imports or export more. If not successful, they have to take a loss of income. In some cases, however, the reduction of labour inputs relative to the increase or decrease in the use of the other factors of production may increase the return to labour and therefore income. This is what happens when farms are consolidated. The local service industry will lose if it caters only to the declining population or does not find ways to reduce its costs or to expand its market. Loss of income resulting from a decline in population is the price one has to pay either for immobility or for immobilism.

We are mostly interested here in regional or inter-regional mobility. But this cannot be examined independently from occupational or industrial mobility. In practice, the individual himself will decide and rightly so about which job he will like best, at what wage and where. If he is a logger, say in Quebec, he may have to go to British Columbia to find a job in his regular occupation. He may not like to go to British Columbia and therefore, to be employed, have to change his regular occupation and work say as a taxi driver in Montreal. Offering him a subsidy to go to British Columbia may be profitable for the British Columbia forest industry and for him but may not be the best thing to do for society as a whole that has to pay the subsidy and which does not really care as to whether or not there are sufficient number of loggers in British Columbia as opposed to the number of taxis in Montreal. The maximum of welfare will be achieved by having the British Columbia industry attract its own labour force through higher wages.

There is, in my view, some considerable elasticity of substitution as between unskilled occupations. It is a reason why, some good results may be achieved by having a mobility policy at the regional level as well as at the national level. Another argument that militates in favour of a regional policy is the sociological one. People will be ready to accept another job in their region rather than moving to another region. The movement should then be perhaps from a given rural area

to a more central town and then from this town to the larger city. The movement between big cities will then be easier to achieve. Of course, this does not
exclude the other patterns of movements which a National policy could promote.

To the mobility of labour must be added the mobility of goods and capital.
The last one presents very few difficulties except in so far as the regional savings
are usually badly channelled. A lot of improvements are still needed though when
we come to goods. There are some industries — agriculture and transportation, in
particular — where the markets of producers in a given area are limited by legislation to the market in that area. This does not lead to long run efficiency, but
creates injustices.

Having said so much of mobility, I now pass to economic policies designed to
promote growth. In the present world context, nearly everybody will agree that
Canada has to envisage its growth problems in a new perspective and design suitable growth policies. These policies should in my view be more along the general
line of thought of the liberal economists. This would be a market departure from
the tradition which looked at economic policies as a way to keep in proper balance
the divergent interests of the different groups and regions of the country. Contrary to this view, the liberal economists propose a mechanism by which those
interests can be adjusted one to the other. I think that there is sufficient evidence
to support this view. What is even more important is that not only will these
policies lead to a greater rate of growth for Canada as a whole but they will also
favour the catching up of the disadvantaged regions. Existing policies — our commercial and transportation policies in particular — have tended too often to
discriminate against those regions. Coming back to more liberal policies will end
this discrimination and add more.

Among government policies, I would equally favour those that would have
the effect of producing a more uniform level of public services of all kinds across
Canada. This, of course, means a higher level of equalization payments for
certain areas. There are some intricate difficulties here but on the whole these can
be ironed out over time. Such policies would help to maintain the level of income
and growth in certain areas at the same time as producing a higher level of welfare.

Government policies either promote growth or the bill has to be footed in
some other ways, namely through welfare payments. I am going to deal with this
by referring to a specific case.

My only experience in the study of regional problems was in the Gaspé
area. This is an area which at most could be called stagnant compared to other
parts of Canada. This area had first been settled in the normal way by people
looking for the best land around where they could establish themselves with their
family and make a decent living. This was at the end of the last century. When
the railroad appeared, it developed a little more and some commerce began to
flourish. Everything went rather well until the Depression. With the great amount
of unemployment then prevailing the Government decided that it should open more
land to cultivation. The region was chosen as one that in that respect offered
good prospects. Of course, no land-use study was done. A great number of new
settlers were thus established on new land, with no resources except a little government money. Actually very few farmed. They cleared a little land but were
mostly interested in getting some income from their wood. When the lot was
cleared they went to work in the neighbouring forests or on the North Coast. Very
few farmed, sometimes to get the many Government premiums. Everything went
rather well up until the end of the war. But soon the forests were depleted and

with the sluggish demand conditions that affected agriculture after the war and with the extremely rapid technological changes that took place in Canadian agriculture, changes which favoured good and/or well located land, the whole agricultural economy of the region was imperilled. Having done what it had done it was now difficult for the government to retreat. It intervened in a massive way through various forms of welfare payments and different types of expenditures on roads, schools, public works, agriculture, fisheries, etc. . . . The latter were very often not justified. The result was to keep the population in the region. Yet unemployment of the open or disguised varieties continued to be present everywhere. As a result, a great many people suffer. Few prosper. The taxpayer has to foot the bill and is deprived of other much needed public services.

This example shows that government policies can have a very bad effect on the movement of people and may prevent the maximization of per capita income, which in the end we should all be striving for. It appears to me that welfare payments should not be used in an undiscriminated way like this. As I said earlier, there is to be a price paid for immobility. Only people who are permanently injured, who cannot move, should be helped. The others should perhaps be aided to move but not to stay unless such a policy is temporary and in the expectation of something better to come.

All of this of course points out to the many facets of the regional problem and to the various ways in which Government policies and the evolution of the economy itself have a bearing on it.

I now come to the question of industrial decentralization or decentralized industrialization whatever you may wish to call it. This is a result of growth itself and therefore of government policies having regard to growth. In turn, it produces growth. It is highly desirable to achieve a balanced growth as between the various regions of the country. Up until now, industry has had too much of a tendency to locate in the central areas of Canada to the detriment of the outlying regions. To redistribute industry however, we nevertheless have to have more of it and the right conditions have to exist. These are a result of policy. I agree with Mr. Brewis that industry will tend to agglomerate, to follow the leaders. This is especially what we need if decentralized industrialization is to take place. But for this, good transportations and trade policies have to be put into effect together with good public services of all kinds. To have an effect on regional economic growth, an industry has to be big, big enough to have forward and backward effects. It should be in a position to export or to compete effectively with imports.

The argument about Southern Ontario industry that Mr. Brewis advances is in my view hardly to be applied to the whole of Canada. These industries could perhaps have been spread on a wider area of Central Canada — but not in the West and in the Maritime Provinces where they are most needed. Industries of that variety will have to locate close to the largest markets.

In conclusion, I want to say that I am very much in favour of Mr. Brewis' argument for restricting aid to these areas that have some reasonably good growth prospects. It is then a matter of accelerating a development which would take place, but over a longer period of time. But I still say that regional growth depends on the whole arsenal of Government policies; Federal and Provincial growth will be concentrated at certain focal points. Mobility has to be assumed. Canada has more than 1,500,000 people to absorb in its labour force between now and 1970; it is a very high rate of growth of the labour force to achieve. This will not be done by thinking small.

COMMENTS

DR. W. R. DYMOND,
Assistant Deputy Minister,
Department of Labour, Ottawa.

I should like to comment on Professor Brewis' paper indirectly rather than directly by telling you about the background thinking which led to the selection of Designated Areas under the Area Development Program of the Federal Government.

The purpose of the Program can be derived from the statement of the Minister of Finance in introducing his budget last year. In assessing Professor Brewis' quotations, I would not treat all written or oral statements which emerge from Ottawa with equal weight.

The Minister of Finance said: "It is important that the new employment we are seeking to achieve in the Canadian economy, and the new investment required to produce it, be directed wherever practicable to areas of slow growth and surplus manpower." Recently the Minister of Labour has said: "This Program is an effort to stimulate growth, particularly in those areas in Canada where unemployment is high. It is designed to equalize opportunities for Canadians in all parts of Canada." These objectives then set the framework within which we worked to recommend to the government areas of slow growth and high unemployment where it is neces-sary to bring jobs to immobilized workers.

With respect to employment and unemployment, the main concern of the Department of Labour is with the development of manpower policies and programs which will prepare workers and potential workers for the kinds of employment which our economy offers and which will increase the efficiency of the operation of the labour market. The present Area Development Program is only one means of achieving these objectives and can only be assessed in relation to other government programs; for example, those designed to stimulate the general growth of the economy, expand foreign trade, to develop the manpower resources of the country through increasing education and training, to reduce seasonal unemployment, to cope with the manpower dislocations which are effected by technological change and to encourage a greater geographical mobility of labour.

The Area Development Program should also be reviewed in relation to the operation of the Atlantic Development Board, which was established to stimulate development on a regional basis. In short, the Area Development Program is part of a total pattern of programs which, from a manpower point of view, is in a considerable measure designed to improve the total utilization of Canada's manpower resources.

How then did we go about selecting areas for designation under the Program?

While some consideration was given to various kinds of geographical districts and boundaries, it soon became evident that the only practicable basis of selection — given by the statistics with which we had to work — and the objectives of the Program, were the areas administered by the National Employment Service. In addition to these practical considerations, this particular geographic unit has several advantages.

The N.E.S. areas, because they are used to administer the work of the employment exchanges, approximate the real boundaries of functioning labour markets; that is, they represent areas in which workers can commute from their homes to their employment. Also, in many parts of the country, the areas embrace a major centre with a number of satellite communities. In addition, they have the virtue of being relatively small in size in populous parts of the country and large in size in areas of scattered population. A consideration of major importance to their use as a basis for an *objective determination* of areas for the purpose of the Program, is that they are the *only* local areas for which statistics on employment and unemployment are available on a current basis.

The use of N.E.S. areas as a basis for designation and the Government's general approach to area development has been the subject of comment and criticism as illustrated by the Brewis paper. It has been said that the selection process does not take into account the industrial potential of an area. Rather it ensures that it is biased towards the selection of areas least likely to lead to the kind of expansion of area employment that is desired. It is argued that the boundaries of designated areas should be large enough to support an industrial complex or growth centres or that the designation should be on a provincial or regional basis.

The basic answer to most of these criticisms is to make the point that the objective of the present program is one of bringing employment *to* immobile and unemployed workers. To reach this objective, it is necessary to bring jobs to *within* commuting distance of workers within the most serious pockets where immobile unemployed workers are resident. This is not to say that policies of labour mobility are not important for they too must play a role in moving the more mobile of the unemployed from these areas to areas of greater employment opportunity. However, no matter how successful policies to stimulate labour mobility are, there will always be a significant residual of workers over the age of 35 for whom programs of labour mobility will not provide a realistic means of secure employment and for whom jobs must be created in their *local* area. It would not be possible either for the government to ignore areas of high unemployment as having little potential by refusing to designate them under the program.

Employment expansion in so-called "growth points" does not provide employment or income for unemployed workers in outlying areas far removed from these centres even if they are in the same province. It is not difficult to find a great many instances of unemployed workers who are unwilling or unable to accept a job that is beyond commuting distance, or even to find groups of workers who have transferred, from areas of high unemployment to jobs in other parts of the same province only to return to their homes and unemployment within relatively short periods of time.

The difficulties involved particularly for older people in pulling up roots are often very real and substantial. Our research on labour mobility has generally shown that in areas of declining job opportunities, there is a substantial core of workers who are unable or unwilling to move. This core of immobility may be obscured by a high rate of total out-migration as is true in many areas of the Maritime Provinces. Studies of labour mobility reveal, however, that the bulk of migrants are young adults. Migration rates in the over 30 age group, where unemployment rates are highest, have been quite low. This is the primary group of unemployed manpower that the present program is designed to assist.

Given the selection of an appropriate set of geographic units such as the N.E.S. areas, the choice of an objective standard for selecting areas of high persistent unemployment and slow rates of growth still raises difficult problems.

First, high unemployment does not necessarily mean slow growth, nor does slow growth or even a decline in employment necessarily result in high unemployment. Vancouver, for example, experiences continuing heavy unemployment, but the rate of employment increase has usually been at or above the national average. Renfrew, Ontario, on the other hand, has experienced a less than average growth of employment while the number of unemployed has been relatively low. Our first criterion was a measure of the depth and duration of unemployment in local areas.

A further point is that the program is primarily concerned with long-term employment and unemployment trends and not with short-run variations in employment due to cyclical or seasonal factors. The solution to seasonal and cyclical employment problems is through different policy measures than those encompassed by this program.

Within this framework of considerations, there are a number of kinds of situations in which the Area Development Program can prove useful. The *first* one is that in which employment has failed to keep pace with the growth of the labour force. For this reason, unemployment tends to accumulate over the long-term and remains high.

Second, is the situation in which there is a basic change in industrial structure which causes employment in the area to decline over the long-term. Even though out-migration may prevent the accumulation of very high levels of unemployment, the waste of social capital involved justifies an attempt to attract new industry and employment to the area. This type of situation is recognized in the designation program by relaxing the unemployment criterion and imposing a requirement that employment must show a decrease over the long-term.

A *third* kind of situation takes into account the development of a severe employment dislocation over a relatively short period, as in the case of Springhill and Elliot Lake. This kind of problem area is encompassed in the program by shortening the time period on which the criteria are based and imposing a requirement of a sustained decrease in employment.

Of the 35 designated areas, 27 were designated under the first criterion, six areas qualified under the second and two under the third.

As I indicated earlier, statistics used to measure unemployment have a number of weaknesses of which I am sure many of you are aware. Similarly, statistics on the trend of employment through time in the N.E.S. areas are based on statistics which though generally reliable have some unavoidable weaknesses. At the moment, however, there does not appear to be any satisfactory alternative measures of employment and unemployment for geographic areas of this size.

Probably the most significant limitation of the present statistical criteria for the designation of areas is that they do not explicitly take into account *under-employment* and low income which is the main problem in many areas of Canada. We have been investigating a number of series that reflect this phenomenon and which are available on a suitable geographic basis. We have examined wage-earner income, family income, labour force participation rates and the number of hours and weeks worked during the year. All of these series are from the 1961 census and are therefore available at only ten year intervals.

Although no firm decisions have been made as yet, it is fairly clear that some measure of underemployment and low income will be necessary to improve the selection of areas in which major manpower resources are under-utilized. At the present time, our investigation suggests that family income may be the most useful measure of this phenomenon, although, of course, low income does not necessarily result only from underemployment.

As you will see, it is not correct as Professor Brewis has suggested that unemployment is the only criterion which has been taken into account in the selection of areas.

I would not regard the criticism as valid — that because the areas are relatively small, many of the benefits of local expansion accrue to other areas. It would be impossible to design a program where the multiplier effects of income generation were restricted to a single area of the country.

I would also question the placing of much direction in the hands of administrators as to the kinds of industries which should be attracted to various areas. In the present program, this decision is left to entrepreneurs as to what areas they wish to bring their industry. Presumably they will only enter areas which in their view have economic potential. In this sense, all areas are treated alike by the government's policy, although the economic results will differ markedly from area to area.

PART III

POLICIES IN THE UNITED STATES AND THE UNITED KINGDOM

- Federal Redevelopment in the United States: Concept and Practice

> Mr. Gordon E. Reckord,
> Assistant Administrator for Program
> Development,
> U.S. Area Redevelopment Administration.

Discussants:

> Dr. Sar A. Levitan,
> W. E. Upjohn Institute for Employment
> Research,
> Washington, D.C.

> Professor Maurice J. Boote,
> Department of Economics,
> Trent University.

- Areas of Economic Stress: The British Case

> Professor Gerald Manners,
> Department of Geography,
> University College, Swansea,
> (1964-65, Resources for the Future, Inc.,
> Washington, D.C.).

Discussants:

> Dr. E. P. Weeks,
> Executive Director,
> Atlantic Development Board.

> Professor Richard Lawton,
> Department of Geography,
> University of Liverpool,
> (1964-65, University of Southern Illinois).

FEDERAL REDEVELOPMENT IN THE UNITED STATES: CONCEPT AND PRACTICE

GORDON E. RECKORD,
Assistant Administrator for
Program Development,
U.S. Area Redevelopment Administration.

Area Redevelopment Act

The Need:

During the Decade of the 1950's, while the U.S. economy was gradually moving upward to new levels, people who lived in certain regions of the United States failed to share in this net growth.[1] This individual failure was characterized by localized high unemployment rates, low local income, and heavy out-migration, and was accompanied by changes in the labour force not clearly understood. Unemployment in some areas during 1950 was running at levels that brought to mind the general depression of the 1930's when 25 to 30 per cent of the national work force was unemployed.

In 1959, in the areas which later became rural development counties, 44 per cent of the families had incomes of $3,000 or less. This compared to 20 per cent for the Nation as a whole. The unemployment rate for all redevelopment areas in 1961 was 10.4 per cent, as contrasted with an unemployment rate of 6.7 for the whole Nation.

These facts and others which outlined the reality of economically stale areas, became a matter of widespread discussion and public concern. The concern on localized unemployment which had been expressed in the Employment Act of 1946 was now more widely acknowledged by observers of the post-war national economy, including the Joint Economic Committee of the Congress. By the mid-fifties the Federal government was being urged to react to this corrosive problem and to seek measures with which to bolster the remedial measures which were being undertaken by State and local economic development groups. The Area Redevelopment Act, Senate Bill No. 1, (Public Law 87-28) was signed into law by President John F. Kennedy on May 1, 1961.

Program Accomplishments

Community Participation:

Since the passage of the Act, some 1,108 counties of the 3,054 counties in the United States have been designated as redevelopment areas. Of the areas currently designated for redevelopment all have either submitted individual Overall Economic Development Programs to the Area Redevelopment Administration or have participated in or are represented by OEDPs covering two or more designated areas.

The OEDP and the process of putting it together have had several kinds of community effects. For many areas — particularly in smaller communities — this was the first time that community leaders had looked at local economic and

---

[1] There had been a general awareness of these areal discrepancies; but the locational pattern showed up on the manpower statistics developed for Korean War planning and other purposes since, supplemented by known information on income distribution developed in the national decennial census.

employment problems in an overall way. For many this was the first estimate of the range of needed local actions needed to reverse local decline. Problems associated with these plans will be referred to below.

Financial Assistance:

The Area Redevelopment Administration has participated in financing projects in almost every major industrial category in over half — 561 — of these areas. Many of ARA's loans have been made to labour intensive industries — wood, food, apparel, tourism and recreation. There have also been loans to capital intensive industries — chemicals, machinery, paper and primary metals. A total of 382 projects for industrial and commercial loans have been approved, totaling $167,306,000. It is expected that these projects, on the basis of the applicants estimates, when fully operational will be responsible for the creation of 42,702 direct and directly related jobs. Close to $100 million of the total industrial and commercial loans have been made in small labour markets and rural areas.

In addition to commercial and industrial loans, ARA has approved 150 loan and grant projects related to ten residential and commercial projects for public facilities, totaling $88,604,000. It is expected that commercial and industrial activity supported by these new facilities will create an additional 31,397 direct and directly related jobs. When we consider that direct and directly related employment generates other indirect jobs at the rate of about 65 to 100 direct jobs, and I apologize for the known inadequacies of this formula, one expects that ARA's loan and grant program will generate over 120,000 new jobs in these depressed areas. This record has been accomplished through the cooperative efforts of other participants with ARA — private banks, 13.7 per cent; local development companies, 10.8 per cent; applicant companies, 8.0 per cent; other private investors, 6.5 per cent; and State, county and city governments, 3.3 per cent. A total of 280 banking institutions in 44 States and Territories have loaned $42,500,000 on 253 ARA projects. Local development companies have provided $31,000,000; applicant companies, $22,000,00; private investors, $18,000,000; and State and local governments, $9,400,000. Of all ARA commercial and industrial loans, 225 or 59 per cent were to new business firms. Although many of these projects were considered marginal or "high risk" ventures when they were made and some are presently inoperative, most are turning out to be highly successful.

Technical Assistance:

ARA has approved 395 technical assistance projects which will cost $13 million. This special program tool has advanced job-producing projects and enterprises within local regions that otherwise would never have occurred or brought new ideas for economic development to local areas, using experts in a great variety of fields to provide technical assistance. ARA has utilized the services of consultants in various fields, engineering firms, universities, and public and private research institutions to help solve the problems of redevelopment areas and to break bottle-necks holding back economic growth.

ARA has launched a broad technical assistance experimental program to create jobs by increasing business knowledge and management techniques in redevelopment areas and hard-hit areas of major cities. We are providing this help through economic development centres at colleges and universities.

The amounts appropriated thus far for technical assistance have only partially met the demand for help by local redevelopment agencies and State and regional groups. Over 800 individual requests for technical help have been submitted to ARA, amounting to a total of more than $40 million. Although it is impossible now to judge the net impact of the technical assistance program enough evidence is emerging to indicate that a relatively low dollar investment can produce extensive job dividends. Benefits from the findings of technical assistance projects accrue to others in addition to the applicant. When the results are such that they may be of use to other areas with similar problems, either because of methodology or technology, publication is made to accomplish wider dissemination. Through ARA's publication of these technical assistance reports, case books, handbooks and brochures, ARA's relatively small investments are being multiplied.

A study is needed to outline the differences and similarities of overseas and domestic technical assistance. We have found that because of differing conditions many of the program ideas used overseas have not worked at home. I am sure that many of our technical ideas would not work overseas. We speculate on these differences but I confess we have not been able to determine precisely why they occur. This would be a useful procedural research task.

Worker Training and Retraining:

As of the end of 1964, 844 projects costing $21,267,000 and involving 37,891 trainees had been approved. Training and retraining resulted in jobs for the unemployed and better jobs for others. Upgraded employment for an employed person opens an opportunity for one less skilled to find gainful employment.

In all, 1,771 projects costing $290,536,000 have been approved under the Act since May, 1961.

Research on Area Economic Distress:

When Congress created the Area Redevelopment Administration, it wrote a requirement for "continuing a program of study and research designed to assist in determining the causes of unemployment and underemployment, underdevelopment and chronic depression" into the Act. The economic and social research undertaken by ARA under this Section (27) of the Act is directed toward important questions of fact or policy, some of which are: measuring the extent of structural unemployment; geographic mobility of labour; moving costs; differences in mobility among different groups; transferability of skills; effects of technological change and industrial composition of depressed areas; cyclical behaviour of employment in redevelopment areas; and others. The ARA research program has been designed to answer questions important in carrying out the Agency's tasks, and to suggest new ways to reduce or alleviate unemployment and promote development and economic growth. ARA's research program is less than two years old. It has obligated over $800,000 in research contract funds to investigate problems which cost the United States billions of dollars each year in unused resources, social decline, unemployed human resources, and lost income. Most of these study projects, incidentally, require between one and three years to complete. The results of some of our earlier projects are just now becoming available, and anyone interested in getting these studies should write to ARA's Publication Division.

Redevelopment Practice

Accomplishments of the Area Redevelopment Administration have been substantial. It was inevitable however in a new national effort such as this that all goals would not be achieved. Difficulties which could not be anticipated arose due to lack of proper tools, unexpected turns from policy application, or ineffective local participation. The variety and complex nature of these problems was anticipated only by those with extensive experience with community and project development.

The experienced public servant is well aware of the information gap that sometimes hinders public understanding of what he is trying to do. Even given public acceptance of the need to do something positive as voiced by the Congress, complete public understanding of the program in action is not always possible, particularly if the program is new and untested, or if it bears heavily upon a traditional way of doing things.

Problems Stemming from the Initial Rush to "Get the Show on the Road":

The Area Redevelopment Administration was "on the spot" when it first opened for business. Great results were expected and in a hurry. An ARA type program had been debated for almost a decade before the bill finally passed the Congress. Naturally the supporters of ARA in an effort to sell the program overemphasized its probable accomplishments. Many Americans traditionally feel that virtually every community has potential for growth, given time and proper "promotion". Many expected their Federal government to assume this responsibility for them. Thus many thought that ARA would spark this growth. When ARA became law there were high hopes that it would accomplish wonders overnight. Not everyone felt this way. Those with community and economic development experience knew the nature of the problems and something of the difficulty of changing local economic trends.

The ARA was expected to move rapidly as well as to accomplish much. ARA was a new try at area development on a vast scale. No doubt post-war experience of the Marshall Plan and expenditures on subsequent foreign aid programs supported an assumption that massive aid would work at home even though the difference or similarities between foreign and domestic economic development were not known. Although the Office of Area Development, an existing unit of the Department of Commerce, had earlier assigned part of its small staff to policy planning for an ARA-type operation, there were, on the whole, few guidelines for operational procedures. Community industrial development programs of the American design were quite extensive. The new Act was based on them but they were essentially local or State-wide and not Federal in either design or expectation. Earlier Federal programs were specific in character and with few exceptions looked at problems not in a regional context but as integral parts of national problems. Regionalism as such existed in only a few separate cases such as TVA, metropolitan planning or river basin investigation. In each of these there was a strong subject bias. Technically trained people fit to work on the program in Washington as well as in the field were in short supply; moreover many of those with experience were not available for reasons of interest or price. Much discussion was necessary before the program could be presented in the field. In the beginning virtually no time was available for preparing usable guidelines for handling loans, for developing a comprehensive and well-planned research program or for formulating a series of guides and information brochures that were needed by local development groups or to train the ARA staff.

But local committees were not interested in ARA organizational problems. They wanted the agency to move rapidly in certifying their OEDPs and in approving development projects which they thought would put people to work or would provide a new public facility such as a sewer or water distribution system. In short, the pressures to get money committed were so great the new agency did not have time to tool up. It was off and running before it could determine whether the right pace was to sprint or to trot.

Problems of Designation:

The selection of areas that would participate in the program is one of the most troublesome aspects of administration. Since designation meant the difference of whether or not a particular area would benefit from Federal lending and assistance, the rules adopted for designating the areas were most critical. And criticism was expected. The ins and outs would never agree and the umpire was assured of only a little good will whichever way his decision went.

When the Congress was debating the ARA bill in early 1961, unemployment was increasing. Accordingly, the Act spelled out the eligibility criteria in terms of unemployment averages which were available at that time for the major labour areas of the country. When time came for passage, the Congressmen from rural counties and from small towns were able to gain admission for their constituent areas. But which rural areas? The Congress offered several guidelines such as level of family income, participation in other programs, percentage of low class farms and others. These were substitute measures of distress and at the time there was no assurance that the cross comparison of unemployment and income was either meaningful or fair. There were other difficulties with the data as well. For example, in a few cases estimates of local income later were shown to be both too low and too high.

There was great interest in the new legislation by those Congressmen who represented low income groups living in the centres of some of the big cities. But the designation formulae cited in the Act made this difficult since unemployment rates were determined on a metropolitan average which normalized out the central city unemployed. Formulas were later devised to designate larger cities as parts of larger labour areas but not to designate parts of these cities. These city designations have been limited to cities of 250,000 population or larger all with serious problems of minority unemployment. Problems of program scale in these large cities are apparent.

Dispersal of the Available Program Resources:

Problems of designation introduce what some commentators consider ARA's major problem, that is, the spreading of its resources over a large number of counties so that its relatively small resources could not possibly meet the demand or have a significant effect.

Meeting the demand was contingent upon more than a single condition — not just a single decision of the Administrator as to how many areas he would serve. On the demand side were the instructions of the Congress in Section (5) of the Act as to which areas were to be included. On the supply side were instructions from the Congress as to how much money would be available to handle problems of these areas. And certainly these two should have some relationship to each other.

The decision as to how much money would be available was made by the Congress before the number of participation areas was decided upon. As a matter of fact the decision on the amount to be appropriated was based primarily upon considerations of unemployment in urban areas alone, not those urban areas in combination with rural areas. Did the Administrator designate too many areas — even with Congressional instruction — or perhaps the Congress did not appropriate adequate funds?

An important development which affected the number of areas participating in the program was the expanded number of area labour surveys conducted by the Department of Labor, which showed for the first time that many areas not covered in previous surveys were eligible under the Act on the basis of the Act's unemployment criteria.

Prior to the passage of the ARA legislation, estimates of area unemployment were based on reports to the U.S. Department of Labor from approximately 500 counties which included the 150 largest labour areas and some 150 smaller areas. Shortly after the Act was passed, approximately half of these 500 counties (about 190 labour areas) were made eligible for participation in the ARA program because of their chronically high rates of unemployment. Rounding out the original group of designated areas were some 475 more rural counties designated primarily because of low income or their previous participation in the rural development program of the Department of Agriculture.

In the two year period between August 1961 and July 1963, the number of eligible areas rose by 410 to a peak of 1,074. This increase was almost entirely due to the upsurge in very small labour areas designated on the basis of Labor Department surveys, and that Department's declaration of eligibility based on rates of unemployment that were substantially and persistently above the U.S. rates. These declarations have been accepted by ARA in the same manner as the declarations concerning the larger labour areas. The actual increase in the number of small labour areas was 390.

It is apparent, therefore, that the overall increase in the number of ARA areas is due almost entirely to the increased activity of the Department of Labor in identifying smaller areas which have experienced chronically high unemployment rates. Little or no information was available from these smaller pockets of unemployment prior to the passage of the Act.

It is interesting to note that the entrance level of income used in the program —1,887 or 1/3 the average U.S. income — is significantly lower than the $3,000 level now generally accepted as the standard for determination of poverty within the United States.

Relating Development Assistance to Need:

In passing the ARA Act the Congress recommended that the new agency make every effort to "avoid the duplication of existing staff and facilities" by calling upon other Federal agencies to assist whenever feasible.

"While these arrangements have probably resulted in certain savings by eliminating or avoiding potential duplication of staffs and activities, they have, because of their inherently cumbersome and awkward nature of administration and coordination, contributed greatly to frustrating and discouraging delays and confusion in the processing of project proposals. It is difficult, at best, for an applicant and a supporting local redevelopment group to understand the difference between ARA and either SBA or CFA, not to mention the need for dealing directly with both agencies. The resulting confusion in the mind of the applicant, and much of the delay, is accentuated by the unfortunate fact that personnel with varying, and sometimes conflicting, viewpoints, represent the different agencies. Though it is recognized that this difference in attitude and approach is, for the most part, the outgrowth of differences in personal experience as well as the prevailing philosophy and procedures in the various agencies (whose own primary function often differs greatly from that of ARA), it is a difference, nevertheless, which tends to make itself felt as a real barrier."[2]

Inability of Local Groups to provide the 10 per cent Local Financial Participation:

Most redevelopment organizations find it difficult to find the 10 per cent local financial participation required under the law. As noted earlier, the ARA can loan up to 65 per cent of the money required for an industrial project and in repayment this Federal money takes precedent over all other loans. Thus participants in the 10 per cent local investment will receive no returns, other than interest, until the Federal loan has been returned and this may take up to 25 years. An investment that ties up funds for so long a period is not very attractive. This matter is complicated by the fact that these funds generally must come from individuals least able to raise them. Some State funds have been used to satisfy ARA's 10 per cent requirement but this is not satisfactory since it defeats the purpose of State revolving fund legislation.

Lack of Incentives to Attract Blue Chip Industries:

In a nation where an estimated 14,000 organizations are actively seeking new industry and where there are many splendid industrial sites available in attractive and well-located communities it is extremely difficult to sell a substantial industry on locating in a Redevelopment Area. The latter have so many obvious shortcomings that a four per cent loan is no special inducement to a successful corporation.

Improving Federal Redevelopment

The Redevelopment Act has been called by Sar Levitan "An Experiment on Trial". This implied that a new idea was being tested and presumably that changes would be made as the tools provided in the Act were used against the problem.

This is the plan. The Administration is aware that changes are necessary to make the program more effective. Numerous changes have been made under the powers available to our Administrator. Loan policy has been modified and strengthened. Regulations covering the approval of overall plans have been revised. Organizational arrangements have been revised. Technical assistance practice has been strengthened by feeding-back management experience.

There are other strictures or instructions, however, written into the language of the Act that cannot be changed without legislative action. The following section outlines the nature of some of the changes that have been suggested. Most of these will require action outside the Agency. They are listed here not as policy conclusions of the Administrator but as subjects for discussion.

Limiting the Number of Recipient Areas:

The Administrator and others are aware of the need to concentrate available resources on a smaller number of redevelopment areas and on other adjacent

---

[2] Report prepared for the National Public Advisory Committee on Area Redevelopment, September 1, 1964.

areas that have some alternate growth potentianl. This is especially so if the program continues at its present scale.

Our basic research program has explored the question of whether the use of the two basic and available criteria on which to base designation — current employment plus annual unemployment rates over a two-to-four year period and median family income level — had produced approximately the same broad rankings of counties that would have been obtained had a dozen socio-economic variables been used. The answer was affirmative. A comparison was made of (1) the competitive employment shift data of the Perloff, Dunn, Lampard type, (2) median school years completed, (3) per cent of population 20-34 years of age, (4) public welfare expenditures per employed person, (5) educational expenditures for employed person, and many others.[3]

Apart from some data deficiencies which confronted us in the early years of our existence, we conclude that our initial efforts were in line with Congress's wishes in so far as it was stated in the Act. Still, the dividing line between designated and non-designated areas might have been drawn differently. Experience has shown that some groupings, especially of rural areas, would have been desirable for a number of reasons, including delineation of more viable areas, easier avoidance of duplication of public facility construction, more efficient utilization of ARA's limited field and planning assistance staffs.

Under suggested changes, the number of counties designated by ARA would be reduced from roughly 1,000 to 750, through the application of new criteria for designation. These criteria, based *solely* on measures of unemployment rates and income, would distinguish different classes of counties, ranked from the worst-off to the better-off.

The distinction between 5(a) urban and 5(b) rural areas would be abolished and the numerous designation criteria presently used would be eliminated. To the extent that they do not qualify under the above criteria, RAD counties — counties included in the program by virtue of the fact that they had been part of the Rural Areas Development Program — counties of low production farming, and areas of low median farm family income (unless they were also areas of low median family income, i.e., unless the proportion of farm families to all families was relatively high) would be eliminated. Use of multiple designation criteria often resulted in different handling of contiguous counties which had the same measures of unemployment or median family income.

More importantly, several steps would be taken to encourage formation of multi-county development regions among designated areas. These steps would adopt a permissive rather than a mandatory regional approach. For example, ARA would, according to one proposal, make funds available to ask the States to delineate regions according to broad standards specified by the ARA, and to support the planning staffs of each region for the early years of the staff's work. In addition, potentially wasteful duplication of public facility expenditures would be achieved by narrowing the location of such expenditures. An additional incentive would be allowed for *regional* public facility projects which are integral parts of the regional plan and serve a regional, as opposed to a local, end. Still further, otherwise non-designated counties which could serve as growth centres could be made part of a region provided the otherwise non-designated population did not

---

[3] Mattila, John, "A Test for the Validity of ARA Designation of Counties", ARA unpublished report, 1964.

exceed half the population of the region. That is, an effort would be made to try to bring aid to depressed areas through more prosperous growth centres which are made a part of a region. These growth centres would be permitted to apply for public facility grants for a share of the cost of *regional* public facility projects. Examples of regional projects are regional libraries, hospitals, certain highway or transportation projects, and the like.

Concentrating Limited ARA Funds:

The above proposal is designed to attack criticisms to the effect that with too many areas, given ARA funds have been spread too thinly. But there is the additional problem that all areas have been equally eligible for aid, thus tending to prevent concentration of aid in areas of greatest need.

Some thought has been given to possible use of a lower interest rate on commercial and industrial loans in severely hampered areas. ARA statistics show that funds flow to areas of all degrees of depression and since the interest rate is only one of the many factors influencing investment decisions, it seems likely that a change would have only a minor effect.

An important related question is that of loan-project selection. ARA's task has been primarily the passive one of reviewing and appraising projects developed by private entrepreneurs in response to the initiative of local development groups. The underlying assumptions have been (1) that local development groups understand the resources, advantages and capabilities of their area best, and (2) that entrepreneurs exercise sound judgment. But entrepreneurs are not infallible in their judgments, which are sometimes based on provincial attitudes and prejudices which restrict unduly the range of choice of plant location sites. Hopefully, ARA will at the minimum broaden the areas of choice. Some will go further and argue that ARA's role should be the more active one in seeking specific projects for specific areas. ARA has adopted the position that it is far better to allow the entrepreneur and local groups the greatest influence on types and location of projects, with ARA's role the important one of providing information on the alternative possibilities and, of course, of review and appraisal of projects.

With respect to appraisal, there is the question of the criteria ARA should use. We are tending toward the British view that there should be no strenuous objections to capital-intensive projects. Progress tends in that direction and often such projects have important secondary effects and they generate still additional projects.

ARA, like the private banks, must be concerned with long-run payouts and prospects for survival and expansion. ARA must in addition, be cognizant of a variety of public concerns.

ARA must be aware of the effects of new publicly financed production on existing capacity — national and regional. Certain types of commerce and industry (i.e., race tracks or gambling casinos) cannot be financed no matter how great the regional economic return. Other things being equal, we would tend to favour labour-intensive projects, but other things are not likely to be equal and ARA's apparent favouritism for labour-intensive projects results primarily from the fact that such projects are often ideally suited to areas of surplus labour.

The Need for More Powerful Investment Tools:

Our investment tools would be sharpened according to proposed changes which reflect problems encountered in the operations of the past 3½ years. One serious problem is that blue-chip companies have not participated in our program and commercial and industrial loan funds set aside for urban areas have not been fully utilized. Because new plants are of necessity the marginal risks which private lenders shun, and because of the fact that tax-loss carry-over provisions will not benefit a fledgeling company with working capital problems, it has been suggested that direct assistance in the form of construction grants to business for plant and equipment cost or use of interest subsidies be considered.

Measuring the Results:

One of the meanest questions faced by the Administrator is how to measure the effect of the program on local unemployment and underemployment. The critics have been most vocal on this point.

The need was for a single numerical index which would reflect program conditions, cover all redevelopment areas equally, be readily available at low cost and most important would relate ARA actions to the index itself.

This was a tall order. One index didn't exist. The only available alternative was to use the several dissonant measures available at the beginning and to improve them over time. In retrospect, this wasn't enough. Especially since those who had reservations about the program at the beginning were not satisfied with involved or conditioned evidence. The result has been public misunderstanding of how the program has progressed.

Some selected samples of the problems are cited below:

1. Local unemployment data is limited to reports on rates as reported by State Employment Agencies. These are unadjusted for seasonal effects. Adjusted rates are available only after the end of the calendar year. Regular seasonal unemployment reports therefore are available only at yearly intervals. They are available only for about 10 per cent of the redevelopment areas. Spot unemployment reports are available for other areas but not on a regular basis.

2. Income data for counties is available only at ten year intervals with the decennial census. The ARA Act covers a four year period. An interesting experiment with income tax data gives promise for yearly data but is at present incompletely developed.

3. The number of jobs developed through loan and grant projects by type and area presumably would be a useful index. Should the report cover jobs anticipated in those projects or be reported when the plant opens? This means a reporting lag of up to a year after commitment of funds for projects so as to cover time for contract negotiation, construction, start-up, etc.

4. Total unemployment in redevelopment areas would be most useful, especially as it relates to national unemployment. It is unavailable. The national employment totals are derived from a household sample. While the sample reflects national conditions it is inadequate for that part of the country included in redevelopment areas. There is no index of underemployment and family income in the generally accepted standard used. (See 2 above.) We are aware of the importance of the relation of unemployment to changes in the work force. We accept however the proposition that the decline of the work force is an alternate to employment generation as a means of local economic adjustment. Our reports so indicate.

In addition to these partial indexes we have used expenditures, purchases of goods and services, construction, number of areas qualified over period, employment rates for areas for which data is available over the life of the program. All suffer from the same inabilities of partial or timely coverage.

Progress reporting is a difficult problem for many individual areas and communities. We have explored techniques and methods for establishing local systems but we are frustrated at the lack of data and the incapacities of local authorities. Our present hope is for a simplified income model such as that proposed by Professor Charles Tiebout and others.

New Management Skills:

Preliminary investigation indicates a deficiency of management skills among businessmen in redevelopment areas. This is not surprising and has been observed informally by many others. Aggressive managers seldom are content in a static or declining situation. Good managers are particularly sensitive to management opportunities and move quickly to more promising situations.

The ARA experience points up the importance of successful private and public managers in regional development programs. Project development and management, community leadership, achievement of agreed-upon goals, compromise on procedure, extension of ideas and techniques, all depend upon the existence and participation of local leadership.

How can we stimulate this type of skill in redevelopment areas? Should we offer incentives to keep managers in these areas? Should we provide training and capital incentives to apt new managers still in school? What other techniques are available? No language change is necessary in the Redevelopment Act — we do intend to actively pursue this question under existing authority.

Improvement in the OEDP Program:

The encouragement of both intra-State and inter-State regions should help fortify what has proved to be one of the unique elements of the program — the local Overall Economic Development Plan approach. The approach is fundamentally sound, has produced some local benefits even when ARA financial assistance has not resulted, and has proved weakest in those areas with inadequate planning staffs and know-how. Regionalization will tend to conserve the personnel pool so that each OEDP will be framed by capable live-wires. It will also permit a full-time development staff financially aided by ARA, as indicated above. It will make possible a more effective job of assisting local planning groups. How much easier the task will be if areas are grouped into a much smaller number of regions!

Conformity with the United States Economic System:

It is well to emphasize a number of points that should already be obvious. The aim throughout has been to disturb the U.S. economic system as little as possible. Private entrepreneurs still make decisions on plant investments, though alternatives are affected by Federal incentives provided. Local development groups are responsible for the basic planning that is required for effective implementation of any area redevelopment program. Local groups still have the job of trying to attract entrepreneurs. It is the intention of the Administrator to continue to encourage local and State developers to improve their efforts at local and regional development and while it may be the longer way, it most likely is the surer way.

Broader Inter-State Regions:

You, perhaps, are aware of the Appalachian Bill now before the Congress. ARA planned the original studies, arranged the initial Presidential meetings and has provided technical assistance that led to the Appalachia Program. This new program is largely an attempt to develop the infra-structure of the region. ARA's loans would supplement the private-investment part of the program. Numerous regional groups and legislative committees have been giving thought to redevelopment of other inter-State regions. Regions have been proposed for upper New England, the Ozarks, the upper Great Lakes Region, the Four Corners, the Northwest, and many others.

Conclusions

In relative terms as a new young and expanding nation, Americans, and Canadians too, for that matter, have acute and abiding interest in local area growth. We have traditionally and perennially equated area success or progress with bigness, with area expansion — with any and all measures that manifest growth, and in particular with increases in population! More people mean not only a bigger market but also a bigger labour force which has persistently throughout our history been a prime factor essential to the harvesting of our abundant material resources.

I cannot believe that the answer to the problems of relating jobs to resources lies only in the creation of jobs in every place where unemployment exists. Neither do I believe that the efficient use of our resources means that unemployment will be controlled by increasing the mobility of people so that they will go to the jobs. The cost of using only one of the alternatives is too great if all the costs are considered.

I do believe that there is a position between these extremes. Some jobs will go to workers with proper investment incentives; some workers will go to jobs if properly motivated. The most efficient way will be to have the jobs meet the workers "half-way". Not half-way but in those growth areas where the jobs can be created at reasonable cost and where the workers will want to work. This means that some areas will adjust to larger population and some areas will need to adjust to a smaller population. The net result will be a more efficient relation of man to his environment within a reasonable opportunity of personal choice.

There is little new in this statement. Others, like Hoover or Harris, have said it more precisely. What is new is the growing acceptance of the merit of the idea by researchers and administrators. It is not a compromise. Both points of view must be pursued to the goal of the most effective area adjustment. The determination of where this adjustment will take place and the stimulation necessary to make it happen is the critical task of the area reformer.

COMMENTS

DR. SAR A. LEVITAN,
W. E. Upjohn Institute for
Employment Research,
Washington, D.C.

We are indebted to Mr. Gordon Reckord for a concise description and analysis of the United States Area Redevelopment Administration activities. I differ with him on some of the interpretations he places on ARA operations and the directions that the program should take in the future.

Mr. Reckord apparently shares the official ARA enthusiasm for community Overall Economic Development Programs. This devotion to community economic programs continues to mystify me. The expectation is that the dialogue of the butcher, baker, and candlestick maker will bring jobs and economic development to the community. We all know that local economic development planning is not new and that thousands of communities have engaged in this process for many years. In some cases these community dialogues have resulted in bringing new economic activity and jobs to their communities. But, I fail to see any new dimensions that ARA brought to this type of activity, even though under ARA auspices the business agent and the urban league representative have been officially added in sharing the community dialogue. We must assume that in this case Reckord relies upon faith. He has not given us any facts to support his faith.

The presumed factual reporting about ARA job-generation activities also leaves much to be desired. Reckord is very careful in suggesting that the 70-odd thousand jobs for which ARA claims credit have not actually been created but will be added at some future date when the ARA-approved projects will become fully operational. But we know that many of the approved projects have not materialized and that some have already gone sour. This is to be expected, since many ARA loans are made to marginal enterprises. It is also to be expected that some of the government-supported projects will fail. Indeed, it would have been a serious criticism against ARA had it advanced venture capital only to successful projects.

I would particularly question the anticipation of a 65 per cent multiplier in ARA areas. To the best of my knowledge, ARA officials picked this figure from a United States Chamber of Commerce publication. But, one may question very seriously whether this multiplier applies to depressed areas where secondary and tertiary industries are already in excess as a result of stagnation or decline of employment in primary industries. I am not aware of any ARA studies which would support the 65 per cent employment multiplier. On the contrary, the only study made for ARA that I am acquainted with, suggesting that the anticipated multiplier in a depressed area would be extremely low, was never released by the Area Redevelopment Administration.

The reason I dwell in some detail on these statistics is my concern with the public policy implications that they suggest. The Area Redevelopment Act is due to expire by the end of this fiscal year, unless Congress acts to renew the legislation. It is my belief that federal aid to depressed areas should be continued and that the present legislation could be improved if not perfected. However, if we took ARA claims as gospel truth, then there would be no need for serious revision of the present law.

Turning to the future direction of the program, the suggestion to reduce eligible ARA areas is most welcome. However, I question Reckord's interpretation of the law, suggesting that ARA had to designate some 1100 counties, or more than a third of the total U.S. areas. Reckord recognizes that even if ARA is left with 750 designated areas, the past and anticipated resources of the agency would still be over-extended to provide any meaningful help to so many communities. His solution is to make some areas more equal than others in qualifying for ARA help. This approach has considerable merit, but the paper fails to spell out in sufficient detail how differentials would be applied. We'll have to await the actual proposals by the ARA before the approach can be evaluated.

Reckord rightfully places emphasis on the need for adequate carrots to attract blue-chip industry to depressed areas. The present law, he suggests, does not have adequate incentives to achieve this end. I would question his proposal that this can be best achieved by offering interest subsidies for new or expanding enterprises in depressed areas.

There is also room to question the present ARA-subsidized direct government loan program. I doubt whether the low interest has been a significant factor in the attraction of new industries or the expansion of existing enterprises in ARA-designated areas. This policy has, however, subjected ARA to considerable criticism and attack. It might, therefore, be worthwhile to consider the wisdom of substituting a loan guarantee program for the present subsidized loan program. This would remove a great many of the business and banking community's objections to ARA. It would also have the effect of expanding ARA capability in assisting enterprises in depressed areas because it would require a much smaller dollar appropriation by Congress to provide for a loan guarantee program than for direct loan policy. I believe that the gains achieved by a loan guarantee policy would greatly outweigh the impact of subsidized direct loans. However, I recognize that in some areas banks do not have the resources or do not customarily advance venture capital, and it is doubtful whether their practice will change even under a federal loan guarantee program. I would, therefore, continue with a modest direct loan program in cases where conventional lenders are not willing or able to offer needed venture capital.

To prevent overloading conventional lenders with industrial paper, the revised depressed area package might also contain a provision establishing a market for long-term loans held by banks or other lenders. This could be achieved by establishing a federal industrial and commercial mortgage association authorized to purchase guaranteed long-term private loans modeled after the present Fanny Mae (FNMA) which has operated successfully for many years in the housing field.

Reckord's paper recognizes the need for establishing gradations of help to depressed areas based upon their respective needs and extent of unemployment or low income. I would suggest a corollary to this excellent suggestion which would recognize that the economic base of some communities cannot be "saved". In such cases provision should be made for encouraging workers to migrate to other areas. I recognize that such a program must be used carefully and with flexibility lest it accelerate the mobility of the more educated and skilled workers from depressed areas and thus further deteriorate the human resources in these areas and make them less attractive to new enterprise.

Finally, consideration may be given to allow depressed areas larger percentages of federal grants-in-aid than are allowed in more prosperous areas. For example, the Federal Government defrays 67 per cent of the total cost of urban renewal planning, but a special provision in the Area Redevelopment Act raised the federal matching share in depressed areas to 75 per cent. The same principle applied to other federal grant programs (including highway and hospital construction, public assistance and education) would increase federal aid to depressed areas.

While I have stressed some divergence of views between Reckord and myself, I want to emphasize that I am in complete accord with him about the need of continuing an effective federal program to aid depressed areas. For more than seven years the United States has been subjected to a high level of unemployment. The ARA experience has shown that, even in an overall slack labour market, the federal program has succeeded in attracting additional jobs to depressed areas, though reasonable people might disagree on the exact impact of this program. But, if we succeed in achieving the ever-increasingly illusive full employment economy, the need for a depressed area program would become even more pronounced. And, as Gordon Reckord has indicated, if past experience is any indication of future developments, depressed areas will remain with us even in an overall full employment economy.

COMMENTS

PROFESSOR MAURICE J. BOOTE,
Department of Economics,
Trent University.

It is widely recognized that the varieties of poverty that exist in the United States form an intractable social problem on a vast scale. The most recent reaction to the problem has been the Economic Opportunity Act of 1964; so far, this program is mainly an attempt to improve the education, skills, and adaptability of young people who have grown up in poverty. In various degrees of severity, the effects of poverty exist in most communities. There are several points to notice about the Economic Opportunity program: it is likely to grow rapidly in scale; it is assumed that it will be complemented by national, aggregate, policies that encourage a high rate of economic growth; every community is eligible — eligibility is divorced from a geographical delineation that is based either on unemployment or on low income; the program is intended to help the neediest families including, for example, migrant workers.

It is now certain that during 1965 the Congress will enact a regional development program. Initially, the program will tackle Appalachia but other regions are likely to be included later. The Appalachian region — parts of eleven states, population sixteen millions — has until recently often been brushed aside as a nearly hopeless case: a region of eroded and exhausted soils, polluted streams, abandoned mines, slag heaps, inadequate public services, county after county of dogpatch. But, given an expenditure of two or three billion dollars on trunk highways, health centres, forestry and other resource developments, and given 80 per cent (or higher) federal grants, instead of matching grants, for existing federal-state programs, the economic prognosis for the region will begin to change. In the face of the facts of life in Appalachia, it is encouraging that it has not been necessary to endure long bickering over the precise course of the line on the map that is to delineate the region; each Governor can, in effect, draw a line for the portion of the state to be included in the region.

The Economic Opportunity Act is directed to the worst cases of individual poverty, the Appalachian program to one of the poorest regions. From Mr. Reckord's paper I conclude that the Area Redevelopment Act may be amended to more definitely direct aid to the neediest, poorest, geographical areas. Since 1961, more than 1,000 redevelopment areas have been designated as eligible for federal assistance but each area is eligible for the same assistance.

In a discussion of eligibility criteria for geographical areas, it is easier to find fault than it is to offer improvements. At present, there are about 490 redevelopment areas designated either on the basis of unemployment rates, or on the basis of approximate rates of unemployment. Thus: (i) there are 140 of the so-called Section 5(a) areas, predominantly urban, each with a labour force of more than 15,000. At least one-third of these areas are multi-county areas. Many of these large urban areas are potentially centres of economic growth. (ii) there are 350 of the so-called Section 5(b) areas, usually single county, rates of unemployment approximately the same as those of the Section 5(a) areas, but a labour force of less than 15,000.

The ARA has not indicated that it intends to recommend to the Congress that the number of areas eligible on the basis of high rates of unemployment be reduced by a change in the unemployment criteria. But the ARA has often pointed out that the criteria now included in the Act have resulted in more than 500 areas being designated on criteria other than unemployment. Thus, there are approximately 140 areas that are now designated because they were included in a development program of the Department of Agriculture that existed prior to the Area Redevelopment Act of 1961. At present, an area (usually a county) is eligible on the basis of low income if the median family income is one-third or less of the national median family income, a cut-off point of $1,887. It appears that many counties suffering this degree of economic stress will no longer be eligible if the number of redevelopment areas is to be reduced to about 750, without a tightening of the unemployment criteria.

I am not convinced that equity is served by the use of two types of criteria; one based on income, the other on unemployment. It forces us to assume that economic distress in an area designated on the basis of unemployment is as severe as in an area designated on the basis of low income. Underemployment and low rates of participation in the labour force in areas of low income can invalidate unemployment data for such areas; income data, on the other hand, presumably are as reliable for areas of high unemployment as they are for areas of low income.

Despite the large number of areas that have been designated, assistance by the Area Redevelopment Administration to private enterprises and to public facilities has been restricted to projects that have immediate, permanent, employment effects. So far, only one in four of the designated areas have benefitted by at least one federal loan to a private business; this is the main incentive to private enterprise under the Act.

The implication in Mr. Reckord's paper that construction grants may be included in the Act when it is amended in 1965 will surprise many members of the Congress. In the past, the conservative House of Representatives would not have tolerated this incentive but it is possible that the current Congress will do something that previous Congresses have balked at.

The Area Redevelopment Act was an extremely controversial measure that languished in the Congress for five years prior to its enactment; on two occasions it was passed by the Congress only to be vetoed by the President. The Area Redevelopment Administration, with over 1,000 areas to be developed, has been faced by a task that is overwhelming in relation to the resources and techniques provided by the Congress. During the past two years the implementation of the legislation has been further hampered by the refusal of the Congress in 1963 and 1964 to vote funds. It is probable that these funds will be forthcoming in 1965 and that the legislation will be amended to complement the Economic Opportunity and Appalachian Development Acts.

AREAS OF ECONOMIC STRESS — THE BRITISH CASE

PROFESSOR GERALD MANNERS,
Department of Geography,
University College, Swansea,
(1964-65, Resources for the Future, Inc.,
Washington, D.C.).

It is now over thirty years since the British government passed its first legislation seeking to ameliorate the problem of localized structural unemployment.[1] This was the Special Areas (Development and Improvement) Act of 1934. Since that date, the statute book has been amended on numerous occasions, the matter has been the subject of a famous Royal Commission,[2] public policy has changed course on several occasions, and a bookshelf of official, semi-official and independent studies of the problem has been filled. In this brief survey, the object is to look back briefly over the past 30 years, to identify the nature of the British problem, to recall and assess the changing nature of legislation and governmental policy, and to single out the principal lessons which might be learned from British experience.

The Nature of the British Problem

Throughout the present century the British economy has been undergoing structural and geographical change. As the country has pulled its resources of capital and labour out of those industries which changing technology and comparative advantages have left as misfits in the modern British scene — in particular those industries characterized by their production of specialized, high quality, almost craft products in limited quantities — the modern industries which have replaced them have been subject to distinctly different location forces than their predecessors. These new industries, founded upon rapidly advancing technologies and concerned especially with the mass production of standardized goods, appeared, succeeded and subsequently expanded in Southern England, the Greater London and West Midlands areas in particular. The consequence was to leave the coalfield-based economies of the north and west with the larger part of the country's old, stagnant and contracting industries; and the considerable resources of capital and labour of these peripheral economies, resources which had been built up in the hey-day of Victorian expansion, thus came to be under- and unemployed.

Historical, economic and social forces were at work to produce these areas of relative boom and prosperity in the south, on the one hand, and the problem peripheral economies — variously called the "special", "depressed", "development" or "less prosperous" areas (Map I) — in the north and west on the other.[3]

---

[1] It is possible to identify three types of areas in Britain which have suffered, or which are still suffering, from "economic stress"; but it is impractical to discuss them all in this paper. The problems of localized seasonal unemployment and rural depopulation, therefore, are neglected and the discussion concentrates upon the issue of localized structural employment.

[2] *Royal Commission on the Distribution of Industrial Population*, Cmmd. 6153, London, 1940 (The Barlow Report).

[3] For a fuller discussion of these factors with specific reference to south Wales, see Gerald Manners, *South Wales in the Sixties*, Oxford, 1964, p. 35 ff.

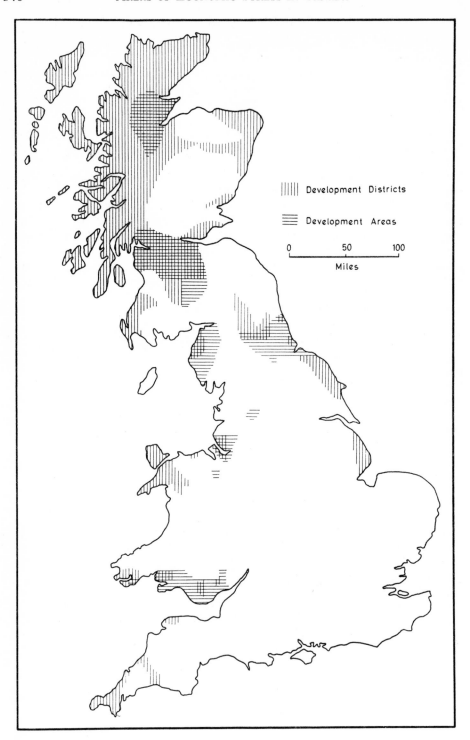

Map 1. Areas of Economic Stress in Britain: Development Areas and Development Districts.

This new and still emerging geography of Britain has been popularly dubbed as "the drift to the south". Yet industry and people also moved away from the west and southwest, and more realistically, the changing industrial and population geography of the country should be recognised as a move towards the centre of the national market.[4] It is only by being aware of the forces behind this changing geography that one can effectively assess the contemporaneous political reaction.

One of the *historical* reasons why a new economic base failed to emerge in the peripheral economies was that many of the new industries grew naturally out of the existing industries, especially the lighter engineering trades, which already existed in the south. It was especially important that the quality of the *labour force* of these trades — the diverse skills, the traditions, and the apprenticeship and training schemes in particular — provided a natural base from which new enterprises could readily develop. The carriage trade of London, for example, was not only a forerunner of the modern motor industry in a technological sense, but it also had built up a labour force with skills which could be easily adapted to the new industry — in a way which the skills of coalminers, shipbuilders or tinplate workers could not. There was, of course, the compensating advantage of the quantity of labour unemployed and hence available in the peripheral economies: this large labour pool could have been cheaply trained and utilized by the new industries. But in the formative inter-war years, when aggregate demand in the British economy was low, adequate supplies of labour were always available in southern England either indigenously or through emigration.

A second historical factor was the lack of *enterprise* on the coalfields of the north and west. It is certain that with a little local initiative, new industries could have been established and many would have succeeded there. The profitability of government-induced industries in the peripheral economies since 1936 amply proves this point. But enterprise was not forthcoming, and one of the reasons lay in the industrial history of these areas, and the nature of the economies and societies which had evolved there during the nineteenth century. With the industrial revolution, these peripheral economies attracted and prospered with industries which by and large were oligopolistic in structure and in which entrepreneurial decisions were concentrated in a few hands. As a result, their societies were denied a widespread tradition of enterprise and contrasted acutely with the highly entrepreneurial characteristics of those in London and Birmingham.[5]

Also stemming from this industrial structure was the relative scarcity of entrepreneurial *capital* in the peripheral economies. Despite the small size of Britain, there is some evidence to indicate that these regions of oligopolistic industry did not develop institutions and traditions which made capital readily available to the small man pioneering a new industry.[6] Unlike London or Birmingham, therefore, where a long tradition of highly competitive, small scale industries had spawned both formal and informal means of making small amounts of capital available to the entrepreneur, the peripheral economies had been left relatively deficient in yet another factor which could have aided in their industrial revival.

---

[4] See Caesar, A. A. L., "Planning and the Geography of Great Britain", *The Advancement of Science*, XXI, 1964-65, p. 1 ff.

[5] See Chinitz, B., "Contrasts in Agglomeration: New York and Pittsburgh", *American Economic Review, Papers and Proceedings,* 50, 1960, p. 279 ff.

[6] *Ibid.*

Once the new industries had taken root in southern England, they had many advantages to gain by staying and expanding there. In the first place, it is invariably cheaper to expand an existing works than it is to move to a new site with all the associated disruption of production, labour and the like. But in addition there was a second group of factors helping to mould the new industrial geography of the country which were *economic* in character and which reinforced the advantages of southern England. The most important of these was the influence of the home *market*. Whereas in the 19th century, Britain in her industrial precocity had been able to open up huge export markets with little difficulty, after 1918 her industry had to face increasingly severe overseas competition. To this was added, in the inter-war years, the phenomena of economic nationalism, currency chaos and a world economic depression. The consequence was that the "new" industries in the first instance grew up largely to serve the home market, and sought to locate as near to its centre as possible. Since they tended to absorb the cost of transporting their goods to market, there was a *transport* cost advantage in such a policy. However, the magnitude of the advantage was small since the cost of transporting most manufactured goods to market in Britain rarely represents more than 2-4% of their total production and marketing costs — even in the case of Scottish manufacture for the English market.[7] More important than transport costs, however, was the fact that a market-oriented factory in southern England could take advantage of the better transport facilities and the general ease of communication there; these lessened the necessity (and the cost) of holding large inventories and facilitated a geographical mobility of labour at every level of the firm, from the workshop floor to the salesman and the managing director. Further, from the point of view of maintaining close relationship by government departments with their research contracts, or — as exports became increasingly important after 1945 — being contacted by foreign buyers or suppliers, and sending goods overseas via the two main ports of London and Liverpool, the transport advantages of southern England were overwhelming as compared with the comparative isolation of the peripheral economies.

As time went on, so did the relative advantages of southern England increase. Particularly was this so in the matter of "external economies". In the growth of industrial complexes, inter-industry linkages, research organizations, specialized transport firms, business services, marketing consultants, specialized brokers and the like are highly important — and invariably they all became available first of all in the new "poles de croissance" of Greater London or the West Midlands. New firms, therefore, could take advantage of them; and the arrival of these new firms enlarged the market and so signalled the possibility of yet further external economies by permitting the emergence of even more specialized facilities and services. Thus, southern England came to have not only the lion's share of the new manufacturing industries, but a wide range of their related service activities too. These were fundamental to the regional growth process.

Reinforcing these economic forces which encouraged the attraction of industry and population towards the centre of the home market were also a number of *social factors*. In the matter of amenities, for example, the Greater London area in particular but also parts of the Midlands, could offer the employer and employee

---

[7] *Report of the Committee of Enquiry into the Scottish Economy*, Edinburgh, 1961 (Toothill Report), p. 72 ff.; see also Luttrell, W. F., *Factory Location and Industrial Movement*, London, 1962, pp. 319-21.

alike more modern social capital and a pleasanter urban environment than the industrial towns of the coalfields. As far as social, cultural, economic and recreational facilities and opportunities were concerned, London reigned supreme. This was not without its influence both consciously and unconsciously in entrepreneurial decisions, and hence in the movement of people and the growth of job opportunities.

Manufacturing in Britain, of course, provides less than one-half of the total number of the country's jobs; and as the economy matures so do service activities become relatively even more important. They, too, have a distinctive and rapidly changing geography. Some services are clearly related to local needs, and *their* distribution tends to parallel regional shifts in manufacturing employment. In addition, however, there are a large number of service jobs which serve regional and national markets — once again for historical, economic and social reasons these have tended to concentrate during the present century in southern England. All service jobs have a tendency to gravitate towards a central place in the market which they serve; and as communications improve so do the market areas of service activities tend to increase and the centralization of service employments ensues. Thus, during the last sixty years, Greater London, the focal point in the British domestic transport network, has come to increase its relative importance as the country's first centre for trade, commerce, banking, finance, government and law. Prestige naturally comes to be accorded to businesses located in such a centre and encourages their multiplication; and the presence in London of the country's largest pool of skilled white-collar labour adds to its attractions. By 1962, Greater London had 115 million square feet of office; its nearest rivals were Liverpool and Manchester with a mere 20 million square feet each. Only too obviously, the opportunities offered by the peripheral economies for the successful functioning of service industries are small by comparison with Greater London.

Such, then, are the major non-political forces which have moulded the economic geography of Britain in the present century. They created a number of difficult economic and social problems in southern England, such as congestion and over-strained public services. In the peripheral economies they showed themselves in declining job opportunities, emigration and at times heavy structural unemployment. The government reacted to both situations. It is to the latter that this paper now turns.

The Response of the Government

The Special Areas (Development and Improvement) Act of 1934 marked the beginning of a new phase in the economic history and economic geography of Britain, and through it the government embarked upon an enduring — though not always consistent — attempt to rehabilitate a number of depressed peripheral economies. A decision was taken to try to lessen the dependence of these areas upon the old, declining industries and to diversify their industrial structure. To this end, the policies of the 'thirties created in the peripheral economies a number of non-profitmaking industrial estates (i.e., industrial parks), and later led to the construction of standard factories by government agencies in advance of demand. These policies amounted to a number of *inducements* to attempt to induce the industrialist away from southern England. This was probably the most that could be achieved in the political climate of the time. With the war, however, the government was able to acquire rather greater powers. In particular, it was able to *direct* industry away from southern England for defence and strategic purposes, a much more powerful weapon for the manipulation of industrial geography.

Seeking a middle road after the war, the government armed itself with a stronger combination of weapons than those available during the inter-war years; yet it rejected the geographical direction of industry as a solution to its problems. Under the Distribution of Industry Act of 1945 and the Town and Country Planning Act of 1947, the government was once again given power to attract industry to the peripheral economies; it extended the system of industrial estates, built factories ahead of demand, and subsidized their rents. In addition, the government was able to offer grants and loans to industrialists locating or expanding in the peripheral economies, and (later) to offer certain tax concessions to new enterprises there. The magnitude of these inducements has varied with time, but by 1964 they represented grants of 10% on the cost of buildings and 25% on the cost of machinery; in addition, the government allowed free depreciation which meant that the whole of the investment could be written off against taxes immediately.

At the same time as offering these inducements to industrialists to locate in the peripheral economies, the government insisted that any new factory over 5,000 square feet, or existing factory extending its floor area by more than 10%, had to obtain an Industrial Development Certificate from the Board of Trade; by this means it was able to *refuse* an industrialist permission to locate or expand in a particular location. In other words, there were "push" as well as "pull" elements to the policies aimed at getting industry away from southern England. In all this legislation, however, the service industries were long forgotten. It was only in 1963 that the Location of Offices Bureau was established to try to *induce* offices away from Central London; then in late 1964 the Office Development Certificate was introduced, a device comparable to the Industrial Development Certificate and a means whereby the Board of Trade could refuse permission for the construction of new office premises in southern England.

Although the government has progressively improved the means whereby it can influence and control the location of employments, it must be recognized that the techniques remain crude and insensitive if for no other reason than the fact that the relationship between floor space and employment is highly variable. Yet even the means at its disposal could have been used to greater effect had they been used with more persistence and rigour throughout the thirty years of "regional protection".[8] Looking back, there have been three main phases during which the government's distribution of industry policy has been really effective. The pre-war years were relatively unimportant. Inducements without controls brought few results, and in any case the economy as a whole was not growing at a particularly fast rate with the result that there were few entrepreneurs looking for industrial sites whose location decisions the government could in fact influence. The war years, however, were different. The dispersal of strategic industries away from southern England was achieved speedily and on a considerable scale. This movement was to be of fundamental importance later, for with it the peripheral economies gained not only a great deal of new capital plant and their labour forces new skills; but they also gained the invaluable evidence that many manufacturing activities other than their traditional ones could be pursued successfully there.

---

[8] Manners, Gerald, "Regional Protection: A Factor in Economic Geography", *Economic Geography*, Vol. 38, 1962, p. 122 ff.

Immediately after the war there was another burst of Board of Trade activity in the peripheral economies. Indeed, the years 1945-47 represent the high point of government influence over these regions in many respects. A high level of aggregate demand in the national economy, and a large number of firms wishing to re-establish themselves after the war meant that factory space, sites and permission to build new plants were at a premium. The result was that the government was able easily to induce industrialists away from southern England, and there was an intensity of new factory building in the peripheral economies such as has never been known since. After 1947, however, the government found it necessary to cut back the level of capital investment (unless industries were producing for export); there was a deceleration in the rate of factory construction nationally; and with fairly high levels of employment throughout the country, a decreasing interest by the government in the whole location of industry policy. By the mid-fifties the use of the Industrial Development Certificate to influence location decisions had fallen into abeyance, and it was possible to obtain one for almost any site in the country.

It became apparent therefore that any success which the government might claim today for having helped to rehabilitate the peripheral economies owes much to the fact that the country had a considerable degree of experience in matters concerning industrial relocation matters from the inter-war and especially the war years; that the Barlow and other government wartime reports had ensured the existence of an effective body of legislation on the statute book immediately after the war; and that there was a government in office in 1945 which firmly believed in influencing the distribution of industrial activity.

After the lapse of a decade, however, industrial location policies were revived once again. With the 1958-59 recession, the level of unemployment in the peripheral economies rose sharply. As a result, the government decided both to issue Industrial Development Certificates with discretion once more, and to start building more factories in the peripheral economies either for lease to specific firms planning expansion or ahead of demand. It was at this time that a major decentralization of the motor assembly industry occurred to Scotland, Merseyside and south Wales. This revived policy, combined with a new interest in a more comprehensive form of regional planning persists to the present day. The magnitude of the effects of all these policies is somewhat elusive. However, between 1945 and 1960 when the Distribution of Industry Acts were in force, the number of jobs created in the development areas directly by government policy was 201,000 (out of a British work force of nearly 22.5 million).

It should also be recalled that the government has supported and helped the peripheral economies by means other than the overt distribution of industry policy. The reorganization and protection of the coal industry, the periodic help given to shipbuilding, the reorganization scheme for the cotton industry and the persistent government influence over the location decisions of the steel industry have all helped to maintain a high level of industrial activity and employment in Wales, north-east England, north-west England and Scotland. Further, partly through government spending, the infrastructure of these regions has been considerably modernized, the devolution of some government departments has increased the number of service workers, and several new towns have been built to help modernize the environment. In these, and many other ways also, the peripheral economies have been helped and the quality of life there improved.

The Results of Government Policies

The distribution of industry policies have been successful to the extent that the levels of unemployment in the peripheral economies have remained relatively low throughout the greater part of the post-war years and net out-migration to the south of the country, although continuing, has been kept down to relatively small proportions. In large measure this is because government policies have helped to transform the employment structure of the peripheral economies, in which the relative importance of the older industries has declined following their continuing decline and the introduction of a large number of new and diverse enterprises. However, major reservations must be made about the success of the policies in removing the fundamental causes of the problems faced by the peripheral economies. The policies were designed primarily to cure one symptom of economic distress, namely, unemployment. But many of the basic causes of the problems which were left by historical, economic and social circumstances, and which must be removed if these regions are ever to achieve unaided, self-sustaining economic growth once again, in many respects were left unchanged by the policies.

With regard to the problem of labour quality, for example, the policies of the government have certainly widened the range of skills as key workers have been transferred with their industries and as training programs have been established by the larger of the new firms; again the quality of training and education schemes available in the peripheral economies today are a vast improvement over the situation 15 years ago. Nevertheless, the range of skills in none of them can compare with the range available to an entrepreneur in, say, the West Midlands; and the Distribution of Industry policy in this regard has missed the real point. As in the country as a whole, there is an urgent need for a complete overhaul of the methods of industrial training and retraining in the peripheral economies. The Industrial Training Act of 1964 points in the right direction with its new training and retraining centres, yet in 1964 the Ministry of Labour was capable of handling only one-twentieth of one per cent of the labour force each year compared with a figure of one per cent in Sweden. Clearly, much remains to be done in this sphere before this labour quality disadvantage of the north and west can be ameliorated.

Again, with regard to the two other problems which the peripheral economies inherited from the past — the relative absence of enterprise and entrepreneurial capital — post-war policies have again missed the mark. The characteristic firm which arrived and succeeded in these areas with government help has tended to be large; it has been a branch plant of a London or Midland firm; the top management and key workers arrived with it; the head office and decision-making has remained in London; and the capital needs have been satisfied either from within the firm or on the London market. Firms such as this, naturally, have made only a limited contribution to the regions' lack of entrepreneurial skills and capital.

In a like manner, as far as external economies and the social disadvantages of the peripheral economies are concerned, a fundamental inter-regional imbalance remains. Certainly a great deal of progress has been made in so far as their facilities and attractions today are much improved over those which were available a decade ago. But the fact remains that although the less prosperous regions offer many advantages and good locations for industrial development, southern England can still offer (in terms of the costs calculated and the factors considered by the entrepreneur) even *greater* advantages and *better* locations.

However, the *economic* disadvantages of the peripheral economies are much less today than they were formerly. This has followed from the changing nature and geography of markets, and changing characteristics of transport facilities and costs. The steady improvement in the country's living standards and hence the growth of markets has meant that since 1945 it has often become economic to establish a variety of manufacturing and service concerns primarily to meet the demands of the regional markets in the peripheral economies. This new market situation is but one aspect of the changing nature of the problems facing the peripheral economies in Britain. Further, better and still improving road, rail and air communications have steadily eroded the effective distance between the peripheral economies and the centre of the British market (Map II). It is true that the transport advantages of southern England remain, more especially since the attention of the new industries has been turned increasingly to export markets, especially European export markets. It is also true that the Ministries and public bodies responsible for transport improvements have rarely taken it upon themselves to consider the implications of their plans and actions in terms of regional development, and that transport improvements could have been better geared to serve the needs of the peripheral economies rather than being built simply as a response to existing and projected traffic flows. It would, of course, be wrong to argue that transport improvements *of themselves* have positively helped to attract new employments away from southern England. Transport is a permissive rather than a dynamic factor in regional economic development. However, the steady improvement of transport facilities undoubtedly facilitates the manipulation of industrial location by the government; and, granted the existence of policies designed to restrain the growth of industry and employment in southern England, transport improvements must be regarded as the principal catalyst in the revival of the peripheral economies.

In sum, government policies to help the less prosperous peripheral economies have been directed at a symptom of their ills rather than the problems themselves and have been considerably aided by changing technological and economic circumstances. These facts together have begun to reduce some of the fundamental barriers to economic recovery and growth in these regions. The factor endowments of the peripheral economies have been much improved. New and vigorous export bases have been created. Indeed, in view of the rather inconsistent application of the government's policies, it is quite remarkable that so much has been achieved. The ease with which a regional economy can be transformed within the British context is all too obvious.

At the same time, it has also to be admitted that the peripheral economies still have a higher than average level of unemployment, that migration from them still continues, that they continue to rely more heavily than southern England upon older industries for their well-being, and that signs of self-perpetuating growth are only occasionally to be found. Significantly, these signs are most frequently to be found in the larger cities within the peripheral economies, and it is to this geography of economic revival that this paper now turns.

The Geography of Revival

From the outset, the government had to define the areas to which its policies would apply. With the 1934 legislation, four "special areas" were created — south Wales, north-east England, Cumberland and central Scotland. Their extent

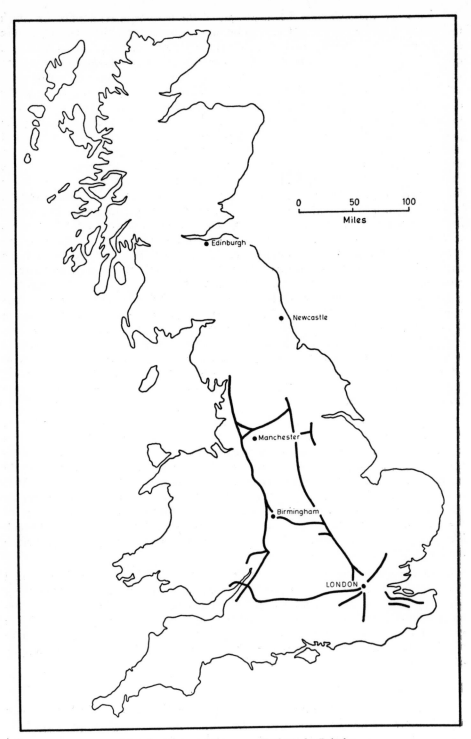

Map 2. Current Motorway Projects in Britain.

was determined by local levels of unemployment; but because the major towns (Cardiff and Swansea in south Wales, Newcastle in north-east England, etc.) recorded lower percentage unemployment figures than their hinterlands, they were excluded from the benefits of the special areas' legislation. After the war, this was changed. The "special areas" became "development areas"; more regions were included, such as Merseyside and the north Wales coalfield; the delimitation of these areas was again determined by their (inter-war and immediate post-war) unemployment records, although by this date their problems were regarded as regional in nature and the major towns within the regions were made eligible for help. By 1958, however, it was realized that there were other parts of the country which were suffering persistently from unemployment, but which, because they were outside the development areas, could not receive government assistance. In response to this situation, the Distribution of Industry (Industrial Finance) Act made help available to any such areas through the Development Areas Treasury Advisory Committee. These additional areas eligible for assistance were nearly all geographically peripheral once again; their unemployment problems, however, were largely seasonal or an aspect of rural depopulation. The greater geographical and functional flexibility in the distribution of industry program which stemmed from this legislation was seen to be so advantageous that in 1960 all the previous distribution of industry legislation was repealed and replaced by the Local Employ- ment Act. Under the latter, any locality (i.e., Ministry of Labour Employment Exchange area) in which unemployment exists, or is likely to exist — and in which that unemployment is thought likely to persist — is eligible for help as a "development district". This flexibility offers certain administrative advantages; but it soon created grave problems for the peripheral economies, for help to them was even less consistent than before (aid was withdrawn from an area as soon as its unemployment rate fell) and their problems were no longer viewed in their proper regional context.

In the immediate post-war years, the Board of Trade had sought to strike some sort of geographical balance within the peripheral economies between taking employment as near as possible to the sources of labour there (that is, to what were often amongst the least attractive localities from the point of view of the industrialist) and insisting that the labour should move either daily or perman- ently towards new sources of employment, sited at the best locations within these regions. Factories therefore were built, and industrialists were induced to locate, in places which, from a manufacturing viewpoint, were certainly not the best within the peripheral economies; yet at the same time they were by no means the worst, and often they did demand of the labour force a certain amount of commut- ing. But with the 1960 legislation, the Board of Trade in fact came to insist that government help was available only to firms locating in the least attractive parts of the peripheral economies, for it was just such localities which persistently had the highest rates of unemployment and which were classified as "development districts". Yet good industrial sites only a few miles from them were ineligible for government help to attract firms and employment.

The weaknesses of this policy, however, were soon exposed; its validity was quickly challenged;[9] and within three years it was virtually abandoned. From 1963 government attitudes towards the planning and development of the peripheral

[9] For example, Manners, Gerald, "The Crisis in Regional Planning", *Westminster Bank Review*, August 1962.

economies, however, have taken on a new look. Not only did regional planning suddenly become respectable with nods of approval from the National Economic Development Council and the Federation of British Industries,[10] but with the publication of the outline development plans for north-east England and central Scotland [11] a new regional approach to the rehabilitation of the peripheral economies came to be adopted. Whilst the 1960 Act remains on the Statute Book, and whilst funds remain available to help the less attractive parts of the peripheral economies, it was decided to channel the greater part of public effort and expenditure into the most attractive — and what are potentially the most rewarding — places from the point of view of economic development. These are invariably the largest and most accessible communities within the regions, towns and cities with the widest range of labour skills, external economies, social amenities and the like. Occasionally they are New Towns such as Livingston, New Edinburgh or Washington near Newcastle. Thus, growth points have been defined in central Scotland and a growth zone delimited in north-east England. It is in these areas that funds will be more readily available to help attract industrialists, that communications will be improved by heavy investments, and that a major attempt will be made to "modernize the environment". It is anticipated that as additional regional planning schemes for other parts of the country are prepared, the same geographical philosophy will be adopted. By taking advantage of the best endowed localities within the peripheral economies, government policies have at last taken on a more realistic, more forward-looking and potentially more successful character.

Following their election to office in 1964, the Labour Government subjected physical planning once again to a major re-appraisal. The ban on further office development in London was imposed through the use of the Office Development Certificate. The planning machine was reorganized. Whilst the Board of Trade still retained its role as the administrator of the distribution of industry (and now offices) policy, and the Ministry of Housing and Local Government remained responsible for the preparation of land-use plans, the former was no longer charged with coordinating all government action with reference to regional development as it had been under the previous Administration. Instead, the newly created Ministry of Economic Affairs was given this coordinating role. In addition, it was announced that in each of the peripheral economies, and indeed in each region (Map III) of the country, two planning bodies were to be established; the first was an Advisory Planning Council, representing both sides of industry, the universities, local authorities and the business community, and serving in solely an advisory capacity; and the second was a Regional Planning Board, chaired by a regional representative of the Ministry of Economic Affairs and representing all government departments concerned with economic and social planning at the regional level. Rival claims on public investment will still be resolved in Westminster, but there is a good chance that the allocation will be less arbitrary than in the past — simply because the regional alternatives will be a great deal more articulate. The

---

[10]National Economic Development Council, *Growth of the United Kingdom Economy to 1966,* London, 1963; National Economic Development Council, *Conditions Favourable to Faster Growth,* London, 1963; The Federation of British Industries, *The Regional Problem,* London, 1963.

[11]*The North East: A Programme for Regional Development and Growth,* Cmmd. 2206, London, 1963; *Central Scotland: A Programme for Development and Growth,* Cmmd. 2188, Edinburgh, 1963.

Map 3. Ministry of Economising Affairs Planning Regions for Britain, 1964.

present proposals, however, still have not created the opportunity of major executive initiatives at the regional level as recommended in the development corporation proposals of Sir Geoffrey Crowther's Steering Committee's Report in *Traffic in Towns*.[12]

British Experience in Retrospect

The policies towards the peripheral economies in Britain over the past 30 years have suffered from an inadequate understanding of the processes and problems of local and regional economic development. In spite of the early appointment — and the many sound conclusions — of the (Barlow) Royal Commission, it is alarming that such a thoroughgoing and continuing attempt to mould the geography of British employment was based upon so scant a body of knowledge. Certainly we now know much more about the costs of industrial movement,[13] and the amount of public expenditure needed to attract industry into the peripheral economies.[14] In the post-war period to 1962, the government spent approximately £1,000 per job directly created by its distribution of industry policies in the peripheral economies, a figure which is almost certainly less than the alternative costs of unemployment benefits and public assistance. It is true that this figure does not take into account many large investments in the less prosperous regions which have undoubtedly aided in their recovery; at the same time, however, it also neglects the additional employment gains in those areas through the local and regional multiplier effects of the new industries. It could well be that £1,000 per job considerably overestimates the costs of the distribution of industry policies; and, granted that the peripheral economies were too large to envisage their complete abandonment, it can be argued that their rehabilitation was fundamentally a sound economic as well as social policy.

Even so, the amount of research which has been conducted into the best means of implementing the policy has remained alarmingly small. For example, there has been no attempt (either generally or with reference to a specific region) to assess the best allocation of scarce public resources in the implementation of the distribution of industry policy. Would it have been better, for example, to put the *emphasis* of public policy upon the creation of industrial training and retraining schemes in the peripheral economies, upon inducements to individual industrialists, upon the improvement of the regional infrastructure and in particular transport facilities, or upon a more generalized attempt to modernize the environment there? Perhaps the introduction of a (subsidized?) geographically-uniform telephone charge throughout the whole country would have been as effective as any other single measure to reduce the entrepreneur's relative isolation of the peripheral economies, and so help in their speedy rehabilitation. But the detailed costs and benefits of these several aspects of public policy (one must stress that they *all* have some part to play) has yet to be subjected to detailed scrutiny.

Again, it is possible that the indiscriminate diversification of the peripheral economies is not only a relatively expensive way of modifying employment oppor-

---

[12]Ministry of Transport, *Traffic in Towns*, London, 1963.
[13]Luttrell, *op. cit.*
[14]National Economic Development Council, *Conditions Favourable to Faster Growth*, London, 1963, pp. 15 and 16.

tunities there but is also one of the least effective ways to steer these areas into a position where they would experience self-perpetuating growth. The strength of these peripheral economies in the 19th century was built upon a considerable degree of industrial specialization, and it was perhaps natural that their 20th century problems should be met by a complete rejection of a comparable employment structure. However, it could well be that the policy has gone too far in the other direction, and that instead of indiscriminate industrial diversification, policies should have sought to encourage the development of related industry complexes in the peripheral economies, such that external economies could accrue as educational and training facilities, mutual suppliers and research organizations and the like became increasingly shared; by this means a setting could possibly be created for the natural attraction of yet more comparable and related enterprises. It might be impossible for a number of years — granted the present state of British regional statistics — to assemble accurate sets of regional input-output matrices along the lines of that proposed by Italconsult for the Bari-Taranto region;[15] but certainly a good deal more thought ought to have been given to the problem of which industries should be attracted where.

Britain's characteristically empirical approach to the problem of localized structural unemployment nevertheless provides a useful body of experience which cannot fail to have some relevance elsewhere. Four points deserve particular attention. The first is the importance of maintaining a high level of aggregate demand in the economy as a whole; for it is only when demand is expanding and new industrial plant being planned that there exists the possibility of significantly influencing the geographical location of industry in a mixed economy. The amelioration of the problems of the peripheral economies in consequence owes a considerable debt in the first instance to Keynes. This might be only a temporary palliative, however, for in the future even with a Keynesian stability superimposed upon an advanced economy it could well be that the problem of structural unemployment will grow simply as a consequence of rapid technological change. The experience of the United States hints at this prospect since each successive boom in recent years has left in its wake a larger core of structural unemployment. A high level of aggregate demand, therefore, might well have relatively less importance in meeting the problems of areas of economic stress in the future than in the recent past.

A second aspect of British policy which is worthy of particular note is the fact that the mechanism for influencing the location of economic activity incorporated "push" as well as "pull" elements, the incentives to industrial development in the peripheral economies being supported by the restraint of manufacturing (and now service) employment growth in the most dynamic regions of the country. Although the evidence is not absolutely conclusive upon this point, what there is suggests that the attraction of new industries to the peripheral economies would have been singularly unsuccessful without both aspects of the policy being invoked at the same time. Certainly, during the early and middle 'fifties when the incentives remained but the restraints were relaxed, the distribution of industry policy had singularly few results.

A third point which emerges from British experience is the ease with which inconsistency can appear in a national economic location policy. This inconsistency has several aspects, one of which — the fact that the policy was administered with

[15]The Economist, November 7, 1964, p. 615.

varying degrees of rigour throughout the thirty year period — has already been mentioned. Equally noteworthy was the failure of both central and local government departments to ensure a satisfactory integration of their various plans. The Board of Trade, for example, only reluctantly accepted its responsibilities in the matter of industrial location policy (it was much more enthusiastically involved in the promotion of exports); and the Board's policies frequently did not harmonize with those of the Ministry of Housing and Local Government — at least until the dramatic arrival in 1963 of Mr. Edward Heath, who for the first time was given the clear responsibility for coordinating all aspects of government policy affecting regional growth. In so far as it is impossible to plan effectively the development of one part of Britain without some fairly detailed reference to other parts, the fate of the peripheral economies has rested to a considerable degree upon the results of public policies towards the growth of population and industry in southern England; in a sense, therefore, it was impossible to have consistent physical planning in the peripheral economies without a thoroughgoing program of regional planning for the whole country. It was only after 1962 that the government showed some recognition of this fact.

The final point to which British policy and experience particularly draws attention is the fact that distribution of employment policies must be capable of recognizing and adjusting to changing economic circumstances. Despite the continuance of the same symptoms of structural unemployment, the problems of the peripheral economies today are, in several important respects, different from what they were thirty years ago. The structure of these economies has already been transformed considerably: some of the industries there which presented major problems in the inter-war years have managed to readjust to contemporary market conditions (the steel industry is an example); the regions which are suitable for effective planning are, on the whole, significantly larger than they once were, and the economic forces moulding the economic geography of the country are very different from what they were thirty years ago. For example, all the peripheral regions of Britain will — if present trends continue — grow appreciably in both employment and population in the next twenty years; and, in some very real senses, it will be the effective planning for this growth which will be their greatest problem. Unless, therefore, the constantly changing nature of the economic characteristics and problems of areas of economic stress are recognized, and policies accordingly adjusted, attempts to solve these problems can easily be either wasteful, or, at worst, ineffective.

British experience, then, offers these lessons in the matter of alleviating localized structural unemployment. Valuable though it might be, however, it is vitally important to remember that this experience was mustered under a set of *distinctive geographical and political conditions*. Distances within Britain are short — and they are becoming shorter. The road distance between London and Cardiff is at present 140 miles, but it will be reduced by about 40 miles with the new motorway and Severn Bridge; London to Newcastle is roughly 275 miles, London to Glasgow 400. It is readily appreciated that these spatial relationships are very different from the continental distances involved in meeting some of the problems of North American local and regional economies. Again, not only does the climate of public and political opinion in Britain allow a degree of government involvement in the matter of economic location which might not be permissible elsewhere, but the political system is unitary rather than federal in structure which in itself influences the range of possible attitudes and actions on the part of the government. It is all too clear, therefore, that not all aspects of the British approach to its problems of localized structural unemployment can be exported equally easily and successfully to other continents.

COMMENTS

DR. E. P. WEEKS,
Executive Director,
Atlantic Development Board.

I.   INTRODUCTION

I have found Professor Manners' paper stimulating, both because of its broad and well organized coverage of the problem, and also of its realistic appreciation of the limitations in applying British experience elsewhere. The British situation is not entirely new to me, since I lived in England for many years, and have had opportunities, both in the spring and fall of 1964, to discuss various issues with authorities in London and Scotland.

It seems to me that any comments should be made against a certain background. If I may turn to the end of the paper first, I would stress, along with Professor Manners, that in assessing the value of the British experience in discussing Canadian problems, we must always bear in mind the many differences between Great Britain and Canada. I should like particularly to stress the following:

(a) even the relatively small Atlantic region is geographically larger than Great Britain;

(b) the rather small Canadian population is dispersed over a 4,000 mile strip along the southern part of the country, with the heaviest concentrations between Windsor and Quebec City;

(c) the Canadian major regions not only have different views on matters of economic policy and political philosophy, but have sufficient constitutional powers to back them up — powers not available in a unitary state like the United Kingdom. For example, Britain has adopted both the "carrot" and the "stick" in influencing the location of industry. This would be difficult in Canada, unless all Governments agreed on a common "stick" and on its common use.

Before referring to specific points in Professor Manners' paper, I should like to mention what I understand to be the purpose or philosophy of regional policy in Great Britain. In several discussions with British officials, and in perusing the literature, I gather that in developing its regional policy, the British consider it desirable to spread economic activity more evenly among all regions in such a way that this will —

— increase the national rate of growth through the better use of resources;

— bring more work to the workers in peripheral areas and check congestion in the south;

— improve the economic and social environment of what Professor Manners calls the "peripheral economies";

— maintain the essential character of the regions; and

— reduce to a minimum the Government support, necessary for social and political reasons, in declining regions.

All the aims may not prove to be mutually consistent.

It would seem to follow from this philosophy, that industry should only be "pushed" or "pulled" to a region if there are some long-term advantages. Otherwise, it is unlikely that regional policy will make any lasting contribution to national economic development or to the region itself.

It is against this background that I wish to comment on certain aspects of Professor Manners' paper. I shall follow the main headings he used.

II.   SPECIFIC COMMENTS ON PROFESSOR MANNERS' PAPER

A) *Nature of the British Problem*

Professor Manners emphasizes the underlying shift in Britain with the expanding industries tending to go to the south, and more particularly to the highly congested London area. In Canada, we have the largest concentration of non-resource based industries along the Quebec City-Windsor axis, particularly around Toronto-Hamilton, and Montreal, although not yet, of course, the congestion which London is experiencing.

The factors responsible for the concentration of industries in both Britain and Canada, are somewhat similar: the availability of a skilled labour force and managerial personnel; access to capital; the external economies of inter-industry linkage; the influence of the home market; the abundance of all sorts of specialized services for industry, as well as the availability of a large variety of social, cultural and educational amenities.

Some of these factors may be grouped under the title of quaternary services, and these are taken to include — quick and frequent travel connections; ease of communication with suppliers and customers; cultural, educational and social amenities, and so forth, in short, those factors which particularly influence executives and their wives in their decision to settle in a particular area. The lack or weakness of such services has tended to operate against the location of certain industries in parts of Scotland, and undoubtedly, in parts of Canada, as well.

B) *The Responses of the Government*

Professor Manners has reviewed British experience from the mid-thirties leading up to the present situation where, on the one hand, the Government can control the location of both industries and offices through Industrial Development and Office Development certificates and, on the other hand, can offer a series of inducements. Professor Manners does not go into much detail on these inducements which include — premises for rent or purchase; 25 per cent grant on the cost of new building or for expansion or adaption of existing buildings; 10 per cent grant on the cost of acquiring and installing plant and machinery in an industrial undertaking; loans for the setting up, expansion or moving-in of a business; free depreciation of certain new plant and machinery and write-off at the rate the company chooses; training assistance and pay allowance for transferred workers. On the infrastructure side in a particular area, assistance may be provided for such things as communications, power and water.

Experience would seem to suggest that the best results may be obtained where all these elements are involved with a maximum of flexibility in their use. Thus, it might well be that after certain minimum infrastructure has been provided, more effort should be devoted to inducements to industry.

C) *Results of Government Policies*

Professor Manners suggests that the policies have been successful to the extent that levels of unemployment in the peripheral economies have remained relatively low throughout the greater part of the post-war years, and migration south was quite small. It is, of course, very difficult to disentangle the various factors which have influenced industries to locate in certain areas, and therefore to measure the real effect of Government action. How important was the "push", and how important was the "pull"? How important were special factors affecting a particular industry? Lionel Needleman, in the January, 1965 issue of Lloyd's Bank Review, is rather critical, and considers that the Government's efforts have been on an inadequate scale.

It should be noted in passing, that a very large proportion of financial assistance has gone to industries already established in the peripheral economies. This in no way reduces the significance which the Government assistance had on regional incomes and employment, but it does cast some doubt on the effectiveness of some of these measures, *if* their purpose was to attract new industries to those regions.

Professor Manners emphasizes that the assistance was intended to reduce unemployment which, of course, is only a symptom of the disease in distressed areas. The assistance left most of the basic problems unchanged. There is no argument against Professor Manners' contention that what regional policy should do is to remove the causes of the disease. This is, of course, fundamental. These basic causes should be identified and their relative importance recognized; and, as far as this is feasible, orders of priorities should be established in taking steps towards a solution. In some cases, the weakness of the region may be the result of inadequacies in transportation, electric power, or industrial water. In other cases, the weakness may be that the supply of labour is inadequate in terms of general education, technical skills, adaptability and attitudes towards mobility and change. And again, it may be that in certain regions, all these weaknesses are present.

D) *The Geography of Revival*

A very important factor brought out by Professor Manners, is the shift in British policy, in the light of experience, away from a simple concentration on areas with a high unemployment record, to the "new look" in 1963, when "outline of development" plans were prepared for N.E. England and Central Scotland. Not only were the regions made larger than before, but it was decided to channel public expenditures and attention to the most attractive points for economic development within the region, where it was believed the external economies and social amenities could best play their part. In short, the "growth points" theory came to the fore.

Obviously it is not always easy to limit public assistance to a comparatively small number of growth areas and Continental experience certainly reflects this. But it would seem to make a great deal of sense to concentrate efforts where there are the best long-term advantages for both the national and the regional economies. This kind of policy can only be successful, however, if special incentives to industries are not withdrawn from the peripheral areas in general, but apply to the growth centres as well. This is what the United Kingdom is doing.

Professor Manners indicates that a fundamental re-appraisal is currently underway, and refers to new planning bodies and to the definition of regions. The present regions set up by the previous government are really Civil Defence areas. It is now intended to determine the regions with more attention to economic factors, but to do this, more statistics will have to be developed. I understand, too, that the regions may be subdivided later into smaller areas.

The British Government proposes to establish an Advisory Planning Council of private citizens, and a Regional Planning Board made up of officials of the relevant Government departments. These agencies represent an interesting organizational proposition. In this connection, I would like to draw your attention to the establishment of a Canadian agency responsible for the development of a specific region. I refer to the Atlantic Development Board. This Board is concerned with the Atlantic region which comprises four provinces, and is considered to be one of the five major economic regions of Canada. The Board consists of eleven private citizens who reside in the four provinces of the region, represent various sectors of the economy, and serve without pay. There is a supporting staff based in Ottawa. In some ways, the Board tries to do the job of both the Advisory Planning Council and the Regional Planning Board. On the one hand, it makes recommendations to the Federal Government for action which may or may not involve the use of its Capital Fund. On the other hand, through its staff, it works closely with both Federal and Provincial agencies concerned with the development of the region. One of its functions is to draw up a regional economic plan in collaboration with the Economic Council of Canada and the Provincial Governments. The full scope of its activity is still evolving, in the light of experience in dealing with regional economic problems within the context of four provincial governments and the Federal Government.

E) *Lessons from British Experience*

We must agree with Professor Manners that a great deal of information is needed for any rational development on a regional basis. The important point, however, is that this information be vital for determining policy, and that time and scarce expert staff not be wasted on collecting data of relatively little significance.

Professor Manners is critical of what has been done in Britain to assess the best allocation of scarce public resources. It is obvious that we should establish an order of priority for public expenditures that would correspond, as far as possible, with the most important needs of the economy. At the same time, it will be recognized that while benefit-cost analysis is theoretically an excellent idea, it is exceedingly difficult to apply in detail in sectors where useful quantification is almost impossible, and where there is no firm basis for statistical comparison. It often becomes necessary, therefore, to rely on the considered judgments of those responsible for developing and implementing regional policy.

The point raised by Professor Manners concerning indiscriminate diversification corresponds with the conclusions of the Italian experts referred to in an issue of *The Economist* last fall. You will remember that the Italians laid emphasis on the need to build industrial complexes rather than isolated plants. It is to be inferred that the complexes would not only provide the advantages of various external economies from inter-industry relations, but would also include social and cultural amenities favourable to the attraction of managerial and technical personnel. But, it also follows that such complexes would either be attracted to quite large existing centres or would require the creation of new towns.

There can be no doubt about the importance of a high level of aggregate demand in the economy as a whole, although as Professor Manners suggests, this does not always make adjustment easy. Professor Manners apparently feels strongly that the movement to peripheral areas would have been unsuccessful without the use of both "push and pull", the "stick and the carrot" and he implies that of the two, the "stick" is the more significant. I have already indicated that the "stick" would not be an easy thing to apply in Canadian circumstances.

The problem of coordinating national and local plans is a major one, and in the Canadian context, can only occur effectively through the voluntary cooperation of the provinces and the Federal Government. Regional planning, where several provincial governments are involved, as in the Atlantic region, should provide an interesting testing ground for both theory and practice.

Professor Manners' final point — the need for maximum flexibility to meet changing conditions — is basic to any realistic development policy. The industries and areas which may appear dynamic today, may become the relatively depressed sectors of the economy tomorrow. But, one thing appears relatively certain. There must be a recognition of the need for the best possible training program, so that workers are prepared technically to move to other jobs, and psychologically to move to other areas. This will require the development of policies that will reduce, not only the financial burden of the individual worker, but his psychological and social burden as well.

"Flexibility" and "adjustment in the right direction" will be basic to future regional development.

COMMENTS

PROFESSOR RICHARD LAWTON,
Department of Geography,
University of Liverpool,
(1964-65, University of Southern Illinois).

Although in general agreement with Dr. Manners' analysis of the British planning situation, I would stress the development potential of many areas outside South East England which are at present within his "peripheral areas". Since the last war virtually full employment in Britain has dramatically changed the general situation from that of the 1930's, yet unemployment rates in some regions obstinately remain much higher than in Britain as a whole (see Table I).

Regions, such as the North Western, Northern, Scottish and Welsh, have relatively high unemployment, especially in times of high unemployment. Moreover their share of national employment has declined as rural depopulation and loss by migration from older industrial areas within them continues. Though less catastrophic than in the 1930's, migration from such areas is higher than perhaps Dr. Manners implies. The north of England (the Northern, North Western and Yorkshire Standard Regions) had a 2.3% loss by migration, 1951-61, as compared with a 3.6% in 1931-51; Wales a 1.9% loss as compared with 6.7%, and Scotland 5.0% as compared with 5.8%.[1] Moreover certain parts of greatest stress within these regions have now declined to the point of dereliction.

---

[1] For a fuller analysis see: Osborne, R. H., "Changes in the Regional Distribution of Population in Great Britain" (a contribution to "This Changing Britain"), *Geography*, 49 (1964), pp. 266-272.

REGION	%age Unemployment		%age Share of National Unemployment		%age Share of National Employment	
	April 1949	April 1963	April 1949	April 1963	1948	1962
London & South Eastern	1.2	1.6	18.2	15.4	24.8	25.3
Eastern & Southern	1.3	1.9	8.3	7.9	9.8	11.0
South Western	1.5	2.1	4.9	4.4	5.3	5.6
Midland	0.7	2.1	4.5	8.0	9.6	⎫
North Midland	0.5	2.0	2.3	5.2	6.8	⎬ 25.3
East & West Ridings	0.9	2.1	4.8	6.5	8.7	⎭
North Western	1.7	3.3	15.1	16.4	14.2	13.2
Northern	2.7	5.1	10.2	11.1	6.0	5.8
Scotland	3.1	5.2	20.2	18.9	10.3	9.6
Wales	4.0	3.9	11.4	6.3	4.5	4.3
GREAT BRITAIN	1.6	2.7	100	100	100	100

TABLE I: REGIONAL UNEMPLOYMENT AND EMPLOYMENT IN BRITAIN

The 1949 figures are representative of a time of low unemployment, those for 1963 one of relatively high unemployment. Both are based upon the *Ministry of Labour Gazette.*

At the opposite extreme the overemphasis upon south-eastern Britain, and upon Greater London in particular, continues, yet creates grave problems of congestion. This over-concentration of jobs and population is the most crucial problem of British regional planning; it is not in the best interests of either the London region itself or of the rest of Britain that these trends should continue.

Many of the so-called "advantages" from which this growth "naturally" springs may, in some measure, be illusory or, at best, only partly valid. Continuing concentration of investment and development on south-eastern Britain detracts from the resources available to other regions and may lead to London's choking itself. The Government's *South East Study 1961-1981*[2] estimated that of an expected population increase of 7 millions in England and Wales during the period 1961-81, 3½ millions would occur in the South East, of which a little over 1 million would migrate into the region. If anything these are under-estimates. Yet already a severe housing shortage exists in Greater London, costs of land and housing are the highest in Britain, labour is expensive and in short supply, and the roads congested especially at the "rush hour". These may be regarded as symptoms of economic overdevelopment.

To effectively "push" economic activity from overdeveloped areas and "pull" it towards underdeveloped areas, planning at three levels is involved, national, regional and local. National economic planning has been much too inconsistent in its population and employment policies, as the Board of Trades' attitude to the granting of Industrial Development Certificates has shown. Moreover it has operated over too limited a sector of the economy. In a country where tertiary and quaternary sectors of activity are of increasing importance, it is surely essential to have some control over the location of office employment. Yet the first bill to control office building in Greater London and the outer metropolitan areas has only recently come before Parliament.

Local planning will no doubt continue to be mainly concerned with physical planning. But many small authorities lack the resources essential for the renewal of housing and other social amenities and for creating conditions conducive to industrial development. Some integration of resources and recasting of local government areas in the light of contemporary conditions is needed and the work of the Local Government Commission which is currently reviewing the structure of local government has been, if anything, disappointingly conservative.[3]

It seems inevitable, if genuine progress towards redevelopment of peripheral areas is to be achieved and effective counterpoises to the South East developed, that more emphasis be laid on regional planning. Such regional planning should involve more than coordination of effort over such local problems as housing and overspill, transport and public utilities, but should have the capital resources and planning powers to play an effective role in regional economic development. The recently

---

[2] Published by the Ministry of Planning and Local Government; H.M.S.O., 1964.

[3] The Local Government Commissions for England and Wales have examined a number of general and special review areas, the latter in the major conurbations, to determine the best means of providing "effective and convenient local government throughout the whole of the review area". It was set up in 1958 and has published a number of reports and proposals, notably those for the West Midlands Special Review Area (Report No. 1, H.M.S.O. 1961) and for the Tyneside Special Review Area (Report No. 5, H.M.S.O. 1963).

Local Government in Greater London was dealt with by the Royal Commission on Local Government in Greater London, 1957-1960, Cmnd. 1164, H.M.S.O. 1960).

constituted regional planning boards set up by the Minister for Economic Affairs are to be advised by regional economic planning councils and will operate from regional "capitals" whose regional needs can be assessed, and passed to the Department of Economic Affairs for consideration in the light of national planning. The necessary regional studies have already been started for most areas and, in some cases, government white papers have already been published.[4]

It is not considered that regional planning of this sort should imply development throughout each and every region of Britain. There are many areas in which, because of declining resources and employment, large-scale outward movement of population should continue. Such include exhausted coal mining areas like West Durham and the marginal farming areas of many parts of Highland Britain.[5]

But neither can whole regions like South Wales, the North East, North West England, and Central Scotland be considered obsolete, with migration the best solution to their economic and planning problems. Such areas have to some degree been held back because of being denied resources to improve roads and other public utilities. Many industrialists and planners in these areas have stressed the need for better communications: for example, a notable potential growth point in the North West will undoubtedly emerge in the area where the new M.6 motorway crosses the Manchester Ship Canal. Similarly, improved communications could greatly assist development in the growth areas designated in the coastal region of North East England. It is ironical that the emphasis upon road improvements in the South East, no doubt justified because of the importance of London and the congestion of approaches to it, diverts scarce resources away from "peripheral areas" equally in need.

If the new Regional Boards are to foster such development, large scale investment in the public sector will be needed in the development areas of Britain. Not only are facilities for developing growth points needed, but an atmosphere conducive to growth must also be established. One of the undoubted attractions of London, especially to the enterprising, is the feeling of being at the centre of things. A century ago, even half a century ago, the large provincial cities were also centres of such enterprise.[6] Although there is some truth in Dr. Manners' belief that they now live in an out-of-date structure and that the centre of power lies in London, the situation is far from irremediable. While there are many advantages to both industry and commerce in concentration, and while London possesses many social and cultural advantages (often subsidized) over the provincial capitals, it does not have *all* the advantages.

Much could be done by better use of local resources and manpower to restore the image of areas of stress not only economically, but in social, cultural and educational facilities. But much more could be done to invest in such development. Many of the new growth industries are footloose, and, given the right facilities and encouragement, could succeed in development areas, as the growth of many of the pre- and post-war industrial estates has shown. I am sceptical of the alleged superiority of labour in the South East. Better facilities for technical education, and more and better industrial retraining schemes could do much to

---

[4] For example, those on *Central Scotland: a Programme for Development and Growth* (Cmnd. 2188, H.M.S.O. 1963) and *The North East: a programme for regional development and growth* (Cmnd. 2206, 1963).

[5] See: Wibberley, G. P., "Some aspects of problem Rural Areas in Great Britain", *Geographical Journal*, 120 (1954), pp. 43-61.

[6] For a vivid account of some such cities see: Briggs, Asa, *Victorian Cities*, 1963.

remedy difficulties in the provinces. Although the motor car industry was reluctantly pushed to Merseyside by Board of Trade pressure, no one now doubts that labour recruitment and training, and the building and bringing into production of the Ford plant near Liverpool has been a great success. Of the present work force of over 10,000 all but 300 key men have been trained locally and are apparently performing efficiently. Nor are entrepreneurial skills lacking in provincial cities: to these, institutions such as the Liverpool Cotton Exchange are a continuing tribute. Moreover, much of the drive for redevelopment in areas of stress has been generated from within and I think Dr. Manners understates the achievement of local authorities like Liverpool, Manchester and in North East England in promoting industrial growth and diversification since, and even before, the war. Many industries have developed vigorously and seem vindicated economically as well as socially. Thus the Ford Liverpool plant is now stimulating medium-sized car component firms to set up plants nearby and genuine growth arising from the major basic industry is emerging around this well-chosen growth point.

In office employment the relatively short experience of the Government-sponsored Location of Offices Bureau which has assisted firms in voluntary dispersal of offices from central London has been that, once removed, employers and employees alike were generally well-satisfied. Furthermore the benefits were reflected in cheaper operating costs, less absenteeism and less strain on staff. However, few of those firms wished to move more than thirty miles from Central London. In the Bill now before Parliament to further disperse offices from an area some 40 miles around Central London by controlling permission to build, it is hoped to produce some decentralization of the massive concentration of office jobs and, thereby, broaden the employment base and opportunities in other regions of Britain.

Such developments can best succeed in truly regional planning. Within the regions now designated[7] planning will be best occupied in promoting development at suitable growth points. The mustering of local effort on a more effective scale in planning re-housing and overspill, in improving transport and public services will greatly assist regional redevelopment, but it cannot provide capital on the scale and at the rate needed to remedy long periods of neglect. For example, Liverpool (with an estimated 43% slum property) has no New Town, although two are now designated; Manchester is a worse case, for the site of its first New Town has not yet been chosen. Indeed of 16 New Towns built since the war, eight have gone to the London region.

Regional investment of the kind urged by Dr. Manners, and strongly supported here, cannot be lightly undertaken. But need it be more costly than investment in the congested London region where diseconomies arising from over-concentration are becoming increasingly apparent and need careful assessment in terms of their social and economic cost? There, the greater costs of housing, transport and living are passed on to employers in higher wages, accentuated by competition for scarce labour, while in other regions advantages in these respects may more than compensate for allegedly uncompetitive locational factors.

---

[7] These are Scotland, Wales and Monmouthshire, and, in England, the Northern (Newcastle), North West (Manchester), Yorkshire and Humberside (Leeds), West Midland (Birmingham), East Midlands (Nottingham) and South West (Bristol) regions. The boards will have office in the cities indicated. There are no plans yet announced for the South East.

Population trends in Britain pose severe problems for the planner. Already crowded, the island's population may well grow by 20 million in the next half century. The peripheral areas of today must retain more of their own natural increase if this "drift to the south" is to be arrested. To do so they need to redevelop their resources now and this may prove to be a wise national investment. It would be indeed ironical if the major preoccupations of British planning continued to be the problem of the drift to the south and of overspill from Greater London!

I was impressed by the similarity of characteristics between areas of economic stress in Britain, with those in Canada as outlined by Professor Graham. Many of the remedies may be similar in concept, if not in scale, not least in the role which integrated public policies may be called upon to play in regional economic development. But the differences are also profound: Britain operates in the context of national social and economic planning in a full employment (and inflationary) economy; we have severe problems of over-congestion in towns, notably in Greater London; the scale of distance involved in relocating industry and commerce is small by Canadian standards. But it is clear to many in Britain that in replanning one is concerned not only with theoretically sound economic solutions but also with concepts and plans that are socially acceptable and politically practicable.

PART IV

REGIONAL POLICIES IN CANADA

- Vital Issues in the Study of Aid

> Professor Edward G. Pleva,
> Head, Department of Geography,
> University of Western Ontario.

Discussant:

> Professor A. L. Levine,
> Department of Economics and Political Science,
> University of New Brunswick.

- Development Policies at the Provincial Level

> Mr. L. O. Gertler,
> Head, Planning Department,
> H. G. Acres & Company, Limited.

Discussants:

> Professor Pierre Harvey,
> Ecole des Hautes Etudes Commerciales.

> Mr. W. Hugh Flynn,
> Ontario General Manager,
> Canadian Industries Limited.

> Mr. Stanley A. Little,
> President, Canadian Union of Public
> Employees and Vice-President,
> Canadian Labour Congress.

VITAL ISSUES IN THE STUDY OF AID

Professor Edward G. Pleva,
Head, Department of Geography,
University of Western Ontario.

I. Introduction

Three interesting reports were released during the same week early in January 1965: the first report of the Economic Council of Canada, the annual report of the Committee for Economic Development, and Dean Wayne A. Danielson's list of the most tired and overworked words and phrases of 1964.

Each year Dean Wayne A. Danielson of the University of North Carolina, using a Univac 1105, compiles a list of the most tired and overworked words and phrases in AP wire copy of the preceding year in order to find the cliche of the year.

Dean Danielson's research found the winner to be "hailed", such as "U.S. election results were 'hailed' in Great Britain, Russia, Brazil and Italy". Runner-up cliche of 1964 was the phrase "violence flared", while "flatly denied" was third. Other cliches included "racially troubled (or divided)", "marched (or went) to the polls", "jam-packed", "in the wake of", "no immediate comment", "cautious (or guarded)", "usually reliable (or informed) sources", "backlash (or front-lash)", "kickoff" (for begin), "grinding crash", "confrontation", "oil-rich nation", "- - wise" (as in "percentage-wise"), "limped into port", "gutted by fire", "death and destruction", "riot-torn", "strife-torn", and "tinder-dry woodlands".

Technical vocabulary taken out of technical reports by students, journalists, and elected representatives often undergoes subtle changes in meaning when used in a new context. Words and phrases with precise meanings in technical journals may take on other connotations when used at a non-professional or popular level. This is particularly true of the words and phrases relating to economic planning and regional development.

A language grows through the additions of connotation which often change a word greatly from its original meaning. This is a normal process and adds much to the vitality of a language. It is important, however, that a continual review of meanings may prevent great misunderstandings, especially where the words and phrases may stand for complex and involved concepts.

The search for meaning of words and phrases taken from technical reports and rewritten in popular language led to an interesting game devised by a small group of professors and graduate students. The term "aid" was, by far, the most controversial word in a long list of words and phrases that had many meanings and implications when discussed openly by a group.

The other terms and phrases on the final list, arranged alphabetically, were: alternate land uses; assistance; austerity; beneficiation; budgets, such as public budgets, regional budgets, administrative budgets; chronic excessive unemployment; centrifugal and centripetal forces; conservation, such as soil conservation, water conservation; decision making; development and redevelopment; disadvantage, such as social or economic disadvantage; dynamic changes, for example automation, foreign competition, shifts in demand; economic growth; economic hazards for the individual, economic stability and economic instability; economic planning; economic policies of the government of its own operations; economic status; efficiency; environmental planning; fiscal policy; management; minimum standards of employment; minimum wages; monetary policy; physical planning; pollution, such as water pollution, air pollution, land pollution, biological pollutions; poverty; program, such as a one-plank program or a program of development; reclamation; regional planning and regional government rehabilitation (habilitation is an archaic word bound to be rediscovered by someone); research; resources, such as water resources; social security; subsidy; system; urban renewal; scope of private enterprise and of government business, respectively; slow growth area; technology; underdevelopment; zoning.

One of the great difficulties in the discussion of aid, in addition to the confusion in the meaning of the term, is the geographical or regional scale in which aid, governmental or otherwise, may be applied. Administrative regionalism, is, and will be, a lively topic of study and discussion in Canada and its provinces. Many expressions of this interest are evident: Regional Government (Ontario), Electoral Districts and Revisions (Canada), Economic Development Regions (Ontario), Metropolitan Government (Toronto, Montreal, Winnipeg, Vancouver) and so forth.

II.   Aid and Regional Government

National aid to any part of the resource base in North America implies a regional approach as well as provincial and state involvement. Geographers are skillful in dealing with the regional concept and have been able to contribute significantly to this phase of planning and development.

During the time this paper was being written, a routine questionnaire on regional government was received. The answers to the questions may serve as a background to a continuing discussion on the regional aspects of aid.

Q.   Is the county a logical base for regional development and planning?

A.   I, as a geographer, recognize the county as politically organized space of larger size than the exploding or mushrooming urbanisms developing across the province, especially the Southern Ontario part. The geographer pleads for space to deal with the growing problems of growth that no longer can be handled by the fragmental pattern of Balkanized local government units.

Q.   Is the county the logical place to start in an effort to expand regional development and planning to larger areas, possibly the economic regions recognized by the provincial Department of Economics?

A.   I believe the economic region is a good device between the sovereign level of the province and the home rule level of local government. The county with an area well adapted to Nineteenth Century conditions is too small for the Twentieth Century. This simple fact of scale accounts for the weakening of the county as an administrative unit. Any agency (governmental, commercial, social, communication, etc.) that has a regional pattern of service will define its own regions. The various departments of the Ontario government right now use over thirty different regional frameworks in administration: highways, hydro, justice, police, tourism, education, lands and forests, etc. Every one of these patterns uses units larger than the county unit. It is significant that only agriculture retains the county unit, thus emphasizing the fact that Ontario was an agriculturally-based economy at the time of the establishment of the county system. I believe the best regional framework to provide an administrative level between the provincial government (sovereign) and local government (grass roots) is something we could call the super-county in that each unit would consist of several counties. These administrative regions would look pretty much like the existing economic regions although several modifications in boundaries seem warranted. Within each administrative region every inducement would be given to the cities and separated towns to "rejoin" the county. Ontario has too many governmental units now and any system of administrative regions must be justified by the number of units it eliminates, not by the number of units it adds. Ontario is probably the "most governed" area in the world. If the democratic process is served by a proliferation of administrative frameworks, I would say "the more the merrier". However, we have reasonable grounds for believing that the "administration of government" can be made more tidy and efficient without destroying the democratic basis of our political institutions.

Q. If the county system is to be used as the regional instrument, what changes, if any, are needed in the form of county government to make it effective?

A. The county form of government is not the goal we are trying to achieve. Perhaps there is much that can be carried on and strengthened. Basically, however, we are interested in larger administrative units and the pattern may be derived from the best of "metropolitan", "amalgamation", "urban district", "conservation authority" thinking. I believe only the areas under the "urban shadow" should be subject to municipal reorganization now. In predominantly agricultural areas, the county has not out-lived its usefulness. It would be preposterous to imagine the "county type of thinking" taking over the problems of an expanding urbanism. What is needed is a framework in which the best brains from both the county and the urban centres can work out solutions to problems that are neither urban nor rural but which are related to something encompassing much more than either rural or urban. We no longer can permit ourselves the luxury of packaging "urban" and "rural" into separate boxes. Certainly in Southern Ontario, we no longer can deal with regional development on a "Swiss cheese basis".

Q. Should the Territorial Division Act be amended to make boundary adjustments and territorial exchanges between counties easier to achieve?

A. Municipal government is a responsibility of the sovereign provincial level of government. However, if the Territorial Divisions Act must be amended to make municipal reorganization also operative from the local option or home-rule point of view, then the Act must be amended to make regional government as meaningful and workable as possible. Certainly no framework of government will be effective unless it has the consent of the governed. My own feeling is that the people are willing to consider new frameworks of administration to achieve more effective administration of government, especially in the field of regional planning. The province has the responsibility of leadership and no one is so naive as to believe the task is an easy one. Careful study is necessary and the province must make a proper presentation. The citizens' financial stake in the most effective use of his "provincial dollar" is at least twenty times greater than his financial stake in "local dollar". The province has the delicate but important task to show why good housekeeping at the provincial level may require a new thinking about the local administration of government where the provincial stake now outweighs the local stake. No one wants to abolish or "annex" any local responsibilities based entirely on local resources and involvement but when the provincial treasury and the provincial economy are drawn in, the provincial administrative framework must become involved as well.

Q.   The Ontario government is committed to the "grass roots" concept of change — the demand for change must start at the bottom, the principle of local autonomy must be preserved, and so on. Is this adequate, particularly in view of the rapid urbanization of much of southern Ontario and the strains of urban - rural relations within townships and counties?

A.   I have a well justified hunch that much that the "province" is thinking along these lines really stems from "grass roots" origins. I am not saying that the local municipalities are screaming "Help!" but I do believe they are asking "Isn't the province really interested in the state of affairs into which rapid regional economic influences have placed us?"

Q.   Should economic development and municipal planning be grouped in one department of government rather than be divided between two as at present?

A.   I believe an interdepartmental committee on "Provincial Economic Planning and Development" consisting of Deputy Ministers of all departments should be set up under the Prime Minister's office for a three year term to bring about the necessary studies and coordination of effort. I have given up on omnibus departments. After all, the old Department of Planning and Development was set up to do everything everyone has suggested to date on planning and development. You are aware of what happened to P. and D. It is now obvious that every department of government is in a sense a department of planning and development: the only legal coordinating level is actually the Cabinet itself. Therefore it is true that only a committtee of deputy ministers can furnish the necessary technical advice to the Cabinet to bring about the necessary coordination at the effective governmental level of the Cabinet.

Reorganization of Ontario governmental structures is underway. This reorganization is really a directed speed-up of process that has gone on continually but always at a lagging pace. Until recently, this lag was not unduly harmful and often was explained as the slow but sure process of democratic evolution. The rapid acceleration of development in the past two decades has forced a studied attempt to bring governmental organization closer to the needs of the present.

In Ontario, the sovereign level of government is the province itself. Local government is the responsibility of the province. As the province developed, most of the expanding governmental activities were assumed by the province and the money needed to carry out these activities was provided by new sources of tax revenue, sources unheard of a century and a quarter ago.

In the meantime the tax base of the local governments has remained relatively unchanged. Yet many of the financial responsibilities to provide for the needs of 1965 Ontarians remain with the local governments. An elaborate system of grants has evolved to bring provincial revenues to the local level. These arrangements were adequate and successful to a surprising degree, but there are certain indications that governmental structures well suited to meet the needs of an agriculturally based society are no longer adequate to deal with those parts of North America, and certainly Southern Ontario, that are undergoing rapid urbanization.

Thus the problem becomes complicated. The administration of aid, obviously, has a regional expression. The question remains, "What kind of regional unit shall be used to administer a given type of aid?"

III. Concentration in the Canadian Economy.

Canada is a highly urbanized state with a high degree of urban concentration.

The degree of concentration can be illustrated best by reference to the Grand Trunk Corridor from Quebec City to Windsor, a distance of 700 miles. This corridor, with an area less than 1 per cent of the total area of Canada, has approximately three-fifths of the total population of Canada, approximately four-fifths of the industrial activity of Canada as measured by the value added by manufacture, and approximately two-fifths of the agricultural production of Canada as measured by the value of crops and animals sold commercially off the farms.

Significantly, the degree of relative concentration is increasing in the Grand Trunk Corridor. The rate of growth in most of the measures of economic development is higher in the Corridor than for Canada as a total country.

Agriculture, likewise, tends to be concentrated with 3% of the total area of Canada producing almost all the agricultural production of the country. The pattern of agriculture, however, is widespread from the Atlantic to the Pacific. Agriculture is the most widespread, dispersed, and decentralized form of economic activity in Canada in which owner-operation is a factor. Other widespread forms of primary industry such as mining, power generation, and forestry have centralized control as a major characteristic.

Aid, in the ultimate analysis, must always have a relevance to the individual in a democratic society that subscribes to a free enterprise system. Thus aid to a concentrated industrialized urban area may be expressed in a way that has individual relevance through corporate persons such as municipalities, crown corporations, industrial combinations, and transportation organizations. Aid to a dispersed agricultural area may be extremely difficult to carry out under existing procedures. The agreements between Canada and the provinces for the carrying out of the terms of the Agricultural Rehabilitation and Development Act reflect the difficulties involved in aid to agriculture.

The second round of agreements in 1965 show clearly that progress through experience is being made but the basic difficulties still exist.

Economic aid is usually justified as a device to stimulate, maintain, or develop a definable part of the national economy. Aid, however, tends to affect the equilibrium of centrifugal and centripetal forces always present in a free or relatively free economic system. Aid, therefore, can be a positive factor in the development and redevelopment of a region through its multiplier effects. To ascertain what kinds of aid will have the desired multiplier effect is the problem that must be solved by the economic planner.

Unfortunately, much that is called aid really is a form of relief to maintain life in an area with a meager resource base. Sometimes aid is really a poorly disguised form of "share the wealth" program on a regional basis. It is certain that our national, provincial, and regional budgets will always include items for relief, care, and per capita allocations for public works, but it is imperative that economic aid for development or redevelopment have a separate categorical entry for itself on the budget.

There are many kinds of aid with multiplier effects to accelerate regional development and redevelopment. Social scientists have an obligation to assist in the identification, the devising of policy, and the operation of programs to meet regional needs in resources development.

The ultimate issues in the study of aid, then, are few in number but important in significance. First, what is the definition and meaning of the term aid? Second, what will be the regional expression of an aid program as carried out at federal, provincial, and local level? Third, what will be the machinery of change in regional government to make aid more effective?

COMMENTS

PROFESSOR A. L. LEVINE,
Department of Economics and
Political Science,
University of New Brunswick.

As an economist, a perusal of Professor Pleva's paper brings to mind the Great Unwritten Paper which continues to circulate among the community of economists, a paper entitled "On Pushing Back the Frontier of *Ceteris Paribus*".

This Great Unwritten Paper has two main themes. First, there is the point that in spite of the change in nomenclature that took place seventy or more years ago, our subject is still *political* economy. Professor Pleva provides us with a sharp reminder of this in his brief disquisition on problems of regional economic growth — however one defines region — and local autonomy. The problem may be stated in stark terms by looking at one of the extreme positions (presumably an extremity which the Ontario Government views favourably). We are all for economic growth at the local level; we are all against retardation at the local level. But the *will* to do something about either of these must *originate* at the bottom, and should probably express itself in such things as local-level policies designed to enhance locational advantages. At the same time, the principle of local autonomy must remain inviolate. Professor Pleva, while recognizing the inadequacy of such an approach, nevertheless insists that "No one wants to abolish or annex any local responsibilities based entirely on local resources and local involvement". But there *are* a few abolitionists — people who incline to the view that "local responsibilities based entirely on local resources and involvement", or simply, "local democracy" or "local autonomy", is to be equated with concentration of same in the hands of local mercantile-professional elites whose last and least concern is with *balanced* development of local resources, including the all-important human resource.[1] And the prospects may continue to be bleak or even nightmarish, with the nightmare retaining all the familiar components — the persistence of pockets of poverty; failure to solve certain hard-core problems of education; and excessive concentration on keeping local tax rates down and retaining archaic assessment criteria without ever a thought to structural or other optima or to

---

[1] There is currently (January, 1965) a proposal before the City Council of Moncton, New Brunswick, to raise the property qualifications of members of Council and of the electorate. The promoters of this measure are to be congratulated for their candour. The local dialogue of butcher, baker and candlestick-maker — apropos of Mr. Levitan's observation — is not to be drowned out by democratic excesses!

questioning the basic tenets of a property tax creed in the first place. And so on *ad nauseum*. (Incidentally, it is to be hoped that the Government of New Brunswick will become the first provincial government in Canada to give the lie to the "local autonomy myth" by adopting the report of its Byrne Commission.)

The nightmare provokes a query which pushes the frontier of *ceteris paribus* in yet another direction and provides the economist's Great Unwritten Paper with its second main theme. Local elites are, among other things, sociological phenomena and must be studied as such. Are there sometimes present in retarded areas vestiges of a colonial administered society — vestiges which have something to do with the perpetuation of low levels of aspiration and the proliferation of social-economic ineffectives on the margin of human existence? Here, too, Professor Pleva strikes an apt note in his mention of "environmental planning" and the "totality of the social environment".

In short, there are a variety of social interstices that must not be neglected by the economist interested in regional development. In addition to those factors already mentioned, the following might also be considered. One wonders how many real insights into problems of regional economic stress are to be gained from analyses such as that undertaken by Harvey Perloff into "Lagging Sectors and Regions of the American Economy"[2] in which the chosen bundle of possible determinants is such that the major causal factors are almost bound to be things having to do with markets and the location of material inputs. One also wonders how many additional insights are to be gleaned from multiple regression analyses such as that undertaken by Victor Fuchs into the changes in the location of manufacturing industry in the United States.[3] Here the relative growth of manufacturing in a given state was taken as the dependent variable and a number of economic and non-economic factors as the independent variables. Within the matrix of his variables, Fuchs found, interestingly enough, that the factors "most significantly related" to the redistribution of industry away from the Northeast and toward the South and West were (1) considerations of space, (2) climate (or average monthly deviation from 65 degrees F.), and (3) relative extent of unionization. In each case the relationship was negative — not surprisingly, in view of the *type* of industry which features prominently in the continuing industrial growth of the areas in question. Consumer demand, or market considerations, are given far less weight than in the Perloff analysis. Although high coefficients of correlation were found to obtain between relative shifts in manufacturing and growth of population and personal income, Fuchs points out, quite plausibly, that it could be that the prime mover behind rising income and population was a *prior* growth of manufacturing. But the intriguing consideration, at least in so far as the present context is concerned, is the relative influence, in the Fuchs study, of a certain socio-economic factor — the extent of trade union organization, which rated somewhat higher in the hierarchy of possible determinants than either market factors or wage differentials. Unfortunately, the apparent negative relationship between extent or density of trade union organization and manufacturing growth rates is accepted, so to speak, at its face value by Fuchs. This is precisely where hueing to the traditional frontiers of *ceteris paribus* may lead to distortion, for it may well be that the extent of unionization is not a determinant of manufacturing growth rate differentials at all.

---

[2] *American Economic Review*, Vol. 50, May 1960, pp. 223-230.

[3] Fuchs, V. R., "The Determinants of Redistribution of Manufacturing in the United States Since 1929", *Review of Economics and Statistics*, Vol. 44, May 1962, pp. 167-177.

More particularly, it is entirely possible that certain *underlying* labour force characteristics which have a bearing on differences in extent of unionization also have a bearing upon differences in manufacturing growth rates; and, furthermore, the latter may be more likely to influence, than be influenced by, unionization.

Other examples of relative neglect of social interstices by students of regional economic problems might be found among studies of unemployment. N. J. Simler's recent paper on "Long-Term Unemployment, the Structural Hypothesis and Public Policy",[4] although not a regional piece, has sufficient regional connota-tions to be of relevance here. Steering a mid-course between the structural hypothesis on the one hand and the deficient aggregate demand argument on the other, Simler attempts to identify the principal factors behind the increase in long-term unemployment rates in the United States, and presents the following hypothesis, based upon regression analysis. An increase in persistent, long-term or structural unemployment relative to all other types of unemployment can occur (and, moreover, can become increasingly concentrated among older workers) without any underlying structural change in the economy at all. More precisely, a rise of structural unemployment can be the *result* of an increase in *overall* un-employment and not a *cause* of it. In short, *inadequate aggregate demand* can be *the* cause of an increase in overall unemployment and this in turn can generate an increase in structural unemployment. But all of this is veering perilously close to the tautological, unless structural employment can be fitted into a broader *industrial-sociological* context, which is not done in Simler's paper.

Admittedly, Simler's analysis might suggest plausible proposals in the policy sphere. Thus he argues that fiscal and monetary policy unaccompanied by labour-market policies (for example, policies directed to structural unemployment by introducing new skills to the unemployed) might not succeed in reducing unemploy-ment without also driving up prices, if the increase in the demand for new units of labour is the same as the increase in the supply of new units and if, at the same time, the internal composition of the increment in demand differs from that of the increment in supply. On the other hand, labour-market policies by themselves, without appropriate fiscal policy, cannot reduce unemployment. However, to set such policy considerations in a regional context, one has misgivings (already alluded to) about the point of departure, about the constricting framework of the analysis. One is dealing with a *society* that is retarded, in an area of so-called economic stress, not merely with an *economy* that is retarded.

This interdisciplinary note might be pursued a bit further by making refer-ence to the results of a recent productivity study of eight New Brunswick manu-facturing industries.[5] A comparison of the gross value productivity of labour in these eight industries with the gross value productivities for the same industries in the country as a whole showed that in almost every case, and extending over a twenty-year period, there was a fairly consistent New Brunswick productivity disadvantage. How to account for this? New Brunswick-Canadian differences in output mix were marginal. There was a *prima facie* case for assuming no signifi-cant differences in the qualities of the labour and materials inputs. Partial and

---

[4] *American Economic Review,* Vol. 54, Dec. 1964, pp. 985-1001.

[5] Levine, A. L., "Toward an Analysis of the Effectiveness of Economic Effort in a Group of New Brunswick Manufacturing Industries". (Paper presented at the 1964 Conference on Statistics of the Canadian Political Science Association, Charlottetown, P.E.I., June 14, 1964.)

multiple regression analysis indicated that those hardy perennials, differences in scale or plant size, and differences in capital intensity, were not associated with the observed productivity differences. In the end, it was concluded that qualitative differences in managerial and entrepreneurial inputs were both highly probable and important determinants of the productivity differentials.

One final observation: it is surely time to "de-emphasize" resource endowment differences as strategic factors in retardation. I have for some years been intrigued by the productivity disadvantages, *vis-à-vis* the United States, which were assuming significant orders of magnitude in important British industries during the last quarter of the nineteenth century — becoming significant, that is, at a time when the *resource endowment gap* between the two countries (although still very substantial) was probably *narrowing*, not widening, as a result of more rapid rates of resource depletion in the United States. This juxtaposition might suggest that the important and relevant avenues to be explored, in retardation situations, are not the usual ones which end on the convenient side of *ceteris paribus*, but, rather, those avenues that extend through a variety of social, social-psychological and other stretches of unfamiliar territory that lie on the far side of *ceteris paribus*.

DEVELOPMENT POLICIES AT THE PROVINCIAL LEVEL

L. O. GERTLER,
Head, Planning Department,
H. G. Acres & Company, Limited.

I

The author wishes to begin with an apology, for which he makes no apologies. He believes that the concept of this paper in the minds of the "architects" of this conference was of a broad comparative survey of the economic development programs of the provinces, with special attention to their effect on areas of economic stress. The assignment conjures up a neat catalogue of each province in terms of Objectives, Structure, Program, Progress and Problems, to which would be added an overall Evaluation. The material would be assembled from published sources which would yield the official facts, and from discussions with major protagonists in each provincial capital which would provide insight into the underlying philosophy and spirit, and general policy directions.

This paper, the author regrets, does not fulfill these expectations. For reasons, which may need no elaboration, it has not been possible to carry out the necessary extensive research. Consequently, this work can only be regarded as a brief sojourn along the alignment of a road that has been projected but not built.

This paper will set out some of the major forces underlying and shaping the present provincial preoccupation with economic development, indicate some of the variations in approach to problems of provincial economic development, and attempt some tentative assessment of the relationship between provincial economic policies and, in the Wilsonian sense, "a national policy for growth". While distinct policies and programs for areas of economic stress may exist, it is assumed that these will be better understood in the context of the general framework of economic policies at the provincial level.

II

It will be taken as demonstrable that this period of Canadian development is characterized by an extraordinary interest of Provincial Governments in policies and programs of economic development. The industrial loan fund and the economic council are ubiquitous.

To understand this phenomenon and the special accents and significance of the provincial policies, it is necessary to appreciate the forces at work.

The first and most basic fact is that a great part of the incidence of Canada's structural economic problem (expressed nationally as a too heavy reliance on primary resource industry) is felt, economically and politically, at the provincial level. The regional variations in unemployment and labour participation are the most conspicuous expressions of this. Symptoms of chronic unemployment have their roots in regional imbalance. Regional differentials in unemployment levels of 5 per cent and 7 per cent have been common since 1957. The labour participation rate expressed as the ratio of employed working force to population, which is a rough reflection of the level of education, technical skills and industrially created opportunities, differs strikingly from province to province. For example, in 1961 when the Canadian average was 35.5 per cent, it was 38.4 per cent in

Ontario, 33.5 per cent in Quebec and in Nova Scotia and New Brunswick respectively 32.1 per cent and 29.8 per cent.[1] It is not surprising that, where the shoe pinches, there is a response.

A second force of importance is that some of the critical structural adjustments that have to be made in the Canadian economy involve changes in the pattern of resource use — agricultural shifts away from marginal lands to alternative uses, increases in size and capitalization of farm units, improvements in the inventories, management, organization and marketing of resource-based industries and retraining of labour for new skills. The Provincial jurisdiction over resources places a heavy onus on Provincial Governments to participate actively in fostering structural changes.

The character of these changes and their severity are illustrated by the case of Prince Edward Island, which epitomizes this problem. The Census shows a negligible increase in employment between 1951 and 1961 — a mere 1.8 per cent. This, however, masks the underlying structural change — substantial increases in the managerial, professional and technical, and clerical categories which were offset by an approximately 30 per cent decline, a total 3,755, in the "farmers and farm workers" group. Nor is the end of this process in sight. Seventy-nine per cent of the provinces 7,335 farms are of a size which is below or on the margin of an economic farm unit, that is, below 179 acres (on the assumptions of a recent P.E.I. Study requiring 114 acres of improved farmland for an annual farm income of $6,000). The author has recently been involved in an examination of employment trends in the Atlantic Provinces and has found that a closer approximation to optimum farm sizes in P.E.I. would involve the loss of an additional 3,880 jobs in farming out of a total of 9,188 employed on farms in 1961, within the next 15 years.[2] The release of people employed in primary fields on this scale inescapably involves a Provincial Government in a process of adjustment which is double-edged — on the one hand, towards changes in the rural patterns of use and production, and on the other hand, towards facilitating integration in urban employments and way of life.

A third condition which affects the goals and scope of Provincial development policies is an increasing preoccupation with environment — the qualitative element in our standard of living. This has various roots. In part, it is an expression of the maturing of our society, of the effects of being freed from pioneer tasks and mentalities, and having the capital accumulation for other than directly productive investments. The character of our centennial projects is a conspicuous example of this. In part, it is an expression of incipient crisis. While Scott's demonstration of the substitutability (although not unlimited) of natural resources, by other forms of capital, does hold, it does not apply to the environmental resources — land as scenery and park and open space, water as a potable and a recreational resource, and breathable air. The causes and symptoms of the pressures on these resources in our time are well known, and their effect on our way of life is increasingly felt.

Galbraith claims that the economist establishment in the early thirties was still fighting the battles of turn-of-century economics, focussed on the efficiency of

---

[1] Camu, P., E. P. Weeks, Z. W. Sametz, *Economic Geography of Canada,* Toronto MacMillan of Canada, 1964, Appendix 3.

[2] Census of Canada, *Agriculture, Prince Edward Island,* Ottawa, Dominion Bureau of Statistics, 1961.

the firm, and that Keynes was a maverick going against the stream. And he raises
a somewhat uncomfortable question: Are we repeating a similar mistake today,
focusing on employment and income aggregates, when we should be concerned with
the "quality of life", which is inherently regional, because the quality of life is
meaningless outside of a specific environmental context? If Galbraith is right, he
puts an entirely different complexion on economic development policies. If the
policy of maximizing returns to the factors of production has the effect of creating
urban behemoths, which we find increasingly difficult and costly to manage and
make livable, is there not some point in looking at the total standard of living —
monetary and non-monetary — and devising a policy to capitalize on both environmental and productive assets. Perhaps, at this time, we need not a General
Theory of Money, Interest and Employment but a General Theory of Satisfactions,
Motivations, and Living Standards.

The provinces with their prime responsibility for resources, land use, and
environmental planning will not easily escape involvement in the policies affecting
"the quality of life".

Another factor of considerable consequence shaping Provincial development
policies is the fact that they are, as a group, becoming fiscally more important.
An OECD Study points out that the Federal Government is at present directly
responsible for only about 40 per cent of the total expenditures on goods and
services of the public sector. The reason for this shift in relative roles is mainly
due, of course, to the fact that the provinces, by virtue of economic growth and
the termination of the "tax rental" agreements with the Federal Government, have
more revenue. The Provincial plus Municipal expenditures are together approximately in balance with Federal expenditures — 16.6 per cent of the Gross National
Product being spent by the first group and 15.4 per cent by the Federal Government (1962). These facts indicate increasing opportunity, and concomitant responsibility, for policies affecting the level of economic activity.[3]

The final factor which the author believes to have an important impact on
provincial development policies is the existence within provinces of substantial
economic and general cultural disparities between regions. This is true for both
the "have-nots" and the "haves". In fact, because of intra-provincial centralization of growth, the disparities tend to be sharpest in the more prosperous provinces. This is illustrated by a recent ranking of the ten economic regions of
Ontario in terms of eighteen selected indicators of "economic health". The
results, which admittedly cannot and should not be taken at face value and are
only an indication of differences, showed disparities of this order: the region
with the best score was five times as "healthy" as the worst, the second best was
only one-half as "healthy" as the best, and the median rank was about one-third
as "wholesome" as the first. These differences may be important materially. The
author has no doubt, after recent discussions in each of the regional "capitols",
that they are important psychologically. The Bay Street stereotype has an astound-
ing durability. One who has had the experience of working there and enjoying the
company of its denizens on the Rosedale Bus knows that they are just a lot of
well-meaning and tragically misunderstood boy scouts. But to the man in the
North and the East and the West, they symbolize the proverbial ogre, draining off
all the riches and depriving others of their legitimate birthright. As long as this

---

[3] Organisation for Economic Co-operation and Development, *Canada,* Paris, 1963, p. 15.

image persists, and Bay Street has its parallel in other provinces, inter-regional disparities will be a source of political tension and find expression in the policies of government.

III

This paper has identified five major influences on Provincial development policies: (1) the impact and regional incidence of Canada's structural economic problem; (2) the necessity of making structural adjustments by changes in the pattern of using resources, which fall largely within the jurisdiction of the Provinves; (3) the emergence of a concern with "the quality of life" and environmental resources as a major preoccupation of economic thought and policy; (4) the increasing scale, and importance for fiscal policy, of provincial expenditures; and (5) the unequal participation of the regions within provinces in economic growth and opportunities.

These influences do not operate with equal force within each province. The particular mix of influences in effect, and the relative weight of each factor, tends to create a bias in each province towards one of two approaches to the subject of economic development: towards either an integrated, provincially-oriented structure and program, or a decentralized, regionally-oriented approach. The integrated approach, under the impact of the first two policy influences — structural and resource use adjustment — is preoccupied with overcoming the handicap with the rest of Canada. Internal regional differences are not overlooked, but they are secondary to the main effort. Provinces in this group will share the general concern with questions of environment, but the intensity of the interest and effort will vary with the size of the growth centres. There will be a tendency to use new-found fiscal strength to round out infrastructure, diversify and strengthen industrial development, and provide employment.

The decentralized approach is strongest in those provinces which do not receive the major impact of Canada's structural and resource adjustment difficulties, and within which the primary motivation of policies is to cope with significant internal regional disparities in economic growth and general well-being. The preoccupation with problems of environment tends to be greater than in the first group because rapid and large scale urban growth creates inescapable pressures, and because of the sophistication of consumer preferences, and the availability of wealth. Comparative financial buoyancy supports an intricate system of current and capital grants to municipalities and regions, and tax measures and other fiscal devices receive consideration as ways of encouraging the development of areas of lagging potential.

The first group includes Quebec, Manitoba, Saskatchewan, New Brunswick, Nova Scotia and Prince Edward Island, and the second group, the regionally-oriented, includes Ontario, British Columbia and Alberta. Newfoundland shares many of the features of the integrated approach, but, as will be explained, it is in a class by itself and requires separate comment. This paper will outline the approaches to economic development in Ontario and Quebec, as assumed prototypes of the two approaches, and will make only illustrative references to the experience of the other provinces in each group.

IV

The locus of economic policy-making in Ontario is the Department of Economics and Development — notwithstanding the functions and services affecting development which are the responsibility of other departments. This is evident in the terms of the *Ontario Statistics Act*,[4] which require that every proposal or action under the Act by any department be reviewed by the Minister of Economics and Development, and in the recent appointment of a Chief Economist, an entirely new position, who will be responsible for advising on Provincial-Federal relationships and for the coordination of government policies and programs related to economic development. Associated with the Department of Economics and Development are three special purpose agencies — the *Ontario Development Agency* which provides loans mainly for working capital to private industry, the *Ontario Research Foundation* which—in close alliance with industry—undertakes applied research on industrial problems (and amongst other things has played a major role in the control of air pollution in the Sarnia petro-chemical area) and the *Economic Council of Ontario*, which is a body of appointed citizens, representing a cross-section of the economic community, with a full-time chairman, and which performs an advisory role in the whole field of economic policy.

The broad objectives of policy on economic development in so far as one can surmise from performance, which in the final analysis is probably the best indication, is (1) to back up and support private industry with information, studies and promotional efforts related to the major concerns of the day, and (2) to provide a framework within which the groups of municipalities constituting the ten economic regions of the province "may explore and work toward solutions on common problems of economic growth and development".[5] The specific focus of the first objective will inherently vary with the rise and fall of major issues. In recent years, there has been emphasis on export promotion and import replacement, and on the impact of automation.

The second objective is more long run in nature and is deeply imbedded in both the departmental and regional structure. Recently, a number of papers have described the formal aspects of the system: the division of the Province 10 years ago into ten economic regions on the basis of the SFPM formula;[6] the establishment within nine of the regions of Regional Development Associations representing the constituent municipalities, interested individuals and groups, and the Department; the division of Regions into county Zones; coordination of regional efforts by a body representing all Associations, the Ontario Regional Development Council (which in turn has representation on the Ontario Economic Council); and the support of the Province through annual grants and the assistance of a special division of Regional Co-ordination.

The Department's interest in regional affairs is reflected, as well, in various statistical and research services which inevitably mirror the general drift of policies. Some of the more important statistical projects accomplished and planned are: Regional Economic Surveys of each region (of which six have been completed) which is part of a long range program to "integrate the individual regional surveys into a comparative economic analysis on an inter-regional basis for pur-

---

[4] Schnick, O. M., "Development and Use of Statistical Data for Economic Analysis on a Provincial and Sub-Provincial Level", *Canadian Political Science Association, 1964 Conference on Statistics,* p. 16.

[5] *Ibid.,* p. 19.

[6] This refers to a method of defining regions described in the recent *Economic Geography of Canada,* and based on Structural, Function, Production and Marketing Factors. *op. cit.,* Camu, Weeks, Sametz, Chapter 10.

For another assessment of regional development in Ontario see Kreuger, R., *Ten Years of Regional Development in Ontario,* 6th Annual Regional Conference, Niagara Regional Development Conference, Grimsby, 1963.

poses of government policy formulation"; economic feasibility studies on a regional basis; time series on regional income as a step towards the development of regional accounts; the determination of differential regional growth rates; analysis of inter-county shifts of manufacturing employment, production, input costs, etc., as a means of understanding "the nature and causes of the changing locational patterns of manufacturing"; estimates of the flow of intra-provincial migration; determination of Ontario's wage structure by industry on a regional basis; decomposition of monthly retail sales by economic regions; exploratory studies "for designing a composite series" to determine the regional incidence of economic fluctuations and so on.[7]

It has been the thesis of this paper that Ontario's emphasis on the regional approach is, to a large extent, based on the fact of inter-regional differences in income and rates of growth. Recently, this has received dramatic emphasis in a publication by the Ontario Federation of Labour, in which it is shown that there are only three counties out of 55 in which less than 10 per cent are under the poverty line (family income of $3,000 or less), that in 28 counties the poor families constitute 10 per cent to 19.9 per cent of the total, 20 per cent to 29.9 per cent in 13 counties, 30 to 39.9 per cent in 7 counties and 40 per cent or over in 4 counties.[8] This situation, together with the differences in general "economic health", has resulted in the issue of the location of economic activities, particularly of new growth, being forced up towards the top of the list of major public issues. This in turn will, the author is convinced, result in the crystallization of a need to evolve a general pattern of future Provincial development, in both sectoral and spatial terms — not only because of economic compulsions but because the pressures of environment in some regions are becoming near-critical.[9]

The development of a tenable concept of the Province's future development could be achieved either my centralized activity at Queen's Park, or by decentralized effort in each of the economic regions. It seems likely that Ontario will follow the latter path. There are four main reasons for this judgment: first, there is the general observation that highly integrated, provincially-oriented efforts at shaping the composition, pace and pattern of economic development occurs only in those provinces where there is a strong drive to "catch up" with the rest of the country. This is clearly not the Ontario case. The disinclination to move in that direction is evident in the role of the Economic Council of Ontario. It assumes increasing importance as a body to which problems are referred, and as an initiator of objective studies of difficult questions. But unlike its counterparts in some of the other provinces, it does not appear to be moving in the direction of indicative planning.

Second, the decentralized regional approach is politically more acceptable. This is not just a matter of expediency, of a "let the regions fight it out" approach. There is wisdom in the recognition that the absence of an over-riding provincial cause does not provide a climate for acceptance of planning from the centre. By the same token, development policies hammered out at the regional level with local involvement will be more acceptable and have a greater chance of success.

---

[7] *op. cit.,* Schnick.

[8] Ontario Federation of Labour, *Poverty in the Midst of Plenty,* Toronto, 1964, pp. 8 and 9.

[9] For a discussion of one environmental problem in Ontario see: The Conservation Council of Ontario, *Water Pollution in Ontario,* Toronto, 1964.

Third, the existing economic regions in Ontario provide a useful framework for meeting the problems of economic stress. Wilson's critique of the selection criteria for the Federal Employment Service Districts is relevant. By making the level of unemployment the test, he argues, assistance is denied the very centres, the growth centres, that could precipitate the regeneration of their regions. He states, "It will not do simply to select a number of scattered districts with particularly heavy unemployment and to offer certain inducements to industrial expansion without reference to the scope for expansion that these districts offer. If the policy is really to succeed, particular strength must be laid on the existing industrial centres or on the scope for creating such centres. What is needed is a plan for regional development rather than piecemeal measures for small scattered districts."[10] The defined economic regions of Ontario, each of which is broad enough to include a variety of resources and centres, qualify for this development role. They could become the focus for the efforts, of ARDA and the Provincial departments, designed to encourage necessary resource-use adjustments, provide essential public works and generally strengthen the regional economies.

Finally, at this stage in the development of the Province, the economic problems and opportunities that occur at the regional level are matched by a number of environmental and service problems. To the province-wide forces that underlie the issues of regional economic location, are added the pressures from below, from the municipal level, to cope more effectively and on a more appropriate geographical scale with problems of air and water pollution, land use planning, the reservation of regional recreation space, conservation, transportation, water supply, sewage disposal, library service and so on. The coincidence of these needs at this time reinforces the regional approach.[11]

The structure for a serious regionally-based approach to the problems of economic development in Ontario already exists. Opportunity for the necessary articulation of regional proposals into a sensible Provincial development concept is provided by the Ontario Regional Development Council, which has links with the Economic Council. Although the machinery exists, it does not at present attain its potentials. A clearer sense of direction and strategy is required at the centre; more strength, particularly the means of assuring consistently competent research as a basis for development programs, is needed in the regions. That these matters are receiving earnest attention is evident in the Government's calling for February, 1965 of a major conference on *Regional Development and Economic Change,* conceived as a means of pooling from North American and other Western countries the thought and experience on regional development, most relevant to conditions in the Province.

V

One of the most striking demonstrations of the difference between the Quebec-type approach to problems of economic development and the Ontario-type is the relative importance placed by each on Research in their ARDA programs. In the figures released by Federal ARDA this past summer on projects at the end of the first full operational year of the Federal-Provincial program, Quebec projects are shown to include an amount of $1,203,546, or about 23 per

---

[10]Wilson, T., *Financial Assistance with Regional Development,* The Atlantic Provinces Research Board, Fredericton, 1964, p. 18.

[11]For a recent examination of pressures for regional services in the Niagara area, see Mayo, Henry B., *Local Government Units of Lincoln and Welland Counties,* Niagara Regional Development Association, Grimsby, 1964.

cent of the total, for research, while the amount for that purpose in Ontario was $187,405 or about 6 per cent of the total ARDA expenditures in the Province. The descriptions of the Quebec research projects indicate that the greatest effort is being made in comprehensive studies designed in the Brome region to evaluate resources "with a view to increasing income, employment opportunities and the standard of living of the population"; in the lower south shore of the St. Lawrence "to study the physical resources and their social-economic impact so that a first draft of an overall plan of action can be prepared", and so on.[12]

The ARDA projects are not isolated phenomena, but are part of what appears to be an increasingly systematic approach to the basic problems of economic development in the Province. The exposition of a set of interrelated policies that together express a Province's approach to economic development is, at best, a hazardous task. To do this, for the dynamic Quebec situation, with which the author has had little contact, may be positively dangerous. One can only attempt something impressionistic, something highly tentative.

There have been a number of government-initiated changes within the past five years which, taken together, assume a deliberate pattern. These are the establishment of public power,[13] educational reform, the creation of the General Investment Corporation, the planning of a steel complex, the decision to institute a universal funded pension, the creation of a single administration for the North, and the establishment of the Economic Advisory Council (Conseil d'Orientation Economique). While each of these seven pillars of contemporary Quebec play a role in economic and social progress (Frere Untel is not only concerned with "joual"), the most important of these for future economic development — the one that is most load-bearing — is the Economic Advisory Council.

The membership of the council is similar in nature to its other Canadian counterparts — a cross section of the economic and related professional community. What is of particular interest from the point of view of its role in policy-making, is its integration with Government, and its role in economic planning. The first is achieved in a number of ways: (1) by including in its membership certain individuals who have important oblique relationships to government functions — such as Jean-Claude La Haye, a planning consultant who is also a member of the Provincial Town Planning Commission and Paul Normandeau, a senior official of General Investment Corporation; (2) by adding to the Council five associate members, representing key government activities, namely the Deputy Ministers of Trade and Industry, Agriculture, Natural Resources and Youth, and the President of Hydro-Quebec; (3) by making the Council responsible to the Cabinet through the Prime Minister; (4) by requiring Council recommendations to be submitted first to a Permanent Ministerial Committee composed of the Ministers of Trade and Industry, Natural Resources, Forestry, Agricultural and Colonization, and the Provincial Secretary; (5) by the establishment of "working groups" made up mainly of officials from government departments, aided by "university consultants", to initiate, undertake and supervise the studies required by the Council.[14]

[12]Agricultural Rehabilitation and Development Act, *ARDA Projects*, Ottawa, Department of Forestry, June 1964.

[13]For the economic role of public power in Quebec see Sauriol, Paul, *The Nationalization of Electric Power*, Montreal, Harvest House, 1962.

[14]*The Financial Post*, February 22, 1964, pp. 17, 18.

The contacts that develop on the basis of this complex of links are sometimes intricate. For example, one of the "working groups" is a Subcommittee on Regional Development — "Subcommittee" of the Permanent Committee for Resource Development which is the interdepartmental group that advises on ARDA work and all aspects of multi-purpose resource development. The Chairman of the Subcommittee, which has a permanent secretary, is Elain Nantel who is Secretary of the Provincial Town Planning Commission. Another member is J. Y. Papineau, Director of Regional Development, Department of Trade and Industry. The Subcommittee initiates proposals for the Economic Council and evaluates regional development work such as the south shore ARDA project. In this way, the Subcommittee provides a link between the Economic Advisory Council, the Committee for Resource Development, the Town Planning Commission, a key regional development agency, and all the on-going rural development work under the auspices of ARDA.

This kind of articulation with Government, at the working level and at the decision-making level, has particular significance for the Council's primary function of advising on economic problems and preparing an economic plan. What it apparently means is that the Council will eventually produce a plan that will build in the contributions of the specialized departments of government, and because of their involvement, will stand a greater chance of receiving the sympathetic cooperation of the departments in the implementation of the plan. What this can mean for the quality of the plan is indicated in a recent paper by Raymond Gagné of the Quebec Bureau of Statistics.

Mr. Gagné has indicated that one of the principal reasons for the extension of the role of the Bureau is "the initiative the Government of Quebec has taken towards economic planning", and he goes on to relate the specific statistical projects this will require, including a system of Quebec accounts, to supplement the Canadian accounts, that "will enable us to study Quebec's reactions to certain changes in our export markets and to the state of the "balance of payments" between our economy and that of the outside world, i.e., the rest of Canada and foreign countries . . . to show the degree of integration of certain industries into our economy . . . to gauge the impact of financial investments made by various governments in Quebec . . . to analyse the direct and indirect effects of newly established industries and the results of demographic expansion". The significance of this kind of service to the Economic Advisory Council does not need to be laboured.[15]

One can anticipate some of the beneficial effects of this kind of integrated planning. Presumably, it should be possible to place the provincial regional development program (which is the responsibility of the Department of Trade and Industry), and aid to areas of stress in the context of a long range program of public investment, that balances costs and benefits and indicates regional priorities.

This may, in fact, be assuming too much. The author is frankly not certain whether the "economic model" that the Council will prepare is confined to industrial sectors, or whether it will extend to the spatial structure as well. On this point, the observations of the Austrian, Walter Stohr, merit some consideration:

---

[15]Gagné, Raymond, "The Quebec Bureau of Statistics, Its Function and Its Future", *Canadian Political Science Association, 1964 Conference of Statistics*, p. 12.

"For each (development) strategy, there will have to be a set of economic (sec-toral) and spatial goals, the latter referring primarily to the distribution of regional centres and their functions, the location of the main arteries, the pattern of agri-cultural and recreational areas, and so forth. The two aspects of economic and spatial structures are closely interwoven."[16]

There is one further feature of the Quebec program that is of interest for its contribution to the technique of administering and developing frontier regions. This is the establishment in the Department of Natural Resources of the office of the Director General of Quebec North (in the person of Mr. Eric Gourdeau), and the concentration in that office of jurisdiction for all necessary government func-tions, with the exception of justice. While policy and decision-making, backed up by the requisite senior professional help, is the role of Quebec North, the facilities of the established departments, e.g., health, highways, education, etc., are available to carry out policy. Thus with a bold stroke, the Government has overcome the dilemma of attempting to develop a region through a multiplicity of agencies, and has prepared the way for a highly coordinated and focussed administration of the North.

This paper has postulated that the Quebec-type of province will be pre-occupied in its program with direct economic issues, and will minimize environ-mental problems. There appears to be some reflection of this in the recent public letter of fourteen priests in Montreal on the housing conditions of their parishes, which provoked the comment from Le Devoir that housing was "the great forgotten problem in the quiet revolution", and from Mr. Laporte, the Minister of Muni-cipal Affairs, that "in four years we have done a lot in many fields, in some up to a revolution — like in education. Now we are opening this area, and within a few years, you will see the result."[17]

Quebec's experiment in economic planning appears to be firmly rooted. To the general conditions that lead to an integrated, provincially-oriented approach, is added the effect of French Canadian nationalist feeling. It has been observed that nationalist sentiment bolsters economic planning because many in Quebec see it as a way of obtaining greater French Canadian participation in the economy of Quebec.

VI

The case of Newfoundland merits some separate, if brief, comment because of its unique development problem. The point of special interest is that it joined Confederation at an economic level that is associated with semi-colonial status, and within 15 years has made substantial progress. Perhaps, a single symbolic statistic will indicate the breadth of the change — in 15 years 550 new schools have been built. The technique and program that fostered such change is of more than passing interest.[18]

Newfoundland shares with other provinces striving to close the economic gap, a propensity for a strong, highly integrated, provincially-guided effort. This has been present, not so much in the shape of a formal system, but, principally, in the person of Premier Smallwood, who as Prime Minister and Minister of Economic

---

[16]Stohr, Walter, "Development Planning for Depressed Areas: A Methodological Approach", *Journal of the American Institute of Planners*, 1964, p. 127.

[17]Lamarche, Guy, "Slum Clearance Neglected", *The Globe and Mail*, January 9, 1965, p. 8.

[18]*The Financial Post*, June 20, 1964, p. 53.

Development has, in his economic role, been the Kemal Ataturk or Munoz Marin of Newfoundland.

Progress, however, has not been accomplished without a program of some substance. In response to a request of Professor Thoman on the author's behalf, an outline of the Newfoundland program for "areas of economic stress" has been received from Mr. Arthur Johnson, Deputy Minister of Economic Development. It presents the Newfoundland approach with a lucidity, penetration, and grace that would be difficult to match: "I am taking the liberty of defining these areas (areas of economic stress) in the Province of Newfoundland — along the following lines: Income, Education and Opportunities. In applying these guidelines to Newfoundland, we may show these areas of lagging potential as areas devoid of opportunities and with a low per capita income and level of education. In Newfoundland those areas coincide and require intensive governmental or other assistance to overcome an economic and social inertia which is the result of a centuries old reliance on a primary product — Fish!

"Without going into a long and detailed history of Newfoundland, I feel a short reference should be made to the very important part history has played in establishing these areas of economic stress.

"The settlement of Newfoundland has followed a well-defined and historic pattern. Small boats and primitive fishing methods forced settlement close to a productive fishing ground, while the limited range of small homemade craft limited the population to the level which production of the available fishing grounds would support. This resulted in the surplus population establishing other small communities. The result is that today Newfoundland has a large number of small, poor communities — approximately 1,100 — incapable of providing an acceptable level of subsistence for their inhabitants.

"The basic industry of these communities has been the catching, processing by salting and drying, and marketing of fish. This was carried out by family groups and created a demand for strong backs and busy hands. As a result, education became a luxury few could afford or utilize. Children received training in their father's fishing boats and passed their skill on to their sons.

"It is apparent that with a community depending on an uncontrollable source of raw material for its existence and with a low or non-educated population, trained in a single trade, opportunities for progress were not forthcoming and these communities fell into an economic and social way of life that has changed little since they were first settled. The areas of Newfoundland and Labrador in which these communities are located are, of course, the coastal areas of the Province. These areas are considered by us to be our areas of economic stress and lagging potential.

"Basically, any program to assist these areas must have three approaches — geographic, social and economic and be designed to overcome many years of stagnation. In other words, we must provide a leap into this century. In such a situation any programme of government, from building roads to the provision of health services affects these areas. Therefore, I am assuming that you are concerned with programmes designed by the province to upgrade the level of education, to develop and adjust resources, to increase income and any other project related to the overall object of assistance to these areas."[19]

---

[19]Letter from Mr. Arthur Johnson, Deputy Minister, Department of Economic Development, St. John's, December 29, 1964.

The appendix to this paper presents Mr. Johnson's detailed outline of the Newfoundland Program in terms of Research, Development and Adjustment of Resources, and Education.

VII

In conclusion, the author wishes to raise as a question, the implications of an enhanced provincial role in economic development for national economic policies. Only recently we were reminded by the Economic Council of Canada of some of the staggering challenges that face the entire country. And we can probably deduce from the moves of Alberta and New Brunswick to establish alliances with their neighbours in broad economic regions that at least some of the provinces have a desire for some economic "lebensraum".

There is a manifest need, for everyone's sake, to work out the theory and practice of Federal-Provincial relations on economic development policies. There have been some interesting forays into this field. It has perhaps been overlooked that within the smoke of the Coyne affair, there was a proposal, in a statement on *The Requirements of Economic Policy Today,* for a national regional development program. Mr. Coyne put forward three propositions: (1) that to ensure greater uniformity in rates of economic development in the various regions of Canada, concrete measures are required to stimulate regional development; (2) that a relatively small number of industrial establishments could transform the regional economy of the Atlantic and Prairie areas, diversify their employment opportunities, and provide them with the economic base for approximating the central Canadian level of government services; and (3) that this could best be achieved by setting up a special department of government, public corporation, or board, at the Federal level, that would study problems of regional development and make recommendations, to be implemented at the appropriate level, for stimulating economic activity in the lagging regions of this country.

More recently, Professor T. Wilson in his work for the Atlantic Provinces Research Board has sought to demonstrate that "regional policies need not be regarded as simply an extravagant extension of the welfare state, but rather as part of a national policy aimed at greater prosperity and a faster rate of growth". And he has set out the proposition that financial aids and incentives to regions within provinces can be reconciled with national goals if such aid is focussed on growth centres — centres which can, on the basis of sound analysis, be expected to respond to external inputs.

Before we can expect consistently sensible policies on this question, we need some common theoretical and philosophical ground. Paradoxically, the author finds inspiration on this matter from the South — in the work of the sociologist, Howard Odum, who developed a concept of regionalism which sought to make the nation strong by the cultivation and integration of its diverse regions.[20]

There are some highly suggestive and germinal ideas in Odum's approach, for Canadians. As a person who identified himself with the South, he saw planning at the regional level, as a means of integrating the Region into the Nation, permitting it to digest the benefits of advanced technology, without destroying the positive things in its heritage — and reducing the country to homogenized uniformity. Regional planning, for him, becomes a device to preserve "folk culture", the

[20]Odum, Howard W. and Harry Estill Moore, *American Regionalism,* New York, Henry Holt and Company, 1938.

traditional social and moral order, against the onslaught of "state civilization", the advancing technological order, while people in their own way move ahead towards the satisfaction of their basic needs. In a sense, he anticipated Galbraith's "quality of life" by a generation, but sees its attainment through a national structure of regional planning that articulates goals and programs, and gradually reduces the tensions that arise from excessive regional disparities. The relevance of this approach for us who have regional differences that we wish to preserve, and others to reduce, will hopefully, not be lost.

APPENDIX

A Program for Areas of Economic Stress, Newfoundland

DEVELOPMENT AND ADJUSTMENT OF RESOURCES

PROJECT	DETAILS	AGENCY
I Subsidized Land Clearing	Program commenced operations 1949. From that date to end of operations 1964, 13083 acres of land have been cleared and brought into production. The province pays a grant of $125.00 per acre, with a yearly limit of 5 acres per person. The object is twofold, to reduce the imports of farm products and to supply alternate means of livelihood.	Federal-Provincial (ARDA) (Department of Mines, Agriculture & Resources)
II Public Pasture Development	Program commenced operations 1958. From that date to end of operations 1964, two pastures have been developed: (1) Bay Roberts 700 acres and (2) Goulds 2500 acres. The object is as in I above.	Federal-Provincial (Department of Mines, Agriculture & Resources)
III Bogland Reclamation	Program commenced operations 1956. From that date to end of operations 1964, 2480 acres have been reclaimed. The object is as I and II above. Cost varies between $135.00 and $165.00 per acre depending on use of reclaimed land. Grant of $125.00 in I above may be applied.	Federal-Provincial (Department of Mines, Agriculture & Resources)
IV Recreation (Public Parks)	Development of public parks and wilderness areas to attract tourists to low potential areas. To date two wilderness areas have been established and 20 sites reserved for provincial parks. Main obstacle — funds.	Province (Department of Mines, Agriculture & Resources)

PROJECT	DETAILS	AGENCY
V Wildlife Management	To maintain existing stocks of wild-life and to introduce new species to supply meat, hides and employment as guides. To date new species of game birds and trial herd of buffalo have been introduced. Other species such as elk are under investigation. Main obstacle — time involved.	Province (Department of Mines, Agriculture & Resources)
VI Community Fishing Stages	To provide modern working areas and facilities for the handling of fish. To date 42 units have been completed and another 14 are under construction. Each community stage consists of building with fish handling facilities and a boat unloading area. Average cost is aproximately $50,000.00 per unit. Object of the program is to improve the quality and reduce the cost of processing fish.	Federal-Provincial (Department of Fisheries)
VII Sales Tax Exemptions	All fishing equipment and fuel purchased for the operation of the fishery in Newfoundland is exempt from the provincial sales tax of 5 per cent. Object is to reduce cost of production.	Province (Department of Finance)
VIII Special Financial Assistance	(1) $160.00 per ton for construction of larger boats. (2) Synthetic gill nets, fish traps, smaller boats (24-35 feet). (3) 50 per cent of cost of synthetic nets, etc. (4) $50.00 towards the cost of water pumps. Object is the improvement of fishing gear.	Province (Department of Fisheries)
IX New Methods and Equipment	(1) Commercial high speed room fish dryer. (2) Synthetic gill nets, fish traps, trawls. (3) The development of a gill netting boat. (4) Power gill net heads drum haulers. (5) Investigation of Porbeagle shark fishery. (6) Synthetic materials for cod trap construction. (7) The modification of small boats for dragging operations. (8) The exploitation of fish resources on rough sea bottoms. (9) The location of concentrations of off-shore bait fish.	Federal-Provincial Industry Federal-Provincial (Department of Fisheries)

PROJECT	DETAILS	AGENCY
	(10) Modern methods of seining herring. Object is the improvement of the general fishery.	

EDUCATION

PROJECT	DETAILS	AGENCY
I Regional High Schools	To provide high school education for an area which otherwise may find it difficult to support a large efficient high school. High schools are located in key areas and transportation supplied by a school bus system, to small communities in the general area.	Province (Department of Education)
II Regional Trades Schools	To provide training in various trades. To reduce the dependability on fishery training provided in the fishing boats. To provide trained personnel to any new industry as may be introduced. Trades schools are located in Port aux Basques, Stephenville Crossing, Corner Brook, Grand Falls, Lewisporte, Gander, Burin, Clarenville, Carbonear, Seal Cove and St. John's. Although a number of these schools are located outside of an area which may be classified as depressed or of lagging potential, they are so situated to provide service to pockets of economic stress.	Federal-Provincial (Department of Education, Province)
III College of Trades and Technology, St. John's	To provide higher education to those graduates of trades schools and specialized training for high school graduates.	Federal-Provincial (Department of Education, Province)
IV College of Fisheries, St. John's	To provide training in modern methods of fishing to young Newfoundlanders who choose a career in fishing.	Federal-Provincial (Department of Economic Development, Province)
V University Extension, St. John's	Television program "Decks Awash" to provide information directly to the fisherman on new methods and equipment used in the fisheries.	Provincial (Memorial University of Newfoundland)

OTHER

PROJECT	DETAILS	AGENCY
I Research	(1) Investigation into livestock production throughout island. (2) Investigation into the place of agriculture in Newfoundland. (3) Investigation into Recreational Resources Study. (4) Potential forest resources adjacent to rural settlements. (5) Investigation into blueberry grounds, potential and marketing.	Federal-Provincial (ARDA) (Department of Economic Development)

PROJECT	DETAILS	AGENCY
	(6) Investigation into the sociological background of an agricultural, fishing, logging community.	
	(7) Investigation into establishing criteria for growth potentials of settlements.	
	(8) Investigation into means of increasing employment in small settlements.	
	(9) Investigation into market structure for products produced by rural communities.	
	(10) Investigation into rural development in other countries by visits of investigating teams.	
	(11) Investigation into processing and marketing of special foods.	
	(12) Investigation into the geographical, social and economical factors of the NW coast of Newfoundland.	
	(13) Investigation into the establishing of two parks in Bonavista North.	
	(14) Investigation into the conditions of population centralization.	
II Centralization	To reduce the number of small settlements the province offers a grant of $600.00 per family to assist in relocating in other larger communities with better facilities and prospects. The grant is only payable if all the families of a settlement express their intentions of moving and sign a petition to this effect. Approximately 100 communities have ceased to exist as a result of this program.	Province (Department of Welfare)

ACKNOWLEDGEMENTS

In the course of preparing this paper, the author had the opportunity to discuss the issues of provincial development policies with Mr. W. G. R. Cameron, Senior Economist, Department of Economics and Development, Province of Ontario; Mr. Michel Belanger, Assistant Deputy Minister, Department of Natural Resources, Province of Quebec; Mr. Eric Gourdeau, Director General of Quebec North; Mr. Jean Yves Papineau, Director of Regional Development Branch, Ministry of Industry and Commerce, Province of Quebec; Mr. H. Aaland, Secretary, ARDA, Province of New Brunswick; and Miss Z. Linkletter, Director, Economic Services Division, Department of Trade and Industry, Government of Nova Scotia.

The author wishes to express his appreciation for their most generous giving of time and thoughtful consideration.

COMMENTS

Professor Pierre Harvey,
Ecoles des Hautes Etudes Commerciales.

There is not much to challenge in the broad analysis presented by Mr. Gertler of the major forces underlying provincial preoccupation with economic develop- ment, variations in approach and relationship between provincial actions and national growth policies. Due to the fact that Mr. Gertler's contribution is mainly of a descriptive character, and had to be so for reasons stated by the author, the following remarks will be limited to emphasizing the motivation of provincial choices and actions, from the point of view of Quebec.

When Mr. Gertler considers that Quebec, Manitoba, Saskatchewan and the Atlantic provinces all have an integrated provincially-oriented approach to develop- ment policies, due to an emphasis put on reducing inter-provincial differences of economic performance, the classification of provinces is right and the motivation of the type of approach chosen is well justified. But I wonder, in order to grasp the true set of motivations of the stand taken by Quebec, if it is not necessary to look a little beyond the author's broad statement. This can be quickly achieved. First, let us look back to the post-war history of Canadian economic policy.

One can admit, I think, that when, during and after the last war, it was decided, at the Federal level, to give this country an active economic policy, the problems of growth were not of major concern. Economic stagnation was con- sidered a possibility which was to be taken care off mainly by a systematic policy of low rates of interest. Positive public action relied on a permanent process of income re-distribution geared to a short-run budgetary policy. Problems of struc- ture were given scant interest and a continuous process of effective allocation of resources would be achieved by factors mobility. There was thus, by and large, an agreement to pursue a policy for economic change in no particular setting. At the time, almost alone, the late Prof. Harold Adam Innis had underscored in rather strong language the contrast between a national policy and a national activity which were not so closely integrated as one might have been led to believe. He wrote then — in substance — that if it were not closely geared to the regional structure of the Canadian economy, full employment would "become a racket on the part of the central provinces for getting and keeping what they can".[1]

As the years passed by it became clear, however, that what Prof. Innis had considered a racket seemed to be working to the main advantage of only one part of central Canada. For in Quebec, even during periods of national full employ- ment, the monthly provincial rates of unemployment always remained higher than national ones, the relative gap being wider in periods of high level of national economy activity. Long before Quebec could itself reach what might have been considered full employment, in Ontario, by contrast, the provincial economy was already in a state of over-full-employment, draining manpower from other prov- inces and even from abroad. But, at the same time, despite similitude in struc- tures, and due to well known differences in culture, the adjoining Quebec economy could never take advantage of the high level of labour demand in Ontario to get rid of what might be considered a persistent excess supply of labour. It was under-

---

[1] Innis, H. A., "Decentralization and Democracy", *Canadian Journal of Economics and Political Science,* August 1943, p. 329.

lined more than ten years ago that problems of a structural character would have to be taken care of, sooner or later, problems of a much wider importance than what is covered by the traditional concept of the depressed area.

Before going further it is necessary, however, to comment briefly on the very notion of structural problems, with reference to regions here defined in terms of provinces or groups of provinces. I am not inferring in the preceding remarks that if one defines structures in terms of industrial sectors considered across Canada, there is a difference of reaction of employment by sectors in the different regions to the ups and downs of national effective demand. What I mean is that the permanence of regional structure, and the continuity of reactions of sectors to the fluctuations of the National Product, act to maintain differences in inter-regional levels of employment, whatever may be the state of the national economy as a whole.

Mr. Gertler makes reference in his paper to the incidence on provincial employment of the primary industries. In the case of Quebec, this question can be taken as an example of what can be called structural difficulties, in the broad sense of the words. If one considers the Quebec economy outside Montreal, the weight of primary activities appears quite important. These industries have particularities of their own. First, they grow by marked steps: during periods of expansion, they give rise to a strong demand for primary labour, but on a temporary basis only; the labour content of the production proper is much less important, and, after the end of the construction, the local rate of unemployment will necessarily be very high even if the national economy maintains its rate of activity. The high labour demand generated by the building phase of those primary projects, on the other hand, seems to be satisfied, in part, by workers from outside the region itself, but also by local rural populations among which disguised unemployment can be considered an endemic. The main effect of the *sporadic* development of primary industries is then a discontinuous transformation of disguised unemployment in more or less chronic open unemployment, as far, at least, as these workers show a very low rate of inter-regional mobility. On the other hand, the employment policies of the companies engaged in the exploitation of natural resources seem to have resulted, in the past, in an accelerated obsolescence of the local labour force with, among other consequences, a high proportion of permanent unemployment. In such a situation, there is little interest in the classical distinction between cyclical and structural unemployment and the public policies cannot avoid a structural character.

But, even if all this was already well known more than ten years ago, one had to wait till 1958, as far as I know, to read the first mentions of it in a post-war Federal document.[2] The statement which I am referring to was signed by a man named James Coyne: it is no surprise that it was later lost in the turmoil of subsequent battles. I submit that, for Quebec at least, the quasi-global character of the provincial problem on the one hand, and on the other, the combination of a strictly short-run national economic policy with a completely liberal attitude towards the design of the structures are the first explanations of the approach chosen by that province. *At the time*, for best or for worst, it seems that the central government missed a very important bus. The government of Quebec, however, was

---

[2] Bank of Canada, Annual report for the year 1957, Feb. 1958, p. 19.

not itself too alert in filling the gap in economic policy. However, the ground was prepared for a later rooting of a provincially biased planning policy referred to in Mr. Gertler's paper.

Mr. Gertler also mentions the factor of nationalism. This is another factor related to the motivation of Quebec's approach to economic development. Some might be inclined to dismiss that factor as being outside the realm of economics. But, when one considers economic policy rather than clear cut concepts of a theoretical character, the *"ceteris paribus"* formula becomes quite misleading. In the case of the French Canadians, the alternative to unemployment cannot be migration to extra provincial growth points. They are fated to progress inside the Province or accept assimilation. In such a context, national feelings will necessarily make a come-back from the cold outside world of the *"ceteris paribus"* to the heart of strictly economic problems.

The average person in Quebec has been, for a long time, well aware of the small importance of his contribution to the management of the provincial economic life. He has also long been told by his leaders that with hard work and skill the small business he had always controlled would eventually grow bigger and bigger and widen the economic power of the inhabitant of the Province allowing him to reach higher economic-social standing. The young generations, however, seem to have lost faith in such a process as a means to achieve status and power. They seem to be more inclined now to believe that in this modern economic world, he who is born big will stay so, but the small fry will never have his chance to catch up with the bigger brother. Therefore, they tend to turn to the one big power they feel they can control, the provincial government, which they invest with the task of promoting economic growth. The problem of power and status being then of prime importance, the approach has to be of the integrated type with a leftist flavour not to be minimized.

But, in order to draft an effective policy either against persistent unemployment or towards national economic power, the Quebec administration had to rely mainly upon young technical personnel without any previous experience in the tasks to be performed. This made it necessary to find, somewhere, a tested model to follow more or less closely. One can understand that the French experience in economic planning had then the character of an inescapable choice. French planning, prior to the fourth plan, having been strongly centralized in approach, its Quebec counterpart, or imitation, could not avoid being so. This leaning towards the French experience was not, however, without short-comings: a province is not a fully integrated economy and, anyway, prevailing conditions could not be the same in Quebec and France. Radical adjustments had to be made to the model. These adjustments having not always been made, Quebec seemed, for a time at least, to be trying to plan in what one could only say was a foreign setting. This resulted in loss of time and many frustrations. It is now the task of the newly appointed director of planning to start all over again, on sounder basis.

Now, what about policies concerning the so-called depressed areas? I think that Mr. Gertler's paper has been quite generous in the description given of regional actions undertaken by the Quebec provincial government. Regional studies are still few and effective action almost non-existent, up to now. It is not impossible, however, to understand such a state of affairs. First, reliable data, at the regional level, is scanty. When it is available, it is often the product and *property* of Federal agencies, whose cooperation, till very recent times, was less than might be desired. The Provincial Bureau of Statistics has still to establish an effective system for information that could be considered workable at the regional level. Anyhow, it is conceivable, that the provincial approach to development being of the integrated type, regional analysis and policy runs the risk of being left behind, at least during the first phases of the new experience undertaken. One can consider too that the Federal action in favour of depressed areas has been a source of uneasiness for provincial regional planners. The areas selected by the Federal agencies are not exactly the ones that would have been selected as the first by an integrated plan. Their limits are, most of the time, fixed by administrative practice. But, due to Federal-Provincial agreements, and problems of fiscal administration, the provincial government is more or less forced to follow the leader and, perhaps, not without some loss of scarce resources, and often at the cost of a confusion of objectives.

COMMENTS

W. Hugh Flynn,
Ontario General Manager,
Canadian Industries Limited.

My assignment is to give an industry viewpoint on what has been said, but, as I am an accountant, by training, you will appreciate that my personal capsule comments will be more in the financial area than geographic or economic.

I was particularly interested in Professor Pleva's concern about county and regional development. This of course fits in with Mr. Gertler's description of the regional areas organized in the Province of Ontario. You may, therefore, be interested in a submission made to the Ontario Committee on Taxation by the Ontario Division of the Canadian Manufacturers' Association. This deals with only one aspect of the problem: namely, the need to reorganize the administrative units in that Province. I am using Ontario merely as an example but no doubt the situation applies elsewhere. In part, this said:

"Local governments form the roots of democracy. We must nourish and protect these roots. Therefore, local residents through local councils, etc., should, broadly speaking, make local decisions about local problems.

"Unfortunately, the multiplicity of municipal governments and school boards hampers both the efficiency and effectiveness of carrying out the wishes of the local residents. Geographically, most of Ontario was frozen into a pattern of counties, districts, townships, towns, villages and cities many years ago. Politically, the interrelationship between these units (with exception of districts and cities) was established about a hundred years ago. Economically, this province has undergone a complete change in the past hundred years. We feel that it is now time for geography and politics to be brought into line with economics. Boundary lines should be changed, the continued existence of some units should be questioned, the political interrelationship should be re-examined.

"We envisage a redrafting of municipal boundary lines and political interrelationships to incorporate the following views and philosophy.

1. Urban problems should be dealt with by urban councils — rural problems by rural councils.

2. Counties as combinations of urban and rural municipalities should be dissolved.

3. The basic rural unit should be the county. The township as a political unit should be abolished.

4. County boundary lines should be redrawn so that they reflect the relationship between the rural districts and the urban centres where rural people obtain so many of their commercial goods and services.

5. The boundary lines for municipal and school units should be made conterminous.

6. Areas of counties adjacent to urban centres should be designated as "Development Areas" in successive stages. As the density of urban use reached 65% in each area it should automatically be annexed to the urban centre.

7. The kind of program suggested by (6) will require regional planning. Therefore, we recommend the establishment of Regional Planning Boards embracing one or more reorganized counties and all the cities, towns and villages within their boundary or boundaries.

"The end result would be to reduce the 979 municipalities and over 3,500 school boards to approximately 300 of each. We believe that this number is adequate to protect both 'grass roots' democracy and local autonomy. At the same time it will afford the local residents a more effective and efficient form of government."

Professor Pleva has drawn a distinction between aid and what businessmen have come to regard as incentives and he stresses the point that economic aid for development or redevelopment should have a separate category in the budget. Provision has, I believe, been made in Ontario budgets for such things as the development agency and other activities promoted by the Department of Economics and Development, though I doubt if the exact cost is anywhere shown separately. As far as the federal government is concerned, for some years annual budgets have made provision for incentives of one kind or another by way of changes in the Income Tax Act. Until recently such measures were either on an all-embracing basis or applied to certain industries such as mining or for defence purposes. More recently, however, such incentives were provided on the basis of designated areas where unemployment was acute. Thus we find the federal government becoming involved in regional as well as national development. It is not clear yet as to how beneficial these area incentives have been in promoting employment in the areas affected but I think a word of caution might be introduced at this point to suggest that great care must be taken to see that uneconomic enterprises are not fostered by such incentives. Generally speaking, as long as we rely on prices to allocate resources and depend on the profit motive, greater all-round benefits will be obtained by lower tax rates than can be achieved by discriminatory subsidies.

Mr. Gertler has given us a very clear picture of the different approaches being taken by the provinces in promoting regional development — Ontario being more concerned with disparaties between regions in the province, while Quebec is more concerned with that province's over all achievements compared with the rest of Canada. In both cases, however, the emphasis is on centralized planning or direction from the provincial capitals. Is there not a certain anomaly here, as all provinces have been endeavouring to take more authority and money into their own hands opposite the federal government? While much of necessity has to be the responsibility of provincial governments, it seems to me that, in this gradual transfer of authority and money raising capacity from the federal government to provincial governments, we are liable to end up in a balkanized country with even less ability to manage fiscal and monetary affairs than we have had up to now. Admittedly, of late, there does seem to be a better chance of obtaining the cooperation of federal and provincial authorities in these matters but unless firm and decisive steps can be taken at the federal level to achieve a truer national objective, all regional planning and development may prove futile.

The first report of the Economic Council of Canada emphasizes the serious-ness of the task ahead of all of us to provide jobs for the large numbers coming into the labour force in the next few years. Unquestionably manufacturing indus-tries will have to play an important part in providing these jobs. At the present time manufacturing accounts directly for 25% of the employed population and indirectly supports large numbers in the service industries. The numbers employed in agriculture have been reduced sharply in recent years and this trend can be expected to continue, as Mr. Gertler has pointed out by using Prince Edward Island as an example. Resource industries, too, are not expected to give more opportunities for employment due to higher mechanization; automation, of course, also faces the manufacturing industries.

This brings me to one area of economic stress which I think is not receiving the recognition it should by the general public. That is the need for reviewing and revising our educational facilities to prepare the coming generation for the new types of work that will be available. This aspect is receiving attention from the federal government through grants to build technical schools, etc., and in par-ticular the problem is being actively tackled by the Ontario government.

Regardless of all this, however, if we expect the manufacturing industries to provide the required jobs over the next five years, there must be a suitable business climate within which they can operate. Vast sums of money will be required to provide the physical facilities to enable us to achieve the goals set out by the Economic Council. Much of course will unquestionably have to come from abroad, but whether from abroad or at home these investments will only be made if there is a reasonable chance of obtaining an adequate rate of return for the risks taken. This depends, as I mentioned, on the business climate and some assurance that governments will not so increase costs as to make our industries non-competi-tive at home or abroad. A very real economic stress can be created by costing us out of business.

In the recently completed automobile agreement between Canada and the United States we may have a precedent for similar measures affecting other indus-tries and other areas of the country. Whether this will really work to our benefit remains to be seen. However, if successful it may open up the way to solving one of Canada's basic problems — the difficulty of justifying economic-sized, low-cost production units on the basis of our comparatively small domestic market. With-out such facilities Canada is at a disadvantage in penetrating world markets as well as meeting foreign competition in the home market.

Without detracting in any way from the regional development programs being undertaken by the provinces, it is clear that full measure of success can only be achieved if appropriate measures to deal with some of our basic problems are taken at the federal level.

COMMENTS

Stanley A. Little,
President, Canadian Union of Public
Employees and Vice-President,
Canadian Labour Congress.

In taking part in the general discussion of this Conference with special emphasis on the two papers presented by Professor Pleva and Mr. Gertler, I wish to join many of the preceding speakers in expressing appreciation to the organizers of this Conference on Areas of Economic Stress in Canada for making this meeting possible.

As a labour representative I intend to comment on some aspects of the two papers in the hope that it may be of help to the Conference to understand our side of the story. I also accept with pleasure the invitation of Professor Thoman to make a few observations clarifying the role of labour in economic development and our rules of interpretation of the five famous economic goals listed in the First Annual Review of the Economic Council of Canada.

I

First Things First

I found that both papers presented this afternoon deal basically with the same regional approach to problems of economic stress. Purely from a rational point of view I am going to formulate the bulk of my remarks to have general application.

It is impossible to treat all the aspects of Professor Pleva's paper. To be honest, when I first read that the Head of the Department of Geography was to speak, I imagined rather naively that he would come with a huge map of Canada and lecture about terribly complicated theories of geophysical, geotechnical, geopolitical sciences, plus geognosy, geotropy and geopony. I thought that he would show us how these theories are interrelated in finding solutions to our question of areas of economic stress in Canada. I somehow expected to learn why, for instance, the Ottawa Valley is a relatively depressed area while the Grank Trunk Corridor from Quebec to Windsor, mentioned in the paper, is quite prosperous.

I agree with Professor Pleva that "geographers are skillful in dealing with the regional concept and are able to contribute significantly to this phase of plan and development".

However, I realize now that this sort of paper would cover a much larger territory than we can cope with today; it would require an extensive, time- and money-consuming research project.

Similarity of Problems

Both documents contain useful information on past achievements and the present situation and suggestions for future action in order to obtain the results we all expect. The events of the last week — and I am referring to the First Annual Review of the Economic Council of Canada — do not detract from the interest of these documents.

In spite of the fact that Professor Pleva deals in a rather limited way only with the regional problems in Ontario, we can draw reasonable conclusions that the problem is basically the same in other provinces; namely, that the county governments are too small and too great in number to provide a standard of good quality of public services across the province. Last year the Government of New Brunswick published the findings of the New Brunswick Royal Commission on Finance and Taxation. The Report, known as the Byrne Report, reveals that there is a need for changes in the structure of local government. This applies to both rural and urban types of municipalities. The physical capacity of local authorities should be strengthened. This involves an impartial scrutiny of the tax base, a study of the incidence of property tax, a search for a revenue other than property taxes to finance the cost of social services, a practical means of establish- ing reserves, particularly those in the form of revolving capital funds, and a clear control of receivables to minimize losses. In addition, there should be a sound approach to planned spending in order to maintain solvency and to put the tax dollar to the best possible use. The motto of the Byrne Report is essentially: "Centralize to Equalize". The centralizing authority would be the Province.

It is my opinion that the reasonings of the Royal Commission are quite sound. The Commission did a creditable job, except for one thing. Labour was bypassed and almost completely ignored. When this was drawn to the attention of Professor Boudreau, one of the authors of the Report, he recognized our criticism but minimized the danger by saying that they "knew labour could take care of themselves and defend their interests". This re-affirmed our belief in the need for one's own research and reasoning.

Stumbling Blocks in Cooperation

While on the subject of Eastern Canada problems I wish to touch on a case in another eastern province. Mr. Gertler's paper is well documented and he has certainly spent a lot of time talking to influential people in key positions. A pity he did not discuss also certain difficulties with labour, especially in Newfoundland.

I do not like to draw a gloomy picture, but I would be guilty of negligence by omission if I did not tell you that the economic prosperity of Newfoundland is crippled by Premier Smallwood's anti-union laws.

There are at least a dozen sections of the labour legislation passed since 1958 which the unions find objectionable. There are restrictive provisions of law setting down a lengthy list of conditions a union must fulfill in order to be tolerated by the government.

This sort of relation between government and organized labour definitely does not contribute to industrial peace and economic growth. Under the magic spell of the First Annual Review I see every successful project as a tripartite under- taking. This is a condition *sine qua non*.

"But First of All"

They told us in high school that one Roman senator, Cato was his name, used to have a habit of ending every speech, regardless of the subject, with the sentence, "But first of all, we have to get rid of Carthage." Our "but first of all" must be to get rid of any vicious anti-labour legislation such as Section 89 of the Ontario Labour Relations Act, which violates national and international labour standards, or other restrictive and oppressive legislation in Newfoundland, etc.

Three-way cooperation between government, industry and labour, which is the very foundation of the economic well-being of our country, must not be based on suspicion and mutual distrust. We must have imaginative cooperation between labour, management and government. None of the three parties should be afraid to make new efforts and use new techniques to accomplish this.

Aid for the Needy Ones

An interesting observation is made in both papers in connection with pockets of poverty in Canada and about governmental policy through "ARDA" (Agriculture Rehabilitation Development Act). The Federal Act was passed in 1961 and the enterprise has been in operation since January, 1963. ARDA, I would say, is a peculiar Canadian creation. There is not much noise about its activities. As a matter of fact, most people connect the Agency vaguely with soil conservation and drainage schemes. ARDA is the product of two federal administrations (Agriculture and Forestry) and the ten provinces and cuts, for instance, across almost every provincial department at Queen's Park in Ontario. Its task is to reclaim people and land. ARDA hopes to devise new and better uses for the land and to persuade the people to accept them. I understand that they need qualified workers, men experienced in agriculture, forestry, economic geography, industry and sociology. Besides the federal branch, all provinces have ARDA administration and all proposals must come from the provinces. The federal branch sets the ground rules, vetoes unsuitable projects and raises a good part of the cost of the suitable ones.

I think this sort of tool of governmental policy helping the areas of economic stress is much better than another important Act. I am referring to the *Emergency Gold Mining Assistance Act* which makes it possible for high-cost marginal mines to obtain financial assistance and keep the mines open. However, there is one remark of criticism. "The cost-aid assistance more than compensates for operating losses." In other words, the subsidy is used for substantial dividends. While we have no objection to profit, my point is there is no requirement for renewal or modernization of operating equipment or industry improvement.

The Role of the Economic Council

Last week headlines praised the First Annual Report of the Canadian Economic Council. The Report defines the problems to be faced, the objectives to be set, and requirements of satisfactory economic progress in Canada for the rest of this decade.

From now on public opinion will judge policies and actions of governments, the performance of management and labour by this standard measure of progress and growth that must be achieved by 1970, that is, if the Canadian economy is to absorb the prospective increase in the labour force and maintain a rising standard of living.

Surely the Economic Council of Canada is not engaged in economic planning that would be imposed in the various sectors of the country but intends to develop a consistent and logical set of policy recommendations that would promote the best performance of the economy.

Its goals are to seek a concensus among those responsible for making decisions in business, agriculture, labour and government about the best way of encouraging steady economic growth.

What Do We Endorse?

There should be no doubt about labour's attitude towards the Economic Council of Canada and its First Report. We endorse the Report, and our national economic objectives are practically identical with those in the Report. Unions want full employment. They want full production and the highest possible national income. Unions want a more equitable distribution of national income, as well as the elimination of poverty. What we want also is to stress the effect of government policy on the country's economic performance. We expect that government policy (or a lack of it) in the area of public investment will be carefully evaluated in the succeeding reviews.

For the purpose of clarity, I have to make three or four comments regarding the five economic goals.

A. The target of *"full" employment* in the Report is defined as 3 per cent of unemployment. We accepted this figure only because it may be, under circumstances, realistic, but we cannot accept it as a positive even for the balance of the decade. After all, we believe that if government were to undertake a really aggressive manpower policy there would be no need to accept such a high percentage of unemployment.

B. As far as a high rate of economic growth is concerned, we believe that it cannot be achieved without

1) adequate attention to monetary and fiscal policy,

2) attention to manpower policy,

3) attention to immigration and its effect on wage levels,

4) effective policy of the government.

C. Reasonable *stability of prices* is another goal. Increased wages put pressure on business to improve production techniques, to introduce new machinery and in general to increase productivity. Higher incomes help create higher living standards. My submission is that Canada's income level will determine what kind of economic growth we achieve or whether we fail by the end of 1970. Our economy does not depend entirely on stock ownership, capital investment and profit incentive.

The present tendency of prices and incomes has been caused by the struggle for a share in the result of material progress. It means progress in the techniques of production, transportation and conservation of goods, progress in business organization, in education, in moral feelings and political thinking, in legal institutions, in public health and progress in the field of life and thought. Therefore the argument of "wage inflation" is scientifically inaccurate and whoever wants to use it must examine also other inflation arguments such as "profit inflation", excessive advertising, over-packaging, etc.

D. An *equitable distribution of rising incomes* must be understood in the spirit of Section 9 of the Economic Council of Canada Act which instructs the Council to advise "how Canada can achieve the highest possible levels of employment and efficient production in order that the country may enjoy a high and consistent rate of economic growth and that *all Canadians* may share in rising living standards".

Reference to "equitable sharing" as a distribution of rising income among geographic regions, and not among all individuals, would represent a serious departure from the intention of the Act. Unions' economic policy in the last years advocates:

1) tax reduction of low incomes to stimulate consumers' demand,

2) easier monetary policy,

3) vigorous expansion of the public sector,

4) increased exports to improve balance of payments,

5) economic planning.

Rapid expansion of the labour force has been evidenced since 1963. Its origins lie in the number of post-war babies who are reaching age.

1,500,000 Jobs by 1970

Statistics show that private enterprise in North America provided only a small percentage of the needed new jobs created between 1957 and 1963. The major source of job growth between these years has been in the public sector of the economy. This does not come as a surprise to me. Unlike private business, the public sector feels responsible for the community as a whole. It alone can set out to produce things that are needed the most: homes, schools, universities, public utilities, hospitals, roads, parks, without worrying about profit.

Government-Management-Labour

The logical conclusion is that more than ever before *government* must become the designer and architect of the good society. It must take a positive and dynamic role in planning the economy, in planning jobs and in developing the means for meeting the overwhelming challenges of automation.

This is my interpretation of the First Report of the Economic Council. This is how I, as a labour representative and the President of the Public Employees' Union, understand our problems. Anyone who reads carefully must see that if we do not pull up our socks, to use our language, and roll up our sleeves, and if we do not achieve the probable goals, we are in deep trouble by 1970.

Industry and management have their tremendous role to play. Our business must almost double its traditional imagination; find new ways and means of developing our great resources and by resources I mean the natural and human; find new markets and last but not least introduce new products, something, which I would call typically Canadian. Ladies and Gentlemen, this is not some kind of northern vision; this is a serious matter. It struck as odd that we have not actually any typical finished Canadian product (except the Ookpik) which would give us a certain monopoly in the world.

As far as *labour* is concerned, I can say only that we are ready to share the responsibility. After all, in any highly developed society, the unions must play an important role and share the responsibility. Perhaps the time is here for us in the labour movement to accept this burden in return for equitable sharing in a rising income. Our men and women do not look only for more money; they are prepared to work harder to deserve it. They must only be assured that higher demands would produce higher results and that a change of climate of employer-employee relationship is a change in kind and not merely a difference in degree. In other words, I respectfully submit, what is needed is the introduction of an improved new regime based on collective bargaining which would involve the acceptance by the parties of assumptions that the pre-collective bargaining standards are a world which has ceased to exist and that individual begging is entirely alien to an era of collective bargaining.

In short, labour wants recognition, morally, legally and materially speaking. We do not advocate anarchy in labour relations; just the very opposite. We know that the concept of right in a democratic society is contrasted with the concept of duty. For this reason we say that the union must be ready to prove its character of representative, durable and responsible organization.

More

The whole problem could be summed up in a modified formula of Samuel Gompers. When asked at a Congressional hearing: "What does labour want?", he answered, "More."

Yes, more. Labour should ask for more (that is, more skill, more education, more responsibility, more money).

Management should ask for more (for instance, more imagination, more initiative, more research, more productivity).

Government should ask for more (such as more guidance, more rationalization, more programs of public expansion).

Legislative Dilemma: Centralize or Decentralize

Although not a specific recommendation, a serious thought does occur to me, if perhaps not to some of my fellow counsellors. The trend of Canadian affairs suggests that the time may be opportune to give study to the advisability of some form of legislative changes dealing with adjustments in a constitutional division of powers in labour matters.

Admittedly, one can envisage many objections, but labour marketing, manpower training, etc. would dictate a more authoritative voice for the Federal Government as opposed to the existing approximate 7 per cent in labour jurisdiction. A strong voice of the Federal Government in labour matters may bring about economic betterment.

1965: A Turning Point

My task has been both challenging and difficult. I do not hesitate to repeat the well-known advice of the eminent economist, John Stuart Mill, "When the job is to raise the permanent conditions of a people, small means do not merely produce small effects; they produce no effect at all."

In view of our tremendous task as defined in the First Annual Report of the Economic Council of Canada and problems outlined here, I have to conclude that there is no question that we have entered upon a time which requires a far greater degree of sincere cooperation between labour, management and government than mankind has ever known before.

APPENDIX A
CONFERENCE PROGRAMME

QUEEN'S UNIVERSITY CONFERENCE

on

AREAS OF ECONOMIC STRESS IN CANADA

January 21st and 22nd, 1965

In these times of pronounced difference in rates of economic growth, whether within a specific country or among countries, it is increasingly necessary to study the problems associated with regional economic development. Queen's University is pleased to sponsor this conference as one means of facilitating such study.

An expression of appreciation is cordially extended to the Area Development Agency in the Department of Industry, Ottawa, and to the Department of Economics and Development of the Province of Ontario for financial assistance.

CONFERENCE PLANNING COMMITTEE

Professor Richard S. Thoman, Department of Geography
Professor David W. Slater, Department of Economics
Professor W. Donald Wood, Department of Economics
      and Director, Industrial Relations Centre
Professor Stewart Fyfe, Department of Political Studies

Queen's University

Programme

Thursday, January 21

8:30 a.m. to 9:30 a.m. — Registration   — Main Lobby, Ellis Hall

9:30 a.m. Welcome   — DR. J. A. CORRY, Principal, Queen's University.

THE BASIC PROBLEMS —
IDENTIFICATION

— Chairman:
PROFESSOR RICHARD S. THOMAN,
Department of Geography,
Queen's University.

Areas of Economic Stress in
the Canadian Federal Context

— PROFESSOR JOHN F. GRAHAM,
Head, Department of Economics
and Sociology, Dalhousie University.

First Discussion

— MR. S. E. CHERNICK,
Economic Council of Canada.

Second Discussion

— PROFESSOR ANDRE RAYNAULD,
Département des Sciences
Economiques, Université
de Montréal.

General Discussion

11:15 a.m. Identification of Declining Regions:
An Empirical Study of the Dimensions of Rural Poverty

— PROFESSOR BRIAN J. L. BERRY,
Department of Geography and
Center for Urban Studies,
University of Chicago.

First Discussion

— DR. PIERRE CAMU, Vice-President,
St. Lawrence Seaway Authority.

Second Discussion

— PROFESSOR DONALD KERR,
Department of Geography,
University of Toronto.

General Discussion

2:00 p.m. THE BASIC PROBLEMS —
TREATMENT

— Chairman:
PROFESSOR M. C. URQUHART,
Head, Department of Economics,
Queen's University.

Policy for Declining Regions:
A Theoretical Approach

— PROFESSOR A. D. SCOTT,
Department of Economics,
University of British Columbia
(1964-65, University of Chicago).

First Discussion

— PROFESSOR CLARENCE L.
BARBER,
Department of Economics,
University of Manitoba
(1964-65, McGill University).

Second Discussion

— PROFESSOR K. G. CRAWFORD,
Department of Political Studies,
Queen's University.

General Discussion

3:45 p.m. Growth and the Canadian Economy: The Problem of Regional Disparities   — PROFESSOR T. N. BREWIS, Department of Economics, Carleton University.

First Discussion   — PROFESSOR YVES DUBE, Faculté des Sciences Sociales, Université Laval.

Second Discussion   — DR. W. R. DYMOND, Assistant Deputy Minister, Department of Labour, Ottawa.

General Discussion

6:15 p.m. Reception and Banquet   — LaSalle Hotel.

Chairman: — PROFESSOR W. DONALD WOOD, Department of Economics and Director, Industrial Relations Centre, Queen's University.

Introduction of Speaker: — PROFESSOR J. E. HODGETTS, Head, Department of Political Studies, Queen's University.

Banquet Address — Growth and Stress: Some Historical Notes   — DR. W. A. MACKINTOSH, Vice-Chancellor, Queen's University.

Friday, January 22

9:00 a.m. POLICIES IN THE UNITED STATES AND THE UNITED KINGDOM   — Chairman: PROFESSOR RICHARD I. RUGGLES, Head, Department of Geography, Queen's University.

Federal Redevelopment in the United States: Concept and Practice   — MR. GORDON E. RECKORD, Assistant Administrator for Program Development, U.S. Area Redevelopment Administration.

First Discussion   —- DR. SAR A. LEVITAN, W. E. Upjohn Institute for Employment Research, Washington, D.C.

Second Discussion   —- PROFESSOR MAURICE J. BOOTE, Department of Economics, Trent University.

General Discussion

11:00 a.m. Areas of Economic Stress: The British Case   — PROFESSOR GERALD MANNERS, Department of Geography, University College, Swansea (1964-65, Resources for the Future, Inc., Washington, D.C.).

First Discussion   — DR. E. P. WEEKS, Executive Director, Atlantic Divisional Board.

Second Discussion	— PROFESSOR RICHARD LAWTON, Department of Geography, University of Liverpool (1964-65, University of Southern Illinois, Carbondale).
General Discussion	
2:00 p.m. REGIONAL POLICIES IN CANADA	— Chairman: PROFESSOR STEWART FYFE, Department of Political Studies, Queen's University.
Vital Issues in the Study of Aid	— PROFESSOR EDWARD G. PLEVA, Head, Department of Geography, University of Western Ontario.
Discussion	— PROFESSOR A. L. LEVINE, Department of Economics and Political Science, University of New Brunswick.
3:00 p.m. Development Policies at the Provincial Level	— MR. L. O. GERTLER, Head, Planning Department, H. G. Acres & Company, Limited.
Discussion	— PROFESSOR PIERRE HARVEY, Ecôle des Hautes Etudes Commerciales, Montréal.
Discussion	— MR. W. HUGH FLYNN, Ontario General Manager, Canadian Industries Limited.
Discussion	— MR. STANLEY A. LITTLE, President, Canadian Union of Public Employees and Vice-President, Canadian Labour Congress.
General Discussion	
4:30 p.m. Concluding Remarks and Discussion of Questionnaires	— PROFESSOR RICHARD S. THOMAN, Department of Geography, Queen's University.

APPENDIX B

LIST OF PARTICIPANTS

QUEEN'S CONFERENCE ON AREAS OF ECONOMIC STRESS IN CANADA

January 21 and 22, 1965

Abell, A. S.

Economic Advisor, Program Advisory Group,
Department of Industry,
123 Slater Street,
Ottawa, Ontario.

Abrahamson, G.

A/Head, Projects Section,
Department of Northern Affairs and National Resources,
Kent-Albert Building,
Ottawa 4, Ontario.

Adamson, R. T.

Chief Economist,
Central Mortgage and Housing Corporation,
Ottawa 7, Ontario.

Alaurent, J.

Directeur, Institut d'Urbanisme,
Université de Montréal,
C.P. 6128,
Montréal, P.Q.

Bailey, D. J.

Assistant Director, Labour Division,
Dominion Bureau of Statistics,
Scott Street,
Ottawa, Ontario.

Barber, C. L.

Department of Economics and Political Science,
McGill University,
Montreal, P.Q.

Barnes, A. S. L.

Director, Conservation Authorities Branch,
Ontario Department of Energy and Resources Management,
P.O. Box 358,
Downsview, Ontario.

Bedore, B. V.

Regional Superintendent,
Ontario Department of Tourism and Information,
Arnprior, Ontario.

Bergevin, J. B.
>Assistant Deputy Minister,
>Department of Industry and Commerce,
>Government Buildings,
>Quebec, P.Q.

Bernolak, I.
>Chief Economist, Program Advisory Group,
>Department of Industry,
>123 Slater Street,
>Ottawa 4, Ontario.

Berry, B. J. L.
>Associate Professor,
>Department of Geography and Center for Urban Studies,
>The University of Chicago,
>Chicago 37, Ill.

Boote, M. J.
>Associate Professor, Economics,
>Trent University,
>Peterborough, Ontario.

Borland, H.
>Director of Urban Renewal and Public Housing,
>Central Mortgage and Housing Corporation,
>Head Office, Montreal Road,
>Ottawa, Ontario.

Brewis, T. N.
>Department of Economics,
>Carleton University,
>Ottawa 1, Ontario.

Brownstone, M.
>Associate Professor, Political Economy,
>University of Toronto,
>894 Innswood Drive,
>Ottawa 13, Ontario.

Buck, K.
>Chief, Mineral Resources Division,
>Department of Mines and Technical Surveys,
>588 Booth Street,
>Ottawa, Ontario.

Cameron, W.
>Ontario Department of Economics and Development,
>950 Yonge Street,
>Toronto, Ontario.

Camu, Pierre,
>Vice-President,
>The St. Lawrence Seaway Authority,
>Ottawa, Ontario.

Carol, H.
>   Head, Department of Geography,
>   York University,
>   Toronto, Ontario.

Carver, H. M. S.
>   Chairman, Advisory Group,
>   Central Mortgage and Housing Corporation,
>   Ottawa 7, Ontario.

Chernick, S. E.
>   Economic Council of Canada,
>   Royal Trust Building,
>   116 Albert Street,
>   Ottawa, Ontario.

Clarkson, S. W.
>   Deputy Minister,
>   Ontario Department of Economics and Development,
>   454 University Avenue,
>   Toronto 2, Ontario.

Connor, J.
>   Associate Professor of Economics,
>   Acadia University,
>   Wolfville, Nova Scotia.

Collom, F.
>   Associate in Research,
>   Industrial Relations Centre,
>   Queen's University,
>   Kingston, Ontario.

Corry, J. A.
>   Principal,
>   Queen's University,
>   Kingston, Ontario.

Cooke, K. B.
>   Sociologist, Resources Development Section,
>   Economics Branch,
>   Canada Department of Agriculture,
>   Ottawa 4, Ontario.

Cranston, W. H.
>   Chairman, Ontario Economic Council,
>   481 University Avenue,
>   Toronto, Ontario.

Crawford, K. G.
>   Professor of Political Studies, and
>   Director, Institute of Local Government,
>   Queen's University,
>   Kingston, Ontario.

Daly, C. J.
>Director, Economic Studies Branch,
>Department of Public Works, Federal Government,
>Room C341, Sir Charles Tupper Building,
>Confederation Heights,
>Ottawa 8, Ontario.

Daly, D. J.
>Economic Council of Canada,
>P.O. Box 527,
>Ottawa, Ontario.

Davidson, A. T.
>Director, Agricultural Rehabilitation and Development Administration,
>Canada Department of Forestry,
>Room 500, Excelsior Building,
>270 Laurier Avenue,
>Ottawa, Ontario.

Deutsch, J. J.
>Chairman, Economic Council of Canada,
>P.O. Box 527,
>Ottawa, Ontario.

Doxey, G. V.
>Chairman, Department of Economics,
>York University,
>2275 Bayview Avenue,
>Toronto 12, Ontario.

Drummie, F. R.
>Economic Advisor,
>Province of New Brunswick,
>Fredericton, N.B.

Dubé, Y.
>Professor of Economics,
>Laval University,
>Ste.-Foy, P.Q.

Dymond, W. R.
>Assistant Deputy Minister,
>Department of Labour,
>Ottawa, Ontario.

Elder, M. A.
>Industrial Commissioner,
>Greater Windsor Industrial Commission,
>369 Pelissier Street,
>Windsor, Ontario.

English, H. E.
>Director of Research,
>Canadian Trade Committee,
>712 Sun Life Building,
>Montreal 2, P.Q.

Fennell, G. H.
            Economic Studies Manager,
            Canadian Industries Limited,
            Box 10, Montreal, P.Q.

Fletcher, R. K.
            Economist,
            Atlantic Provinces Economic Council,
            175 Bronson Avenue, Apt. 304,
            Ottawa 4, Ontario.

Flynn, W. H.
            Ontario General Manager,
            Canadian Industries Limited,
            130 Bloor Street West,
            Toronto, Ontario.

Foohey, D. E.
            Staff Economist,
            Atlantic Development Board,
            71 Bank Street,
            Ottawa, Ontario.

Frick, H. C.
            Economics Service,
            Department of Fisheries,
            Sir Charles Tupper Building,
            Riverside Drive,
            Ottawa 8, Ontario.

Fyfe, S.
            Associate Professor of Political Studies, and
            University Planning Officer,
            Queen's University,
            Kingston, Ontario.

Garner, J.
            Federal-Provincial Relations Division,
            Department of Finance,
            205 Confederation Building,
            Ottawa, Ontario.

Gathercole, G.
            First Vice-Chairman,
            Hydro-Electric Power Commission of Ontario,
            620 University Avenue,
            Toronto, Ontario.

Gertler, L. O.
            Head, Planning Department,
            H. G. Acres & Company Limited,
            1259 Dorchester Road,
            Niagara Falls, Ontario.

Goldberg, S. A.
>Assistant Dominion Statistician,
>Dominion Bureau of Statistics,
>Tunney's Pasture,
>Ottawa, Ontario.

Goodman, R. V. S.
>Research Officer,
>Department of Labour,
>Ottawa, Ontario.

Graham, J. F.
>Head, Department of Economics and Sociology,
>Dalhousie University,
>Halifax, Nova Scotia.

Grandy, J. F.
>Assistant Deputy Minister,
>Department of Finance,
>Ottawa, Ontario.

Haase, G.
>Chief, Program Co-ordination Division,
>Area Development Agency,
>Department of Industry,
>123 Slater Street,
>Ottawa, Ontario.

Hansen, K.
>Executive Assistant,
>Manitoba Economic Consultative Board,
>Norquay Building, 401 York Avenue,
>Winnipeg 1, Manitoba.

Hartle, D. G.
>Research Director,
>Royal Commission on Taxation,
>88 Metcalfe Street,
>Ottawa, Ontario.

Harvey, P.
>Ecole des Hautes Etudes Commerciales,
>535, Avenue Viger,
>Montréal 24, P.Q.

Haviland, W. E.
>Economist,
>Canadian Pulp and Paper Association,
>2280 Sun Life Building,
>Montreal, P.Q.

Henderson, D.
>Director of Planning,
>Manitoba Department of Municipal Affairs,
>404-1181 Portage Avenue,
>Winnipeg 10, Manitoba.

Henson, G.
>Director, Institute of Public Affairs,
>Dalhousie University,
>Halifax, Nova Scotia.

Hills, T. L.
>Associate Professor,
>Department of Geography,
>McGill University,
>Montreal, P.Q.

Hodgetts, J. E.
>Hardy Professor of Political Studies, and
>Head, Department of Political Studies,
>Queen's University,
>Kingston, Ontario.

Hodges, R. C.
>Chief of Land Use, ARDA,
>Department of Forestry,
>Excelsior Life Building,
>270 Laurier Avenue West,
>Ottawa 4, Ontario.

Honey, P.
>Ontario Department of Economics and Development,
>950 Yonge Street,
>Toronto, Ontario.

Issa, M. J.
>Economist,
>Ontario Department of Labour,
>8 York Street,
>Toronto 1, Ontario.

Istvanffy, D. I.
>Director, Alberta Bureau of Statistics,
>Department of Industry and Development,
>Room 333, Highways Building,
>Edmonton, Alberta.

Johnson, I. E.
>Economist, Program Co-ordination Division,
>Area Development Agency,
>Department of Industry,
>123 Slater Street,
>Ottawa, Ontario.

Jones, D. H.
>Consultant on Research,
>Dominion Bureau of Statistics,
>Tunney's Pasture,
>Ottawa, Ontario.

Kayes, S. B.
> Chief, Incentives Administration Division,
> Area Development Agency,
> Department of Industry,
> 123 Slater Street,
> Ottawa 4, Ontario.

Kelly, L. A.
> Associate in Research,
> Industrial Relations Centre,
> Queen's University,
> Kingston, Ontario.

Kerr, D.
> Department of Geography,
> University of Toronto,
> Sidney Smith Hall,
> 100 St. George Street,
> Toronto 5, Ontario.

Larry, O. W.
> Clerk-Comptroller,
> Corporation of the Town of Trenton,
> 15 Dundas Street East,
> Trenton, Ontario.

Lavigne, W. J.
> Commissioner, Area Development Agency,
> Department of Industry,
> 123 Slater Street,
> Ottawa, Ontario.

Lawton, R.
> Department of Geography,
> Southern Illinois University,
> Carbondale, Illinois.

Lee, H. S.
> Senior Economist,
> Ontario Economic Council,
> 950 Yonge Street,
> Toronto 5, Ontario.

LeMasurier, A. H.
> Chief Co-ordinator, Regional Development Division,
> Ontario Department of Economics and Development,
> 950 Yonge Street,
> Toronto 2, Ontario.

Levine, A. L.
> Associate Professor,
> Department of Economics and Political Science,
> University of New Brunswick,
> Fredericton, N.B.

Levitan, S. A.
> The W. E. Upjohn Institute for Employment Research,
> 1755 Massachusetts Avenue, N.W., Suite 320,
> Washington, D.C. 20036.

Levitt, K.
> Assistant Professor of Economics,
> Department of Economics,
> McGill University,
> Montreal, P.Q.

Linkletter, Z.
> Director, Economic Services Division,
> Nova Scotia Department of Trade and Industry,
> Provincial Building,
> Halifax, Nova Scotia.

Little, S.A.
> President, Canadian Union of Public Employees,
> Vice-President, Canadian Labour Congress,
> 176 Gloucester Street,
> Ottawa 4, Ontario.

Lok, S. H.
> Department of Industry,
> Ottawa, Ontario.

Mann, J. K.
> Regional Statistics and Analysis Staff,
> Dominion Bureau of Statistics,
> Tunney's Pasture,
> Ottawa, Ontario.

Manners, G.
> Lecturer in Geography,
> University College, Swansea.
> (1964-65) Resources for the Future, Inc.,
> 1755 Massachusetts Avenue, N.W.,
> Washington, D.C. 20036.

Marsh, D. B.
> Assistant General Manager, (Economic Research),
> The Royal Bank of Canada,
> Head Office, 1 Place Ville Marie,
> Montreal, P.Q.

Martin, G.
> Director, Economics Research Bureau,
> Quebec Department of Industry and Commerce,
> 585 E. Charest Blvd.,
> Quebec, P.Q.

Massue, W. H.
> General Manager,
> The Lower St. Lawrence and Gulf Development Association,
> 1260 University Avenue,
> Montreal, P.Q.

Matthews, R. A.
> Private Planning Association of Canada,
> 712 Sun Life Building,
> Montreal 2, P.Q.

MacDonald, J. A.
> Assistant Deputy Minister,
> Department of Northern Affairs and National Resources,
> Langevin Block,
> Ottawa, Ontario.

MacKay, A. N.
> Research Associate,
> Institute of Local Government,
> Queen's University,
> Kingston, Ontario.

Mackintosh, W. A.
> Vice-Chancellor,
> Queen's University,
> Kingston, Ontario.

McBain, J. W.
> Clerk-Comptroller,
> Teck Township,
> 99 Government Road East,
> Kirkland Lake, Ontario.

McDaniel, R.
> Assistant Professor,
> Department of Geography,
> Middlesex College,
> University of Western Ontario,
> London, Ontario.

McDougall, D.
> Co-ordinator, Economic Research,
> Royal Commission on Taxation,
> 88 Metcalfe Street,
> Ottawa, Ontario.

McKee, A. F.
> Chairman, Department of Economics,
> Laurentian University,
> Sudbury, Ontario.

McLarty, R. A.
>Director of Economic Research,
>Province of New Brunswick,
>Scovil House, Brunswick and St. John Streets,
>Fredericton, N.B.

Nicholson, N. L.
>Senior Professor of Geography,
>Department of Geography,
>University of Western Ontario,
>London, Ontario.

Nordin, J. E.
>Manager, Montreal Branch,
>Industrial Development Bank,
>901 Victoria Square,
>Montreal 1, P.Q.

Oestreicher, E. A.
>Director,
>Department of Finance,
>Confederation Building,
>Ottawa, Ontario.

Officer, E. R.
>Department of Geography,
>University of Waterloo,
>Waterloo, Ontario.

Papineau, J. Y.
>Directeur, Service de Developpement Regional,
>Ministère de l'Industrie du Commerce,
>585 E. Blvd. Charest,
>Quebec, P.Q.

Pellai, G.
>Research Officer,
>Department of Labour,
>Ottawa, Ontario.

Perry, J. H.
>Executive Director,
>Canadian Bankers' Association,
>50 King Street West,
>Toronto 1, Ontario.

Plaxton, C. G. F.
>Engineering Consultant,
>Program Co-ordination Division,
>Area Development Agency,
>Department of Industry,
>123 Slater Street,
>Ottawa 4, Ontario.

Pleva, E. G.
> Professor and Head,
> Department of Geography,
> Middlesex College,
> University of Western Ontario,
> London, Ontario.

Raynauld, A.
> Associate Professor,
> Department of Economics,
> University of Montreal,
> C.P. 6128,
> Montreal, P.Q.

Reckord, G. E.
> Assistant Administrator for Planning and Research,
> Area Redevelopment Administration,
> United States Department of Commerce,
> Washington, D.C. 20230
> 400 Beechwood Road,
> Alexandria, Virginia.

Reisman, S. S.
> Deputy Minister,
> Department of Industry,
> 123 Slater Street,
> Ottawa, Ontario.

Robertson, R.
> Director,
> Canadian Tax Foundation,
> 154 University Avenue,
> Toronto 1, Ontario.

Rodd, R. S.
> Associate Professor,
> Department of Agricultural Economics,
> Ontario Agricultural College,
> University of Guelph,
> Guelph, Ontario.

Ruggles, R. I.
> Professor of Geography, and
> Head, Department of Geography,
> Queen's University,
> Kingston, Ontario.

Saumier, André.
> Research Officer,
> Canadian Council on Urban and Regional Research,
> 225 Metcalfe Street, Suite 308,
> Ottawa, Ontario.

Schnick, O. M.
> Director, Special Research and Surveys Branch,
> Ontario Department of Economics and Development,
> 950 Yonge Street,
> Toronto, Ontario.

Scott, A.
> Professor of Economics,
> University of British Columbia.
> Graduate School of Business,
> University of Chicago.
> Chicago 37, Ill.

Simmons, J.
> Assistant Professor,
> Department of Geography,
> University of Western Ontario,
> London, Ontario.

Sinclair, M.
> Ontario Department of Municipal Affairs,
> Queen's Park,
> Toronto, Ontario.

Smale, H. R.
> Economist, Economics Branch,
> Department of Trade and Commerce,
> Ottawa 4, Ontario.

Spelt, J.
> Professor,
> Department of Geography,
> University of Toronto,
> 100 St. George Street,
> Toronto, Ontario.

Szabo, M. L.
> Chief, Division of Economic Geography,
> Geographical Branch,
> Department of Mines and Technical Surveys,
> 601 Booth Street,
> Ottawa, Ontario.

Teeter, J. A.
> Deputy Commissioner, Area Development Agency,
> Department of Industry,
> 123 Slater Street,
> Ottawa, Ontario.

Thoman, R. S.
> Professor of Geography,
> Queen's University,
> Kingston, Ontario.

Trotter, B.
> Executive Assistant to the Principal,
> Queen's University,
> Kingston, Ontario.

Urquhart, M. C.
> Professor of Economics, and
> Head, Department of Economics,
> Queen's University,
> Kingston, Ontario.

Wahn, J. D.
> General Economist,
> Canadian National Railways,
> P.O. Box 8100,
> Montreal, P.Q.

Walter, K. W.
> Geographic Advisor,
> Imperial Oil,
> 111 St. Clair Avenue West,
> Toronto 7, Ontario.

Weeks, E. P.
> Executive Director,
> Atlantic Development Board,
> 71 Bank Street,
> Ottawa, Ontario.

Wood, W. D.
> Professor of Economics, and
> Director, Industrial Relations Centre,
> Queen's University,
> Kingston, Ontario.

Woodsworth, D. E.
> Research Director,
> The Canadian Welfare Council,
> 55 Parkdale Avenue,
> Ottawa 3, Ontario.

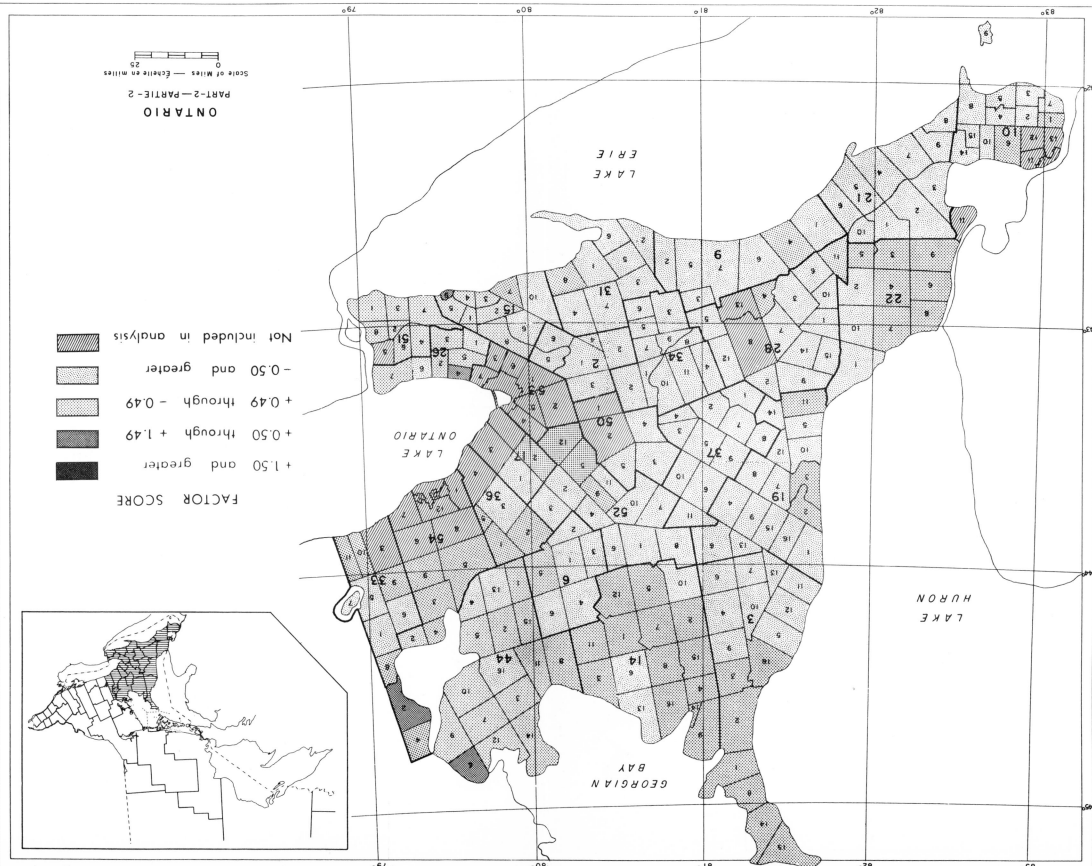

ONTARIO
PART-2 — PARTIE-2

Scale of Miles — Échelle en milles
0   25

FACTOR SCORE

+1.50 and greater
+0.50 through +1.49
+0.49 through −0.49
−0.50 and greater
Not included in analysis

LAKE ERIE

LAKE ONTARIO

LAKE HURON

GEORGIAN BAY

Factor 1

Fig. 2.—Factor one—Southern Ontario.

ONTARIO
PART-1—PARTIE-1

FACTOR SCORE

Not included in analysis

-0.50 and greater

+0.49 through -0.49

+0.50 through +1.49

+1.50 and greater

Scale of Miles — Echelle en milles
0   25

Fig. 1.—Factor one—Eastern Ontario.

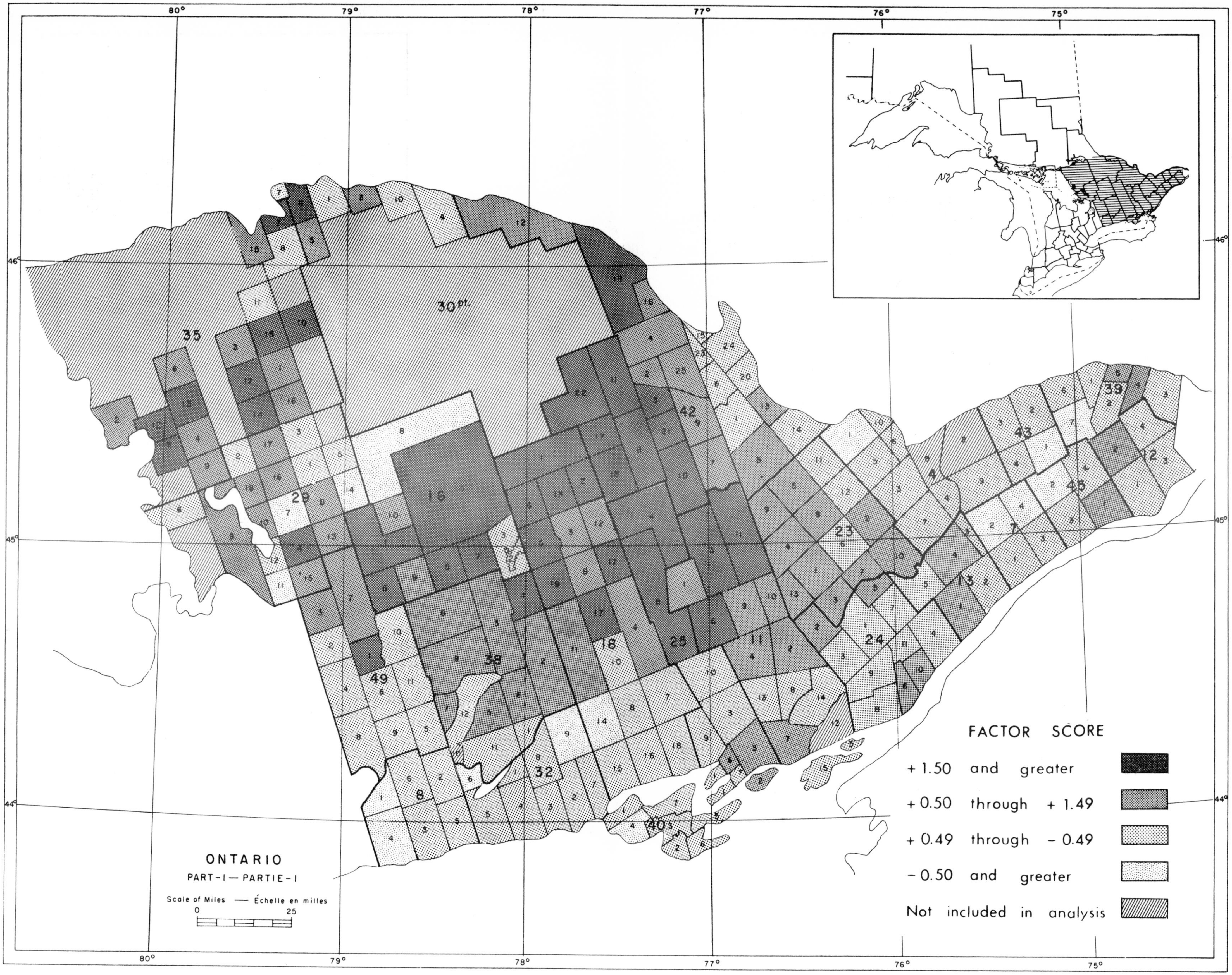

Factor 1

Fig. 3.—Factor two—Eastern Ontario.

Factor 2

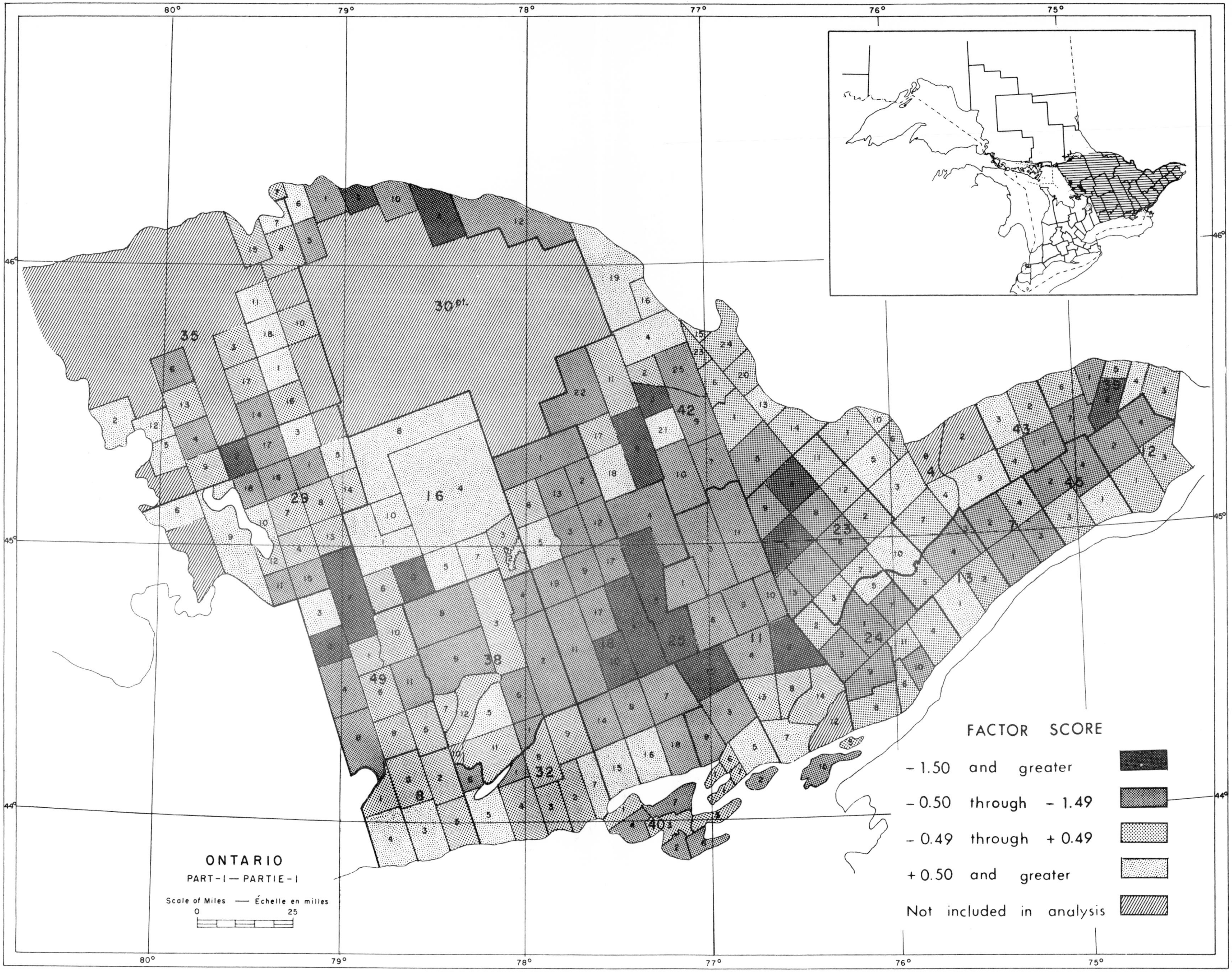
80°
79°
78°
77°
76°
75°
46°
45°
44°
ONTARIO
PART-I — PARTIE-I
Scale of Miles — Échelle en milles
0
25
FACTOR SCORE
- 1.50 and greater
- 0.50 through - 1.49
- 0.49 through + 0.49
+ 0.50 and greater
Not included in analysis
30 pt.
35
16
29
38
49
8
32
40
42
25
18
11
23
24
13
4
43
45
12

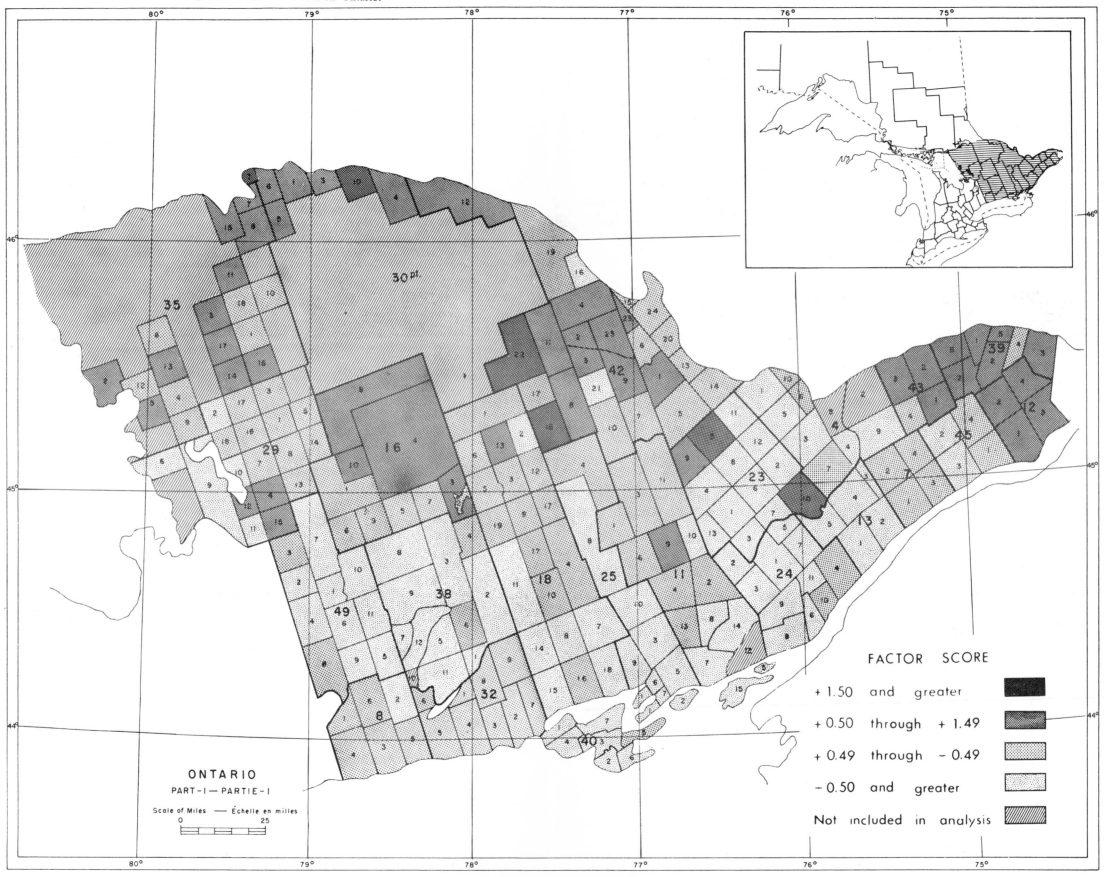

Fig. 8.—Factor four—Eastern Ontario.

Factor 4

FACTOR SCORE

+ 1.50 and greater

+ 0.50 through + 1.49

+ 0.49 through - 0.49

- 0.50 and greater

Not included in analysis

ONTARIO

PART-1—PARTIE-1

Scale of Miles — Échelle en milles
0   25

ITEMS GROUPED

STEP	I	J	VALUE
1	78	86	0.25000E-02
2	75	76	0.74000E-02
3	31	34	0.17400E-01
4	62	92	0.24000E-01
5	91	94	0.40500E-01
6	50	51	0.57800E-01
7	124	152	0.74600E-01
8	99	102	0.95200E-01
9	102	101	0.10630
10	52	63	0.12800
11	66	28	0.14850
12	46	65	0.17713
13	45	47	0.20763
14	133	143	0.23603
15	152	153	0.26610
16	89	97	0.30010
17	131	149	0.33500
18	71	71	0.37190
19	65	71	0.41690
20	81	68	0.45560
21	81	88	0.49790
22	110	115	0.54290
23	14	4	0.58930
24	103	117	0.64370
25	10	12	0.70620
26	138	138	0.76910
27	126	31	0.83660
28	28	13	0.90510
29	28	80	0.97317
30	28	30	1.05697
31	17	22	1.13547
32	14	77	1.21637
33	125	151	1.31337
34	57	62	1.42293
35	138	138	1.56640
36	120	123	1.65508
37	127	150	1.79718
38	150	136	1.94218
39	9	11	2.05665
40	7	47	2.21035
41	113	107	2.35842
42	100	111	2.53726
43	35	40	2.73326
44	63	53	2.91376
45	149	140	3.09884
46	48	54	3.28927
47	7	154	3.48474
48	117	108	3.69131
49	101	106	3.89131
50	34	35	4.10591
51	34	1	4.18624
52	75	130	4.63157
53	125	128	4.4072x
54	134	134	4.85786
55	20	26	5.11825
56	26	25	5.38590
57	143	83	5.65580
58	20	26	5.95480

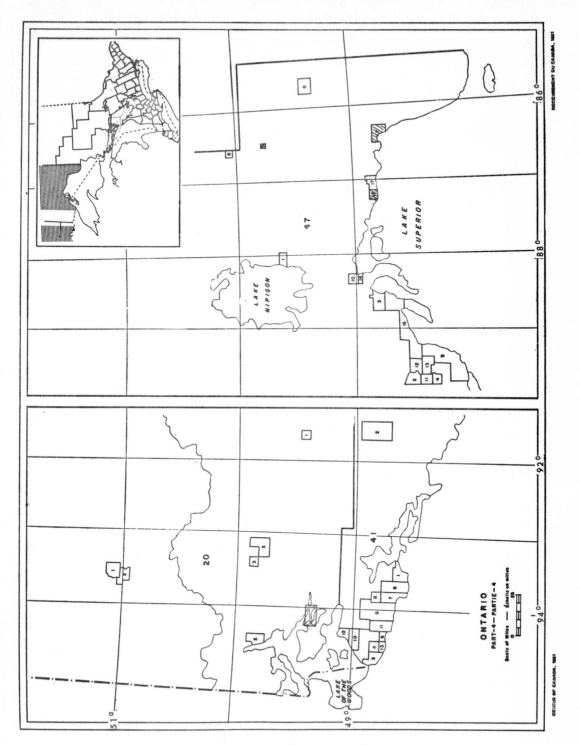

Fig. 11.—Base map—Northwestern Ontario.

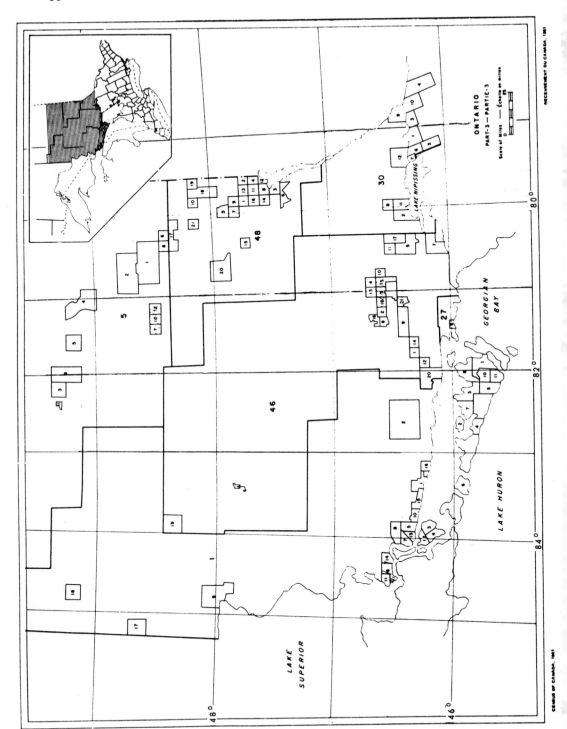

Fig. 10.—Base map—Northern Ontario.

Fig. 9.—Factor four—Southern Ontario.

Factor 4

FACTOR SCORE

+ 1.50 and greater

+ 0.50 through + 1.49

+ 0.49 through − 0.49

− 0.50 and greater

Not included in analysis

ONTARIO

PART-2—PARTIE-2

Scale of Miles — Échelle en milles

0   25